MODERN HUMANITIES RESEARCH ASSOCIATION

CRITICAL TEXTS

VOLUME 7

Editor
MALCOLM COOK
(*French*)

LA DISME DE PENITANCHE

by

Jehan de Journi

LA DISME DE PENITANCHE

by

Jehan de Journi

Edited by

Glynn Hesketh

MODERN HUMANITIES RESEARCH ASSOCIATION
2006

Published by

The Modern Humanities Research Association,
1 Carlton House Terrace
London SW1Y 5DB

© The Modern Humanities Research Association, 2006

Glynn Hesketh has asserted his right under the Copyright, Designs and Patents Act 1988 to be identified as the author of this work.

All rights reserved. No part of this publication may be reproduced, stored in a retrieval system, or transmitted, in any form or by any means, electronic, mechanical, photocopying, recording or otherwise, without the prior permission of the publishers.

First published 2006

ISBN 0 947623 71 X / 978 0 947623 71 5

ISSN 1746-1642

Copies may be ordered from www.criticaltexts.mhra.org.uk

Table of Contents

Manuscript and Editorial Practice 1

Author, Date and Audience 3

Background and Sources 5

The Language of the Text
    Phonology 8
    Morphology 18
    Vocabulary 25
    Versification 26

Bibliography 28

LA DISME DE PENITANCHE 33

Notes to the Text 118

Rejected Readings 183

Glossary 185

Index of Proper Names 203

INTRODUCTION

The *Disme de Penitanche* deserves to be better known to scholars for a variety of reasons. Linguistically, it is a reliably dated text (from 1288) exhibiting many interesting phonological and morphological traits of the Picard dialect and containing a large number of early or unique attestations of lexical items. In terms of its content, it makes a major contribution to the vulgarizing theological literature dealing with confession and penance which flowered in the thirteenth century. Moreover, in his concluding prayer the author details a number of contemporary figures who, like him, were present in the eastern Mediterranean as the crusades drew to their close in the late 1280s and early 1290s. Finally the work contains a hitherto largely unnoticed passage giving significant information about games and pastimes at the period.

MANUSCRIPT AND EDITORIAL PRACTICE

The work is known from one manuscript only, London B.L. MS Add. 10015, a vellum manuscript, dating from around the time of the completion of the *Disme de Penitanche*, or very shortly after. The manuscript measures some 180 mm by 125 mm. The volume contains two works, the *Disme*, followed (on ff. 81r to 200v) by the *Image du Monde*.[1] Our text spans ten quires of four bifolia each, numbered from f. 3r (though ff. 30 and 31 may be single sheets). Pages are ruled in single columns with twenty-one lines per column, the writing block measuring approximately 140 mm by 65 mm. The *Disme de Penitanche* finishes a few lines before the end of f. 80v. The next three pages are rather cramped: the index to the *Image du Monde* begins on f. 81r in two columns with hardly any margin, the left-hand column measuring some 40mm and the right-

---

[1] The first verse version, see H. Hesse, *Studien über die zweite Redaktion der Image du Monde* (Halle, 1932).

hand one the usual 65mm. Folio 81v is similar, but with the wider column on the left. The text of the *Image* proper starts on f. 82r at the top of the wider (right-hand) column, the end of the index occupying eighteen lines of the inside column. With f. 82v, the page reverts to its normal single-column format. A new gathering begins with f. 83r, and the manuscript continues in its previous format to the end, though the ruling is for twenty-three or twenty-five lines. It will be seen that the *Image du Monde* begins on the last two folios of quire ten, which is otherwise occupied by the *Disme*. The two texts were evidently planned as one volume, and not bound together subsequently. The cramped index may suggest some miscalculation on the part of the scribe.

The text of both works is written throughout in the same clear book hand, with very little abbreviation and hardly any correction. Imperfections in the membrane are all written around, and do not obscure the text. In both texts sections begin, usually after a blank line, with a built up dropped capital which mostly descends from its own line onto the line below, with diapered infill that typically extends into the left-hand margin over several lines. The very first initial on f. 3r is three lines deep and highly decorated, and a picture extends from it into the right-hand and lower margins, showing an archer shooting at two birds among foliage, while a dog chases a rabbit and a seated cat looks directly out at the reader. A similar though smaller design of foliage and birds is used to frame the right-hand column at the start of the text of the *Image* on f. 82r, and the usual geometrical and astronomical illustrations appear in this latter text.

There are various pen-trials on the fly leaves and a later unpractised hand tries here (inaccurately) to write *jaspar fert mirrham thus melcior basta* (presumably for *balta[sar aurum]*), and repeats the attempt in whole or part elsewhere (e.g. ff. 95v, 97v, 113v, 120r). This must have been done after the manuscript was bound, since some of the words are blotted onto the facing page. The same hand copies out the superscription from f. 3 (with mistakes). A different hand has written *sancta maria ora pro nobis* on f. 1r, and there is a line drawing of a man's face in cap and bells on f. 1v. On f. 200v, after the *Image du Monde* (and in the same hand), is a colophon: *Mesires sains bodes fist chest romant | benoiete soit lame de li*.

The normal practice in editing the text has been to leave the manuscript reading unchanged so far as possible, even where a very simple alteration might have been thought an improvement (though such alterations are suggested in the Notes from time to time). Metrical grounds, however, have been considered sufficient to justify emendation.[2] Word division has been made to conform to modern practice, as has the distinction between *i* and *j* and between *u* and *v*. All punctuation and diacritics are editorial; the tréma has been added for the reader's convenience, even in a few cases where it might be thought strictly unnecessary.[3] Abbreviations (which are not numerous in the manuscript) have been expanded in accordance with scribal practice. Bold type in the edition represents the use of decorated initials in the manuscript (see above). Rejected readings are listed at the end of the volume, and most are remarked upon in the Notes; in the Rejected Readings the expansion of an abbreviation is shown by the use of italics. All other emendations are enclosed within square brackets, or are made the subject of a note; an -*s* has been added to correct errors of case only where this was necessary for the sake of metre.

The work has been edited once before, by Breymann in 1874 (see Bibliography). His edition is altogether unsatisfactory.[4] It is extremely careless and full of misreadings often of a very elementary kind; it frequently 'corrects' the manuscript quite unnecessarily; on the rare occasions when it tackles genuine manuscript problems, it tends only to make them worse, and its apparatus is wholly inadequate to a proper understanding of the text.

AUTHOR, DATE AND AUDIENCE

About the author, who names himself as *Jehans (sires) de Journi* in lines 29 and 3292, nothing is known except for what can be gleaned from the text.[5] According to his own testimony he wrote

---

[2] Spellings such as *que ele* for *qu'ele* (19), *se a* (66) *le hom* (585), *de aucun* (785), have been left unaltered.

[3] For example on *äa*, *öo*, or *ïon*.

[4] See Foerster's scathing review.

[5] Breymann (p. 105) found one reference in one source (E. G. Rey, *Les Familles d'outre-mer de Du Cange*, Collection de documents inédits sur l'histoire de France (Paris, 1869), p. 594) to a Jean de Jorny who appears in a 'Tableau

the work as an act of penance during a period of illness in Nicosia on Cyprus (4–12, 3287–94). He also claims (12–23) to have written other works prior to the *Disme*; none of these appears to have survived, but his skill at versification strongly suggests that this is not his first attempt at composition. He has quite extensive knowledge about certain people and events connected with the Kingdom of Jerusalem at the end of the 1280s, and the implication is that he had spent some time in the eastern Mediterranean. Given his dialect, it is assumed that he takes his name from Journy in the Pas de Calais, a small village on the edge of the forest of Tournehem, though there is no external evidence for this.[6]

In line 895 Jehan explicitly states that he is a *chevaliers lais*, yet the text would lead us to the conclusion that he must have been a man of some considerable education, almost certainly at university level. Not only is he interested in the technical details of confession and penance as they were then being debated, but he also uses scholarly vocabulary, such as *article* (1882), *determiner* (894), *distinction* (2559), *thëologie* (885); his material often points to a serious Latin source (see, for example, lines 1194, 1320, 2645, 2847), and he adopts the scholastic methodology of division and subdivision (doubtless taken over from his source, see, for example, notes to lines 1545, 1979, 2577), and of citing authorities (Gregory six times, Augustine five, for example, alongside a range of Biblical sources — see the index of proper names). He even claims in line 883 (assuming that he is not simply repeating the claim from his source), to have participated in the kind of

---

généalogique des maisons de Soissons et de Rivet' as being married to Euphemia, daughter of John of Soissons, though he points out that two other sources give the name as de Verny.

[6] The village is apparently first mentioned in the seventh century, when count Wambert de Renty granted it to Bishop (later Saint) Omer in 651, though it seems never to have been of any significance. (See Commission départmentale des monuments historiques, *Dictionnaire historique et archéologique du département de Pas de Calais : arrondissement de Saint-Omer* (Arras: Sueur-Charruey, 1877), tome 1, p. 254.) Several crusader knights took a title from their territories in the crusader states, and there is a town of D'Journi (Journieh, Jounieh) on the coast just north of Beirut, now a seaside resort, which has ruined fortifications dating back to the our author's time. So far as I am aware, this has never been suggested as a possible origin of Jehan's surname.

determinatio that formed the concluding part of the *disputatio*, the fundamental teaching method in the universities of the day.[7]

In lines 3287–92 Jehan states that he started and finished the work in the year 1300 minus twelve years, i.e. in 1288, and there seems no reason to question this date. Jacoby (see Bibliography) describes the context in which French texts were read and written in the eastern Mediterranean at this time, and explains that copyists were active in the region. Though our work was apparently written on Cyprus, it is not known whether it was copied there. If the presence of a Picardizing scribe on the island, sharing a similar dialect to that of the author, seems rather an unlikely coincidence, then it may just be that, having recovered from his illness, Jehan returned to France, bringing the work home with him.

He addresses his audience in the plural as *Segnour*,[8] and envisages his text being read aloud at lines 1465 and 2031, though the possibility of an individual's reading the text for him- or herself is also assumed at lines 1839–45 and 2026–29. Furthermore, various Biblical figures crop up in the text without explanation, not only well known examples such as Cain, Judas, or Jonah and the whale, but also more recondite ones like Hezekiah, Joel, or Tobias. All of this suggests that Jehan had in mind a literate audience with the financial means to have access to books, and with a better than elementary acquaintance with the Bible.

BACKGROUND AND SOURCES

The *Disme de Penitanche* forms part of the great mass of vernacular literature concerned with religious instruction which was produced in the Middle Ages. More particularly it belongs to

---

[7] The two principal university teaching methods were the lecture and the disputation. The lecture involved the reading and explanation of a text by the master. The disputation was a highly formalized debate which took place between students or between student and master. A question was analysed and a solution was proposed; an opponent would raise points against it and expose erroneous arguments; finally, sometimes after several days' disputing, the master would determine a definitive solution.

[8] See 921, 1169, 1529, 2032, 2895, 2949, 3115. This is also the term of address he imagines Joel and Jesus using in lines 1198 and 2340.

the tradition of works designed to help the laity prepare themselves for confession.[9] This tradition was given a particular impetus by the fourth Lateran Council of 1215–16, a large and highly influential ecumenical council under the patronage of Pope Innocent III, which sought to promote ecclesiastical reforms of various kinds. Among these reforms great emphasis was placed on two areas which were to have far-reaching effects on vernacular literary production, namely better education in matters of doctrine (for both clergy and laity), and, most particularly, confession. The twenty-first canon of Lateran IV made it compulsory for every Christian who had reached the age of reason to make confession at least once a year,[10] and in consequence, created a need to teach the people about the faith, particularly about sin, confession and penance. The later thirteenth and fourteenth centuries saw a flowering of instructional literature for the laity which continued to be produced well into the fifteenth century.[11] The earliest examples are mostly from England, such as the *Lumere as Lais* or the *Manuel des Péchés*,[12] to be followed before the end of the thirteenth century by continental works such as the *Miroir du Monde/Somme le Roi*, or the many shorter, generally anonymous texts listed in the *Grundriß der romanischen Literaturen des Mittelalters*,[13] including, of course, our own work.

The *Disme* is a strange hybrid. On the one hand it has many popular features such its presentation of the seven deadly sins using the framework of the Three Enemies of Man (639ff., 2032ff.), its striking images, such as that of the fountain (95ff.) or the likening of contrition to lye (1169ff.), its edifying story from

---

[9] Payen (see Bibliography) gives details of the climate in which these confessional works were written, and (in chapter three) situates the *Disme* in this context (though one might perhaps question his insistence on Jehan de Journi's debt to the *De Vera et Falsa Poenitentia* of pseudo-Augustine).

[10] 'Omnis utriusque sexus fidelis, postquam ad annos discretionis pervenerit, omnia sua solus peccata confiteatur fideliter, saltem semel in anno, proprio sacerdoti…'

[11] On the later literature, see Geneviève Hasenohr in *Grundriß der romanischen Literaturen des Mittelalters* VIII, 1 (Heidelberg, 1988) 272–77.

[12] For these two works, see 1671*n*.

[13] See Segre in Bibliography. While our author concentrates on sin, confession and penance, he is nonetheless aware of the scope of the wider-ranging manuals of instruction, as he makes clear in lines 1827–38.

the *Vitae Patrum* (512ff.), or its abundant proverbial expressions scattered throughout the text.[14] On the other hand it shares many elements with works of *haute vulgarisation* like the *Lumere as Lais*, such as its technical description of contrition, its scholarly distinction between substance and form (2847), its recourse to sources from among the university text books of the day, or its often punctilious citation of the Fathers and the Bible.

Jehan's sources have been identified only partially, and more work needs to be done in this area. However, we can recognize small sections as deriving ultimately from Raymond of Peñafort and others from William Perrault (preeminent authors respectively of a very widely used *Summa de Paenitentia* of 1229 and a *Summa de Vitiis* of ca. 1236),[15] and yet the overall shape of our work is not based in any way on either. This suggests that one source at least might be one of the many compilations made up from such authorities (usually designed for serious students of religion) that were in circulation from the mid-thirteenth century.[16] Certainly, a passage such as 1227–30.[17] would seem to point to such a conclusion, in want of further evidence. There were, of course, compendia of a more popular kind in French and in Latin, the latter often designed to help preachers to compose sermons, and one of these might have provided the material on the deadly sins, the sermon-like exempla, etc. One must also ask how many primary sources are likely to have been available to the author in Nicosia in 1288.[18] The various possible mistaken attributions in the text[19] lead one to wonder whether he was not to some extent working from memory. At all events, even allowing for substantial parts of the

---

[14] See lines 412, 692, 1347, 2160, 2440, 2448, 2452, 2568, 2712, 2828, 3213, 3278.

[15] See, for example, the notes to lines 316, 481, 486, 1320, 1383, 2577, etc.

[16] See H. G. Pfander in *JEGP* 35 (1936), 243–258; L. W. Patterson, *Traditio* 34 (1978), 331–80.

[17] 'Toutes les coses sus noumees | Sont en confession prouvees | Par Augustin et Ysidore, | Bede, Bernart et saint Grigore.'

[18] Unfortunately Jacoby (*op. cit.*) deals only with French texts, and not with Latin ones. However, he records that many French books were imported into the region by the crusaders, and it is clearly not implausible that Latin texts would also have been brought there by pilgrims, priests or clerics.

[19] See, for example, the notes to lines 685, 826, 1452, 2816.

text being original, it seems unlikely that the inspiration for the remainder will be found in a single source, and Jehan has taken pains to integrate disparate material into a coherent whole with a broad appeal.

THE LANGUAGE OF THE TEXT

Phonology

Tonic Vowels

A: The vowel *a* tonic and free develops to *e*; the scribe writes *ei* on only two occasions, *heit* 65 and *seit* 78, probably by analogy with the first person. (Cf. Gossen §1 — see Bibliography.) The endings *-er*, *-é*, *-és* do not rhyme with their palatalized equivalents *-ier*, *-ié*, *-iés*, except that a glide seems to be introduced after *i* in hiatus, allowing *humilïer* to rhyme with *laissier* 259, or *senefier* with *espeluquier* 1867, a pronunciation more clearly attested in the spellings *crucefïiés* 393 and *otrüier* 2690. There is confusion of *ar* and *er* before a consonant, e.g. *sarmon* 495, *enkerquiés* 2207. The suffix *-alem* generally develops to *-el*, e.g. *ostel : ost tel* 641; *corporele : tele* 944; *morteus : entredeus* 551. Very occasionally the etymological form is retained, e.g. *loiaus : rainssiaus* 1606 (and cf. *especïaument* 17, *perpetuaument* 2164), but the Picardism *-iel* does not appear. The *l* normally falls in the spelling of *tes* (e.g. 1301) and *ques* (e.g. 1722, 1503), though the only form at the rhyme is *teus* (: *morteus* 441). The Picard forms *le*, *me*, *te* and *se* appear for *la* (both article and pronoun), *ma*, *ta* and *sa*, though the Central forms are much commoner (see below). (Gossen §5.)

The diphthong *ai* was preserved longer in the North and East than elsewhere, and words spelt *ai* in our text rhyme only with each other. The spelling *e* appears in only one word, *fes* (< FASCEM, : *confés* 2805), an evident licence. This diphthong was sporadically reduced to *a* (cf. *aguise* 1033, *agreté* 1040, *manie* 351), making *a* and *ai* interchangeable for many Picard scribes. Our scribe writes *faic(h)e(nt)* for the present subjunctive of *faire* on nineteen occasions, and *fache* on only three, including the sole rhyme (: *grasse* 2869). He also spells the subjunctive of *haïr* as *hache* in rhyme with *faiche* at 1677. The scribal form is doubtless influenced by the indicative. The suffix *-age* is spelt *-aige* on one occasion (*usaige* 32, against ten examples of *usage*), *apairaument* 1746 vies with *aparaument* 369, *aigrie* seems to represent *agr(o)ie* at 2345, and there is one example of a future stem *air–* (in *airont* 1735), as against twenty-four of *ar–* (e.g. *aront* 1111). (Gossen §6, §7.)

As is usual in Picard texts, the diphthong *ié*, derived from palatal plus *a*, followed by a feminine *e*, is always reduced to *ie* (e.g. *eslongie : folie* 16, *brisie : conplie* 2906, cf. Gossen §8). A much more striking characteristic of our text, however, is that the equivalent masculine ending is also reduced to *ie*, e.g. *peccie : mie* 2209, *pitie : vie* 949, *traitie : Thobie* 2863 (cf. 332, 352, 909, 1160, 1609, 1872, 2409, 2710, 2724, 2868, 2993, 3042). Our author does not rhyme *ié* with *é*, so all the rhyming words spelt *ié* in the edition rhyme only with other words in *ié*. The question thus arises as to whether *ie* is an alternative form for the author to the standard *ié*, or whether it is the *only* form he uses. It is possible that we should read all the cases of *pechié*, *pitié*, etc. as *pechie* and *pitie*. This 'masculine' *ié* is derived from palatal plus *a* on all but two occasions. The rhymes *haitié : pié* 628 and *congié : pié* 2648, if read as *haitie : pie, congie : pie*, would be the only two out of eighteen rhymes involving a reduction of the diphthong *ié* deriving from tonic free *e*, but this scarcely seems a convincing counter-argument. More telling, perhaps, is the involvement of this *-ié* with the second person plural verb ending, e.g. *pecciés : sachiés* 2100, 2508, *: regehissiés* 1888, *proisiés : detrenchiés* 1198, though again, the verb ending enters into no other rhymes than these. Finally one might adduce *pecchiés : meschiés* 1029. On balance, the spelling *ié* has been retained in the edition, but with an awareness that, however convenient for the reader, it may not, in fact, always represent the author's pronunciation.

E: As regards free open *e*, the reflex of DEUS typically appears as *dieu(s)* (222 times), though the Picard form *diu(s)* is found fourteen times (and the anomalous *deu* twice). The rhymes are not sufficient to make it clear which form the author used. MATHAEUS gives *Mathieu* at 2789 (not at the rhyme), *Matheus* (: *eus*) at 352 and *Mathés* (: *matés*) at 300; MELIUS always appears as *mieus*, though the form *miudre* is found at 588. The reduction of the diphthong *ie* to *i* (more characteristic of Walloon than Picard) does not appear, nor does the breaking of *e* from blocked open *e* (in forms such as *tierre* for *terre*), an apparent exception being in forms derived from QUAERERE, (e.g. infin. *aquiere : terre* 2521), where analogical remodelling has taken place. The suffix -ELLUM generally develops to *-iau* (also *biau*), though *oisaus* (167), *ruissaus* (143, 2458, 3105, and cf. *ruissiel* 104) and *vaissaus* (483) also appear. (Gossen §§9–12.) Tonic *e* (open or closed) followed by a nasal and a consonant develops to *en*, which, it is generally held, is in principle not identical with *an* in Picard. Most of the dozen or so apparent exceptions in our text could be explained away by supposing a change of suffix (e.g. *apparant* 558, *couvenant* 1964, *astenanche* 2178, *penitanche* 2212, etc.). At 2990 *feme : diffame* (*: blame* 3253) is probably not a nasal vowel, which leaves only the licence *noiant* (*: gerroiant*) 2037. (Gossen §15.)

Free closed *e* has diphthongized to *oi*, which rhymes with *oi* from *o* or *au* plus yod; the spellings *ai* and *ei* are not found in the text. (In *feble* 852 and *febleche* 1272, Röhrs (see Bibliography) suggests that diphthongization was inhibited by the following 'muta + liquida'.) Of the three typically Picard infinitives, *caïr/keïr, seïr* and *veïr*, only the first appears exclusively in this form (*caïr* 1138, and scribal *cheïr : haïr* 67) *Veïr* rhymes with *obeïr* at 406 and appears again at 2544 (cf. *pourveïr : obeïr* 565), while the Central form *vëoir* rhymes with *mirëoir* at 782 (also with *assäoir* at 486, cf. the anomalous *vöoir : pöoir* 2500). *Sëoir* appears in 272 and 314, in neither case at the rhyme. Closed *e* followed by a nasal develops to *ain*, which rhymes with *ain* from *a* + nasal (e.g. *mains* < MINUS : *mains* < MANUM 799, *plaine : fontaine* 101). (Gossen §§16, 17, 19.) For closed *e* followed by *l* plus a consonant, in ILLOS/ECCE ILLOS, the rhymes sanction only *eus/c(h)(i)eus* (e.g. 474, 586, 1145, 1667), though the scribe normally writes *aus/cheaus/chiaus*.

I: The Picard development of -ILIUS/-ILIS and -IVUS to -*ius*/-*ieus* is reflected by the scribe in *fieus* 1477, *fiex* 3276, *soutius* 778 and *vix* (< VILIS) 672, with its compounds *vieutanche* 1630, *vieuteche* 2054, *vieutés* 1568, along with *chius/chieus* (e.g. 167, 1328), though these forms never appear at the rhyme. It is possible that the form *contrius* (1375, 1380) belongs here, as representing a change of suffix to -IVUS, but again the word is internal to the line.[20] (Gossen §§20–21.)

O: The author does not rhyme the diphthong *ue* from free open *o* with *eu* from closed *o*, though the scribe uses the spellings *ue* and *eu* indiscriminately, e.g. *cuer* 73, *ceur* 1486, *remuet* 1860, *meur*

---

[20] Röhrs suggests (p. 302) that the form might have arisen by analogy with North-Eastern perfects and participles in *iu*.

1074 (cf. Röhrs p. 302). Just as the diphthong *ié* is reduced to *i* before a 'feminine' *e* (e.g. *brisie* for *brisiee*), so *ué* is reduced to *u* in *puent*, e.g. 208, 1290 (cf. *pueent* e.g. 212, 1270, and see Pope §1320(v)). There is also evidence for the absorption of the first element of the diphthong in spellings such as *avec* 2513, *evre* 984, 1412, *preve* 1231, *reve* 1384, *treve* 1306, 2007, 2551, though these forms appear only in self-rhymes (Gossen §24). There are thirty-three examples of open *o* followed by *l* + consonant resulting in the characteristically Picard *au* in both stressed and unstressed positions, e.g. *assaure* 1425, *assaus* 1995 (< ABSOLVERE), *faus* (< FOLLIS) 237, *taut* (< TOLLIT) 381, *tauroit* 375, *vausist* 2708. These words do not appear in our text in rhyme with *au* from *a* + *l*. (Gossen §23.) Open *o* + *j* develop into *ui*, which rhymes with *ui* from *u* + *j*, and also, after a guttural, with *i* (*cuide* : *aïde* 676, *aguise* : *isse* 1033). The same is true of closed *o* + *j*, even pretonic (a Picardism) in *fuison* (e.g. 373). The learned suffix -ORIUM/-ORIA appears six times as *-oire* (*gloire* : *boire* 197, *memoire* : *croire* 2790) and eleven times as *-ore* (*glore* 813, *memore* 2777), though only once in anything other than a self-rhyme (*Grigore* : *Ysidore* 1230). The equivalent form *-are* for *-aire* does not appear. (Gossen §6, §27.) JOCUM gives *ju* (2589) and *geu* (2605, cf. *juer* 2588, 2625), rhyming with *Dieu* (1487, 2609), and LOCUM gives *liu* fifteen times and *lieu* twelve times, again rhyming with *Dieu* (502, 1821) or *cieus* (256, 324). However, FOCUM gives only the Picard form *fu*, rhyming with *fus* (< FUSTEM) at 213. The same reduction is found in the rare spelling *ius* ("eye") at 819, against *ieus* (781, 1062), never at the rhyme. (Gossen §25.)

Closed *o* stressed and free gives *eu*, as in Central Old French, rhyming with *eu* in *eus* < ILLOS and in the reflex of -ALES (e.g. *glorïeus* : *eus* 474, *entredeus* : *morteus* 551, *crueus* : *engigneus* 777). The reflex of -OREM rhymes with *-our* in *creator* : *atour* 807 and *clamour* : *amour* 3149. The remaining cases are all self-rhymes. The scribe writes *-eur*, *-or* and *-our* indiscriminately. Unstressed forms such as *sor/sour*, *por/pour*, *nos/nous* are never spelt with *eu*, the only exception being *leur*.[21] (Gossen §26.)

Before a nasal, the vowel *o* appears both as *o* and, more commonly, as *ou*. Spellings such as *conissanche* (1722), *comnissanche* (2397), and the abbreviated con*n*oist (1938) and *connoistre*

---

[21] And *seure* in the expression *courre seure*, which Röhrs believes is derived from SUPRA rather than SUPER, though cf. Gossen *loc. cit.*

(55) (*gnoist* and *cõnoistre*) sanction the first (and rarer) of these variants, while spellings such as *devouns* (780) or *encontroumes* (726) support the second variant.[22] The typically Picard spellings with *ou* may represent a degree of denasalization (Bourciez's explanation, reproduced by Gossen). The scribe writes the Picard form *pume* (for *pome*) in 1254, but, unlike the examples given by Gossen where the word rhymes with *plume*, here the rhyme is with *home*. There are five further spellings with *u* alone, (*abunde* 1510, *cunkie* 2296, *prenderunt* 3248 and the possibly Latinizing *secunde* 1577 and *sunt* e.g. 141). The scribe always writes *boin* for *bon*, but the only rhyme is with *persoune* in 1531. (Gossen §28a and §28b.)

Atonic vowels

Turning to atonic and countertonic vowels, in the group *c + a*, the *a* is retained in *caïr* 1138, *kaï* 1760; elsewhere the vowel is reduced to *e* (*chevaus* 768, *keï* 2437). Pretonic *a* and *e* in hiatus as the result of the loss of a Latin consonant become *e*, but generally keep their syllabic value, e.g. *seür* 349, *veü* 2438 (though cf. *äaisier* 2267, *gäaingier* 20, etc.). There is, however, a monosyllabic past subjunctive of *avoir*, namely *eust*, e.g. 547, alongside *eüst*, e.g. 69, and cf. *benoit* 106, *miroirs* 1731 (cf. 781), etc. (See Morphology below.) Countertonic *ai* is sporadically reduced to *a*, e.g. *agreté* 1040 (cf. 1036), *manie* 351 (cf. 790), etc., as is *au* in *amosne* e.g. 2416, 2423 (cf. 2386, 2389). The scribe has *travellier* five times and *batellier* once beside the expected forms, though -*ill*- appears only in *millor* 2496 etc. (cf. 586 etc.). In initial syllables *e* near a labial shows a typically Picard development to *u* in *buveroit* 1203, *bueveries* 1768, *fumier* 520, 527 (cf. *femoit* 515), though analogy doubtless has a part to play here. (Gossen §§29–31.) Before *s*, pretonic *ai* is reduced to *i*, another Picardism, in *arestison* 2643, 3093, *comparison* 416, etc., *counissance* 200 etc. and *orison* 1141 etc. Free initial *e* is raised to *i* in *yglise* 3004 (cf. 1349), *iretage* 2160, *criee* 969 (cf. 326), *Grigoire* 1085 etc., *hyraus* 2580, though *infer* (206 etc., cf. 999 etc.) is probably no more than a Latinizing spelling. The *o* of *prometre* passes to *a* in the usual Picard form *prametre* 832 etc.; the superficially similar forms *cambien* 1304 and *quanbien* 2425 are more probably modelled on

---

[22] The suggestion made by Suchier (see Bibliography) and repeated by Röhrs, that all of the (eight or nine) spellings in *onn* and *onm* in the manuscript should be replaced by *oun* and *oum* is consequently not to be followed.

quant (or even QUAM). Unstressed *o* is reduced to *e* in *quemans* 329, 1338 etc., *quemande* 2686 (cf. 2016), *gloutenie* 672 (cf. 1633), *honerer* (3041 etc.), and cf. the odd spelling *queme* for *comme* at 2399 and 2966. (Gossen §§33–37.)

Aside from the doublet *souverain* (e.g. 1018) and *souvrain* (e.g. 1410),[23] the insertion of a schwa between 'muta + liquida' (Gossen §44) appears only in the future stem of verbs (e.g. *perdera* 246, *istera* 844, *renderoit* 584, *responderoie* 2615). It is sporadic (cf. *ardra* 216, *metra* 1966, *rendroit* 571, etc.), the choice apparently determined by the syllable count.

Consonants

C/G: Characteristically for Picard, *c* before Latin *e* and *i* normally appears as *ch*, e.g. *cheler*, 1854, *decheü* 1362, *chité* 2982, *lanche* 178, and the demonstratives *chest*, *chele*, etc. There are a dozen spellings with *c*, e.g. *certes* 2323 (cf. 1516), *prince* 3244 (cf. 3094), *ciel* 1059 (cf. 1089) plus around forty demonstratives (quite common spelt with *c* even in Picard).[24] (Gossen §38). Along with *t* + *j*, *c* + *j* develops to *ss*. The form *grache* never appears even in Picard texts, and in the *Disme*, *grasse* rhymes with *masse* at 2969, consequently, rhymes such as *grasse : face* 2102, *place : face* (1251) may be ascribed to the poet, while spellings such as *grasse : plache* 1439, *faiche* (FACIAT) *: passe* 329, *cache* (QUASSAT) 2292, *glache* 2412, *hache* 1677 are scribal. The reflex of -ICIA/-ITIA/-ITIUM appears as both -*ise* and -*isse*/-*ice* (e.g. *conmandise : eglise* 2039, *avarisse : visse* 1710, *convoitise : atise* 1591). However, these forms also rhyme together, either as a poetic licence, or more likely as a result of a regional pronunciation in which the final voiced consonant is devoiced (cf. Gossen §49), e.g. *avarisce : devise* 1582, *justice : atise* 925, and cf. *aise : abais[s]e* 169, *aiguise : isse* 1033, *conduisent : puissent* 3015. The scribe often spells this ending as -*iche*, but this is not certified by the rhyme (*niches : visses* 1235, or *avariche : couvoitisse* 731, *serviche : delisse* 603, *: frankise* 811). The only anomaly here is *riche : niche* 1585 and *riches : visses* 2180 (see Gossen §41, 2°). The word *riche* does not appear elsewhere at the rhyme. The older form of the suffix, -*esse*, is authorial, though the scribe always writes -*eche* (e.g. *leeche :*

---

[23] And a purely scribal *capiteles* at 3005.

[24] *Ses* appears for *ces* in 1350 and 1789.

e[s]presce 2364, : princhesse 3261, tristreche : apresse 985, destreche : confesse 1891.[25] However, the author apparently allows himself two Picardisms in pereche : teche 1641 and povreche : pecce 1702. The reflex of -ENTIA is likewise mostly spelt -enche, but the only rhyme other than self-rhymes is conscïenche : apense 1869, cf. obedïenssse : apensse 3085. (For rhymes such as branke : penitanche, see below.) Word-finally the scribe has ch in douch 1529, esforch 857, tierch 1573, rench (pres.ind.1 of rendre) 251, 1495, though none of these is at the rhyme, and dous and tiers are much commoner. At 2309 sench (SENTIO) rhymes with sens (SENSUM). Similarly FORTIS gives fors rhyming with effors at 1193, cf. jors, travaus, crois (CRUCEM), vois, etc., all of which suggests the early Picard reduction of ts to s. Apart from Ezechïas and Yzaÿas/Yzaïes, the letter z appears only in hazard 2591 (Gossen §§39–40). Latin c + a is mostly written ca (e.g. caitif 223, escaper 850), though the centralizing spelling cha appears two dozen times, including nine examples of chascun as against twenty-nine of cascun, and nine examples of char (CARNEM) as against three of car. Where this a has become ie, kie is the commonest spelling (e.g. kief 1552, afikiés 1436), though chie is not far behind (chief 759, affichiés 2175), and cf. the rhyme cunkie : peccie 2296. Where a has become e, the scribe has spellings such as bouke, branke, etc. This is the only place where the c sound appears at the rhyme, but in our text these words rhyme only with themselves, or with the three Picardisms penitanche 1169, repentanche 1658 and croissanche 1828 (see above, and cf. rike for riche), though at 1299, the rare rasques does rhyme with Pasches. (Gossen §41.)

The three spellings goie (noun) 191, (verb) 192 and resgoï (497) reflect the Picard development of Latin g + a, but the forms joie (twenty-two times, e.g. 820), joiant (1059, 1457) and resjoïr (820) suggest a likely palatal pronunciation (Gossen §42). The reflex of AQUAM is normally iauge (e.g. 162, but see note to line 345, and cf. Gossen §43).

S: The conflation of s and ss (i.e. voiced and unvoiced sibilants) is mentioned above (cf. Gossen §49). Evidence for the disappearance of pre-consonantal s (= z) may be found in the rhymes blasme : ame (e.g. 201), blasme : diffame (3252),[26] not to

---

[25] Cf. the verb adreche : confesse 1408.

[26] Cf. the conjectural emendation estre : metre (2135).

mention the many scribal omissions and hypercorrections (e.g. *meïme* 4, *list* 1833). The fact that this *s* was silent may have encouraged the scribe in his occasional and idiosyncratic spelling *sr* for *r* before a stressed syllable in *mesra* (for *merra*, future of *mener* with assimilation of *n* + *r*) 197, *asesront* 419, *avesra* (future of *avenir*) 1877, *desrain* 754, *desraignier* 760, *esrrer* 1069, *esrrement* 1734, *esrranche* 2006. The spelling might also be influenced by the sporadic Picard development of *s* to *r* in words such as *varlet*, *dervé* (see Gossen §50).

B/V/W: The suffix -ABILEM normally has the learned form -*able*, though two scribal spellings reflect the distinctive Picard development to -*aule*, namely *couvenaule* (not at the rhyme) 1155, and *coupaules* (: *Dïauble*) 1495. The parallel form -*iule* from -IBILEM does not appear. (Gossen §§52–53.)

An intrusive *v* appears in the spelling of *jovene* 1541, 1708, and *Estievene* 310, presumably a Latinism, and, more mysteriously, in *pechavour* 2709 and *pechevor* 121. In the first three cases the letter cannot have been pronounced; in the last two, Röhrs suggests (p. 321) that it indicates the hiatus, in which case it might have been more sympathetic to print a *u*. Compare *efforchivement* at 499 (see note).

Germanic *w*- generally appears as *g* (*garir* 1777, *gerre* 613, *gile* 651), occasionally as *gu* before *e* and *i* (*guerre* 620, *guise* 2556), never as *w*, a symbol which is not used by our scribe. (Gossen §51, §54.)

R/L: Although the characteristic assimilation of *r* to *l* in *parler* (Picard *paller*) is not found, the scribe nonetheless appears to glance at it with the spellings *parlle* 2821 and *sourparllers* 3213. The *r* falls before a consonant in *herbegier* 843, 2980 and possibly in *inte[r]pretacïon* 1195 and *sou[r]plus* 2553. Compare *rep[r]egne* 1464, where dissimilation may be at work, though this is more likely to be a slip of the pen. Metathesis is found in *aprechevoir* 384, 568, 1265, 1849, 2310, *gouvreneres* 749, 3154; cf. *couvreture* 2313. One might also list here the forms *glouternie* 1550 and *gloutrenie* 2131, which appear alongside *gloutounie* 1633 and *gloutenie* 672, 2348. (Gossen §§55–57.) *Tristre* 922 and *tristreche* 985 have an adventitious *r*, perhaps as an echo of the first syllable. *Legistre* 223 has acquired an *r* to rhyme with *ministre*, and the opposite (and not uncommon) phenomenon of discounting an *r* at the rhyme is seen in *confessent : reverssent* 1337 and *garde : malade* 2224. The rather unusual *seront* for *selonc* appears twice

(503, 913), alongside fifteen examples of the usual form. (For the spelling *sr* for *r*, see above.)

Palatalized *l* is usually spelt *ll* medially: *conselle* 3250, *travalle* 2852, *falle* 710, *valle* 1536, while finally it has the typically Picard spelling *l*: *traval* 2159, *consel* 785, *orguel* 261. (The spellings *ill* and *il* appear very sporadically: *faille* 2851, *vaille* 914, *soleil* 1186). However, this is merely an orthographic convention, and this *l'* does not rhyme with *l* in our text, the only apparent exception being *cele : aparelle* 821, in all likelihood a defective rhyme. (Gossen §59.)

As is characteristic of Picard, there is generally no adventitious *d* in the group *l'r*, though the spelling usually shows a double *r*, e.g. *pourre* (: *rescourre*) 221, *taurroit* 1932, *vaurront* 40, cf. *assaure* 1425, *tauroit* 375; the only exception is *miudre* (MELIOR) 588, which Gossen maintains always has a *d* even in Picard. The same is true for *n'r*, *amenrrira* 2461, *couvenrra* 1946, *tenrrement* 948, *venrra* 1472, 2404, cf. *amenri* 2594, MS *revenries* 2411. The *n* is absorbed in *couverra* 1999, *souverra* (: *couvenrra*) 1945, *terroit* 1206, *verroit* 1205 (cf. *dourra* 198, 831). There are only two exceptions to this: *chendre* 221, 1180 and *remaindre* (: *fraindre*) 2857, of which the former never appears without the *d*, according to Gossen. There are two further rhymes here: *menrre : desfendre* at 645 (where the form seems to be scribal), but also *amenri : Henri* at 3167 (where it must be due to the author). The group *m'l* has the Central form with the intercalated *b* more often than not, e.g. *sambler* 1792 etc., *samblanche* 592, *emblent* 1752, *ensamble* 255, *trambler* 757, as against one example each of *assanllés* 747, *resanlle* 2259, *samle* 1333 and *humles* 2773, and four of *humlement* e.g. 2120. (Gossen §61.)

(See also the comments on the vocalization of *l* in the discussion of vowels above.)

M/N: Except word-finally (and before -*s* and -*t*), where only *n* appears, the scribe writes *n* or *m* indiscriminately after *a*, *e*, and *o*, e.g. *lamgue* 2090, *sanble* 1269, *contemdre* 1972, *menbres* 2269, *omques* 353, *ronpirent* 483, suggesting complete nasalization of these vowels and absorption of the nasal consonant. The case for *i* and *u* is not clear.[27] Final *n* occasionally has a following *t*, *sient* (MS) 485, *dant* 539, and *(a)dont* is the normal spelling of *(a)donc*

---

[27] See Röhrs p. 317.

(e.g. 304, 413; cf. 222 and *dont* < DE UNDE (MS) at 1912). See also the note to line 503. Adjectives in *-ant* form adverbs in *-aument* (*apa(i)raument* 369, 1746, *erraument* 1745, *plaisaument* 2821), perhaps influenced by adjectives in *-al* (e.g. *loiaument* 12).

The palatal nasal appears spelt *gn* (the usual spelling), e.g. *gäagnier* 1165, *ign* (almost as common), e.g. *gäaignier* 389, *ngn*, e.g. *gäangnent* 231, and *ingn*, e.g. *gäaingnier* 20.[28] In final position the spellings *ng* (*gäang* 1587) and *ing* (only in *oing* 2366) appear, as does the noteworthy *ig* in *besoig* (521, 1800, 2074, 2197) and *resoig* (522, 2196). When the spelling *ng* is followed, as it typically is, by *e* or *i*, the possibility of an affricated pronunciation must be considered. An affricate is surely intended in the rhymes *laidenge : venge* (1578) and *laisdenge : renge* (from *rendre*, 22), and one could read *menchongne : alonge* (1916) in the same way, though the spelling *alonge : menchoigne* (1792), might make one wary. Moreover, *alonge* also rhymes with *pardoigne* (1958) and *besoigne* (2117), which rather suggests that in *alonge : longe* (154, the only appearance of the adjective at the rhyme) the author intended the palatalized form *loigne*, despite the scribe's *longue* (2139) *longuement* (1759) and *longement* (2844). A few words do seem to have undergone a double development from Latin, e.g. LINEUM > *linge* and *ligne*, (cf. the doublet in our text of *mengier* 432 and *megnier* 1315), and there is some evidence that Picard favoured the palatal pronunciation in such cases (see Gossen §62). Perhaps this variability gave the author licence for the rhyme *eslongent : plongent* (234), the only other case in the text where a palatal seems to be ruled out. *Besoig* rhymes with *resoig* on two of its three appearances at the rhyme; at the third appearance (2074) it rhymes with *selonc*, which, like *longe* mentioned above, could conceivably be read as *seloign*. The *Anglo-Norman Dictionary* (*AND* — see Bibliography) does list a form *suluing*, but Tobler and Lommatzsch (T-L) do not have a single example of *seloign* in four and a half columns, and this is probably an imperfect rhyme (if the line is not actually corrupt).

---

[28] Cf. the isolated spelling *essoinne* 1455.

Morphology

The Noun Phrase

There are few curiosities of gender in the text: *j(ë)une* is feminine for the author (e.g. 2154, 2355), as is (not unexpectedly) *espie* (659), and there is one apparently feminine *usage* (2974, but see note). *Ost* is masculine at 352 and 648, but feminine at 755.

The two-case system of the noun phrase is generally well preserved, as is so often the case in Picard texts (cf. Gossen §63 end). However there are slips, for example where a word having a correct flexional *-s* rhymes with one that (correctly) lacks such an *-s*, an indication of the true state of affairs in the spoken language, e.g. *seront trop mains lassés De souffrir les qu'autres d'assez* (891), *cheus Qui vers nous sont fel et crueus* (1146), *Soient venïel ou morteus, J'en sui repentans et honteus* (1953). It will be seen that the scribe is generally at least as accurate as the author if not more so. There some two dozen such cases in the text. Cf. 1331, 1405, 1511, 1549, 1556, 1605, 1633, 1882, 2073.

Nouns derived from the Latin third declension (including *(preud)homme, abé, compain, conte, enfant, lerre, pastre, sire*) are generally used in textbook fashion,[29] the only exceptions being *prestre* (eleven examples, all oblique singular)/*prestres* (five examples, all nominative singular) and *fel* used as a masculine nominative plural adjective at 1146 (cf. 777). The comparatives (*menrre, graindre*, etc.) also have the approved forms on twelve occasions, with *gregneur* as masculine nominative singular at 786, *miudre* as oblique singular at 588 and *millors* as nominative singular at 2893. Nominative singular agent nouns *conmanderres, enblerres, gouvreneres* and *pecc(h)ieres* are all used classically, the only exception being *paintëours* at 2871. Elsewhere, forms in *-eur/our* are used 'correctly'. Mostly these are spelt with final *-eur/our*, though three learned forms have the Latinizing spelling *-or* (*confessor* 1395, 1781, *tutor* 2638, *creator* 807, cf. *createur* 326), and the suffix is monosyllabic. Rarely the suffix counts for two syllables, when the scribe writes *-eour* on three occasions (*paintëours* 2871, *pechëour* 972, 1469), and on two occasions just *-eur*, which has been emended to *-ë[o]ur* in the edition for the sake of clarity (*donnë[o]ur* 2452, *peccë[o]ur* 1941). Compare the

---

[29] Allowing for the frequent analogical *-s* on the nominative singular.

aberrant *pechavour* 2709 and *pechevor* 121. *Seur* 1934 and *Evain* 1110 are also used conventionally.

The corresponding adjectives (*grant, cruel, bruiant*, etc.) have the traditional feminine form on 121 occasions and the analogical form with final -*e* on forty-nine. Setting aside the cases where these adjectives appear before a vowel or in self-rhymes, we are still left with one hundred traditional forms to thirty-two analogical ones, a ratio of three to one. Since the analogical forms provide an extra syllable, the demands of the versification must frequently be decisive in the choice of one form or the other. Adverbs are formed only on the traditional stem (e.g. *griefment* 3184, *loiaument* 12), and it is a feature of the text that adjectives in -*ant* form adverbs in -*aument* just like adjectives in -*al* (*apa(i)raument* 369, 1746, *erraument* 1745, *plaisaument* 2821). The synthetic *graindre/ gregnour* appears seven times, compared to ten examples of *plus grant*.

The definite article *li* is always nominative. It is followed by a form with the appropriate flexional ending on all but two occasions (97, 1556). It is always syllabic, even before a vowel. Twice it is apparently feminine; at 355 we read *li mers*, vouched for by the metre, and which could be a Latinism, and at 995 *li premiere* (describing *cose*); cf. *li tiers (cose)* 1750 and the remarks under *un* below. Where *l'* is masculine, it is oblique singular on all but six occasions (*l'abaissier* 171, *l'airs* 344, *l'Orgueus* 746, *l'uns* 1888 and *l'autre* 1559, 1609, cf. 1709 — it will be seen that three of these forms lack the flexional -*s*). Special cases are *l'on* 1889 and *l'om* 2417, and the single instance of the pronoun spelt *l'em* at 25. Compare *le hom* at 585 and 1293 (where *le* is not syllabic), *le estre* 1442, and *le oume* 1938, the only other places where *le* is written for *l'*. Unsurprisingly for a Picard text, *le* is a feminine article on twenty-five occasions, (e.g. 204, 302), as against 254 examples of *la*. It is masculine nominative singular at 2073 (*le coutre : outre*) and 1986 (*le mal*, line internal). Before a consonant, *le* (edited as *lé*) appears three times for *les* (501, 1145, 1691). On the whole, the article combines with prepositions in the usual way; feminine *le*, of course, does not undergo enclisis (*de le* 1050, 2034, *a le* 2562). *En + le* generally gives *u* (twenty-two times, e.g. 80, 313), but there are five examples of *ou* (all in the last third of the text, e.g. 2351, 2863) and six examples of the extremely rare form *un* (see 191*n*). *A + les* is always *as, aus* appearing only as a pronoun (see below).

The indefinite article is usually written ·*i*·. Where it is written in full (used as an article or a pronoun), case distinction is observed in eleven cases out of twelve, the exception being line 830. On three occasions the pronoun *un* refers to a feminine word: 2719, where the antecedent is *maniere*, and 1746 and 1879 where the antecedent is *cose* (and cf. *li tiers* at 1750). The latter two instances are confirmed by the syllable count. *Uns* appears to be plural at 1955. (Gossen §63.)

Among the unstressed possessives, the Picard masculine oblique singular forms *men* (1335, 2609) and *sen* (455, 516, 787, 1137) appear, alongside the vastly commoner *mon* and *son*. In the feminine singular *se* appears six times (314, 732, 1238, 1608, 2214, 2322), though *sa* appears ninety-eight times, and *te* appears once (2276) against three examples of *ta*. *No* appears as masculine oblique singular at 669, 969 and 1142, and as feminine singular at 740, 667, 712, 1314 and 2411 (though *nostre* is three times as common). *Vo* is masculine oblique singular at 1533 and 2624, against one example of *vostre* at 2633. Except for one masculine nominative singular *nos* at 600, *nos* and *vos* are always plural. There are five examples of the analogical plural form *lors* (423, 1153, 1733, 2664, 2857); elsewhere the expected *lor* and *leur* appear (eleven examples). The stressed possessives are rare; there are only sixteen or so in the text, all masculine, and all but two are accompanied by a determiner (381, 1463). They show only expected forms. (Gossen §§66–69.)

The demonstratives (Gossen §70) present rather a complicated picture. Only four forms have initial *i-* (1319, 1484, 1753, 2937 — these are not mentioned separately below); spellings with *c-* rather than *ch-* are commoner among the demonstratives than they are in the scribe's orthography in general, but they are still outnumbered by more than ten to one.

The normal result of ECCE HOC is *c(h)e* or *c(h)'* (167 times), but there are twenty-two examples of the Picard stressed form *chou* (e.g. 75, 177). There are a further five examples of *c(h)e* used as a masculine oblique singular adjective (e.g. 524, 550), and two examples of the rare *chu* in the same function (842, 1645).

Combinations with ISTE give masc.nom.sing. *chis* (e.g. 897, 1463, a typically Picard form); masc.nom.pl. *c(h)ist* (1046, 2024); masc.obl.sing. *chest* (204),[30] *c(h)estui* (35, 1643); masc.obl.pl. *ches* (417); feminine singular *c(h)este* (249, 989), and plural *c(h)estes*

---

[30] Cf. 2029*n*.

(twice, at 721 and 2114). The form *c(h)es* is also used as feminine plural on sixteen of its thirty-one appearances (e.g. 255, 406, 3189), and the spelling *ses* appears at 1350 (masc.obl.pl.), and 1789, 1807 (fem.pl.).[31]

Combinations with ILLE give masc.nom.sing. *c(h)il* (fifty times, e.g. 8, 2165), *chius* (twice at 1328 and 1410), and *chieus* (again twice only at 167, 1476); masc.nom.pl. *c(h)il* (twenty-one times, e.g. 207, 210), *chiaus* (twice at 1703 and 2740), and *chaus* (once at 3009); masc.obl.sing. *cel* (once 1034), *c(h)elui* (thirteen times, e.g. 63, 242); masc.obl.pl. *chiaus* (twelve times, e.g. 39), *chaus* (five times, e.g. 1156) *cheaus* and *çaus* (once each, 2222 and 1752), *c(h)eus* (three times, 1145, 2669 and 3090), and *chieus* (only in 586 and 1504); fem.sing. *c(h)ele* (twenty times, e.g. 190, 199), and plural *celes* (twice, 464 and 1753). Finally, the form *c(h)eli* is feminine at 825, and masc.obl.sing. at 2794 and 2940. It is noteworthy that only the masculine forms in *-eus* appear at the rhyme (with *Dieus*, *crueus*, etc., see above), with the exception of *cheaus : aus* at 2222.

The ISTE-forms are overwhelmingly used as adjectives (89% are adjectival and only 11% are pronominal). ILLE-forms, on the other hand, are 85% pronouns and 15% adjectives.[32]

The personal pronouns offer a few points of interest. There are nineteen examples of *j'* and fifty-five of *je*, of which eight are post-verbal (six *veul je*, one *di je* and one *lo je*). Against this there are four examples of the Picard form *jou* (29, 845, 1458, 1573), two of which are postverbal (both following *veul*). The spelling *ge* also appears in *di ge* at 2681 (cf. 2785) and *tien ge* 2823. *Tu* is once reduced to *t'* before a vowel at 552. The typically Picard forms *mi*, *ti* and *si* do not appear, only *moi*, *toi* and *soi*. Again characteristically for Picard, the pronoun *le* is used eleven times for a feminine object (e.g. 526, 542), as against nine instances of *la* (cf. the use of *le* as a feminine article, mentioned above). The singular masculine stressed pronoun *lui* appears forty-three times; on a further two occasions (both in line 531) it is used with a feminine

---

[31] Cf. *ches* for *ses*, in all likelihood, at 1508.

[32] These figures mask an unexpected difference between masculine and feminine forms: the masculine ILLE-forms are 94% pronouns and 6% adjectives; the feminines, however, are only 43% pronouns and 57% adjectives. Aggregated, these figures give the percentages indicated above. No comparable gender distinction is discernible in the ISTE series.

antecedent. Otherwise *li* is the normal feminine stressed form, though *li* is masculine in some twenty cases (e.g. 327, 376). The form *eus* appears only at the rhyme (five examples, e.g. 353, 403), elsewhere the scribe uses the Picard form *aus* (fifteen times, e.g. 762 1298), including once in rhyme with *cheaus* at 2222.[33] (Gossen §§64–65.)

Among the relative pronouns, *que* (*ke*) is frequently used for *qui* (e.g. 9, 1498), though *qui* is seldom (or perhaps never) used for *que*.[34] *Qui* is used for *cui* (e.g. 1417), though, again, the reverse is not true. *Qui* often appears in the sense "if anyone" (e.g. 443, 1833).

The Verb

Characteristic of the text is the large number of doublets among the infinitive forms: *finer* 893 and *fenir* 2936, *jeüner* e.g. 2141 and *juner* e.g. 2148, *proier* e.g. 1388 and *prïer* 2740, *rechoivre* 2795 and *rechevoir* 3260, *tarder* 1743 and *targier* 1877, *veïr* 406, 2544 (cf. *pourveïr* 565) and *vëoir* e.g. 486, plus, possibly, *gerrier* 797n, and *gerroier* 3207 3228. In addition, both *fuier* and *fuir* are implied at 1252, 1915, 2158. Apophonous verbs almost always have canonical forms (*demeure* 327 ~ *demourer* 862, *treuve* 1383 ~ *trouver* 1251, *maine* 206 ~ *mener* 538, *paine* 344 ~ *pener* 575, *pris[e]* 834 ~ *proisiés* 1197, *lie* 526 ~ *loier* 531), as do the imparisyllabic verbs *aïe* 2709 ~ *aidier* 35, *mengüent* 2384 ~ *mengier* 432. There are a tiny handful of anomalies: *prïons* e.g. 2953 against *proions* 1141 and *proie* 1392 against *prie* e.g. 125 (infinitive *proier* e.g. 1388), and *parlle* 2821 against *parolent* 2273.

Pres.ind.1 has a final -*e* on four occasions (*apele* 203, *prie* 42, 2340, *renoie* 1496, all assured by rhyme or metre, but cf. *apel* 2414, 2441, *cuit* 1677, *lais* 896, *lo* 1461, *pri* 1544, 2278 etc.), but never a final -*s* (see *atent* 1517, *croi* 2309, *di* 248, *requier* 42, *sai* 1446, *vif* 962, *voi* 1509, etc.). The scribe uses the Picard ending -*ch* three times, twice in *rench* (251, 1495, both internal) and once in *sench* (SENTIO, 2309) in rhyme with *sens* (SENSUM). (Gossen §75.) Pres.ind.1 of *trouver* is *truis* 2608, with *trueve* 1232 used as pres.sbv.1 (see below). The pres.ind.3 form *paire* (from *paroir*

---

[33] On *i[l]* versus *i*, see note to line 333.

[34] See lines 2218, 2687 and 3236 (where *qui* may be for *cui*), and cf. lines 240 and 1392.

1178, : *faire*) is anomalous, and is presumably by analogy with the subjunctive.[35] There is a doublet in *va* (nine examples, e.g. 700) and *vait* (four examples, e.g. 98). There is one pres.ind.4 form which has the dialect ending *-oumes*, namely *encountroumes* 726 (: *soumes*, cf. fut.4 *iroumes* 840, and see Gossen §78). The (usually Western) ending *-on* appears three times, always on *faison* (: *raison* 152, : *orison* 1143, 3265 — all three oblique forms).

The first-person form *renge*, normally subjunctive, and commoner in Western French or Anglo-Norman than Picard, is found at line 22 in rhyme with *laisdenge*. It appears after *tant que* in the sense "until, up to the point where", which normally takes the indicative (cf. 702, 2049, 3208). *Trueve* 1232 (: *preve*) seems to be pres.sbv.1. The dialect ending *-aisse* (Gossen §71) does not appear. Pres.sbv.3 of *-er* verbs has an adventitious final *-e* on six appearances (*acorde* 1071, *grieve* 1624, *guie* 2940, *otroie* 3079, *rue* 1183 : *remue* 1184) but retains the traditional form on eleven (*ament* 1071, *barat* 652, *envoit* 3043, *frot* 1184, *gart* 1852, *jeünt* 870, *maint* < *mener* 1656, the curious *maint* < *mander* 3164n, *ost* 2109, *otroit* 789, *prit* 2110); *trouver* shows both *truise* (= *truisse*, cf. *truisent* 3088) 1390 and *truist* 1832. At 125 *sequeure* rhymes with *pleure*, while at 1402 *sequere* rhymes with *s'enquere*. There are four further doublets: *ait* (e.g. 27) and *aie* (1250 and 1852, both : *delaie*), *doigne* (e.g. 2417, cf. *pardoigne* e.g. 1958) and *doinst* (e.g. 2868, cf. *pardoinst* e.g. 1143), *puisse* (e.g. 1314) and *puist* (e.g. 88), *voise* (87) and *voist* (557). The Picard spellings *fa(i)che* and *faichent* (e.g. 2869, 903, 484) rhyme only with *grasse*, *passent*, etc., so the form *hache* (: *faiche*) at 1677 must likewise be scribal; similarly the spelling *meche* appears line internally at 3257, but *mete* appears three times, including a self-rhyme with *entremete* at 2986. Pres.sbv.3 of *escondire* is *escondisse* at 2836.

Imperat.5 of *prendre* shows the Picard dental stem in *prendés* 3130 and *aprendés* 1530, which do not appear in the indicative. Imperat.5 of *oïr* is usually *oés* (e.g. 1883) but appears once as *oiés* (2534), while *oing* is imperat.2 of *oindre*.

In the future and conditional, contracted forms are the norm,[36] generally spelt with double-*r*, e.g. *durra* 2891, *perseverra* 167,

---

[35] T-L has one further example of this form (in six columns) being used as an indicative.

[36] There are two exceptions in *ploureront* 1035 and *rentrera* 1437 (and see 2891).

poursivrrai 1680. The forms *couvenrra* 1946 and *venrra* 1472, *venrroit* 2404, *revenrions* 2411, show the characteristically Picard absence of the glide consonant (see above under phonology), also evident in *vaurroit* 2832, *vaurront* 40, 916 (from *vouloir*) and *taurroit* 1932, *tauroit* 375, 378 (from *tol(d)re* — for the vowel see above), while the commoner *couverra* 1999, *dourra* 198, *dourroit* 831, *souverra* 1945, *terroit* 1206 and *verroit* 1205 (from *venir*, cf. *verra* 1969, *verront* 1036, from *vëoir*), show the absorption of the *n*. The scribe's idiosyncratic spelling in *asesront* (= *asserront*) 419, *avesra* (= *aviendra*) 1844, *mesra* (= *menera*) 197, has also been commented on above. *Souferont* 890 may be a case of metathesis, but is more likely to be the contracted *souffront* with inserted schwa (cf. *perdera*, *istera*, etc. discussed among the atonic vowels, and *souffreroit* 137 — Hasenohr §154 (see Bibliography) suggests that this is a Northern form, cf. Gossen §74). The future stem of *avoir* appears twenty-four times as *ar–* (*ara*, *aront*, *aroit*, etc.) but there is one example of *airont* (: *saront* 1735) a result of the ambiguity of the graphy *ai* (see above). The future of *savoir* appears as *sara* 794, 1409 and *saront* 1736. There are no imperf.4 forms in the text, and only two cond.4 forms, which have two different endings: *revenrions* 2411 and the conservative *metriens* (disyllabic) 2401. The other endings of these tenses are as expected, with the exception of *iroumes* 840 (cf. *encountroumes* 726 and Gossen §78) and the anomalous *feroiie* (perhaps for *feroi je*, see 2716*n*). The dialect ending *-iemes* does not appear (Gossen §79). *Ert* appears twice as a future tense (247, 1594), and *iert* nine times (e.g. 34, 968), in competition with *sera* nine times (e.g. 184, 848). *Erent* is not found as a future tense, and *seront* appears five times (e.g. 420, 891).

Erent does appear as an imperfect at 348, while *estoient* appears at 281 and 3290. *Ert* is imperfect at 342 along with six examples of *iert* (e.g. 294, 1830), in competition with three examples of *estoit* (490, 517, 2145). Otherwise the imperfect endings all contain *-oi-*, there are no conservative *-ei-* forms, and no forms in *-oue*, *-eve* etc. from neighbouring dialects.

In the preterite and past subjunctive sigmatic forms are preserved throughout (*aquisist* 2304, *asesist* 4549, *desist* e.g. 540, *fesist* e.g. 333, *mesist* 1368, *mespresi[s]tes* 2626, *traisistes* 2628, *vausist* 2708, see Gossen §76). *Prendre*, whose past participle is spelt *prins* by the scribe (even in rhymes like *prinse : devise* 2229, though not at 1156 where it rhymes with *pris* < PRETIUM), has the preterite *prinst* e.g. 488, *prinrent* 481, and the past subjunctive *prensist* (manuscript *presinst*) at 1240. The Picard pret.6 ending *-isent* (Gossen §77) does not appear, only *-irent* (seven times). In stem-stressed preterite forms like *eut* 1099, *eurent* 510, *seurent* 1102, *peurent* 1101 we find only the Picard vowel, with the single exception of the interloper *ot* 514*n* (cf. Gossen §72). End-stressed Picard preterites in *-ui* and their corresponding past subjunctives (such as *euimes*, *euissiens*, see Gossen §73) do not appear, except for the pair *fuissiemes* : *ovrissiemes* 2398, which also provide the only examples of the Picard fourth-person ending *-iemes* in our text. In this context *ataquissiés* 2620 is something of an anomaly. Finally we should note the monosyllabic form *eust* used as a past subjunctive at 547, 806, 1367, 2330 (cf. pret.3 *eut* 1099, and the expected *eüst* four times e.g. 69, 1095).[37]

Vocabulary

The vocabulary of the text presents several points of interest. It contains many rare words and collocations, e.g. *amaritude* 995, *apens* 2879, *aqueste* 2582, *aspret* 136, *atendre l'estour* 657, *aval le vent* 220, *conqueste* 2581, *coreument* 2822, *definanche* 737, 1453, *esmanche* 1802, 1806, *estainte* 2513, *grevable* 2392, *pantain* 134, 137, 139, *ploumet* 2873, *point de l'eschequier* 2598, *raconforter* 2138, *resgardëure* 1023, *resoig* 522, 2196, *sire de la rote* 703, *sour esperanche de* 1323, *souräagié* 2737, *soutillanche* 204, *talenter* 2642, *targement* 477, *toupet* 2599, and many words and collocations used with an uncommon sense, e.g. *defenir* ("die") 971, *fraindre* (v.i. "break off, stop") 2858, *grigoise* ("dice game" usually *griesche*) 2592, *lumiere* ("lamp") 2388, *mais* (prep. "except, besides") 1685, *medechine* ("medicinal plant") 929, *mouvoir de* ("be inherited from") 1074, 2545, 3272, etc., *parrochien* ("parish priest") 1383, 1407, *passer* ("break" a rule) 329, 460, 485, *soi passer* ("behave") 469, *portement* ("behaviour") 1733. Indeed some of these expressions are hapax legomena, such as *acorderresse* 1224, *aigrure* 1191, *conqueste* 2581, *cultiverresse* 1223, *encheoir* (impersonal, "befall") 1094, *esperassïon* 1104, *estre en fuer a* ("be valued by") 2765, *maugré sa faiche* 1992, *miseranche* 1422, *outragier* (adj.) 2382, *prestanche* 1629, *puisor* 88, 97, 160, *resgardanche* 1721, *septesme* 1351. Other words are

---

[37] See also 1613*n*.

early appearances (taking a dictionary dating of around 1260 as indicative). Most of these are learned terms, such as *article* 1883, *demonstractïon* 1049, *diffamer* 2989, 3254, *dilatïon* 1237, 1363, 2989, *especialité* 2655, *e[s]presce* 2365, *obeissanche* 590, *passable* ("transitory") 2158, *priver* ("remove") 960, *suistanche* ("substance, not form") 2847, *tutor* 2638, *vaineglorïeus* 236, *voluntaire* 1901, 1988, 2001, though a few, such as *despiter* 2794, *espargne-malle* 2259, *lessive* 1175, 1201, 1370, etc., ·ix· *quilles* 2604, *ratiere* 1598, are everyday words that may have been in use for some time without previously appearing in writing.

Breymann's text has generally been very well read for T-L (and judiciously corrected in various places), but still a handful of expressions or senses have never been picked up, such as *apairaument* ("openly") 369, 1746, *apens* ("thought, reflexion") 2879, ?*apoursuivir* 2028, *apresse* 530, ?*a trie* 1775, *conquerant* ("obtainer") 2577, *despoire* 1086, *(nostre) eure est morte* (?"our hour has come") 1311, *foursser* (v.t.) 473, *medechine* ("medicinal plant") 929, *ordurie* 2723, *Patriarche* ("patriarch") 3153, *poissanche* ("prime") 1444, *restoble* 214, *roi de l'ost* 649, *Turqueman* 3226. All in all, Jehan de Journi appears to have been a lexical innovator of some talent.

Versification

The author avails himself of various doublets for the sake of the syllable count, standard examples, such as *com/come*; *encor/encore*, *grant/grande* etc., but also more idiosyncratic ones such as *juner* 2148/*jeüner* 2141; *miroir* 1731/*mirëoir* 781; *seeaus* (monosyllabic) 151/*seël* 150, etc. The word *seeaus* in the list above is just one instance of the scribe's occasional habit of adding inorganic *e* (with no syllabic value); others are *aversaiere* 2401; MS *capiteles* 3005; *croiere* 2789; MS *deerain* 1339, 1443, 1671; MS *faiere* (the first *e* subpunctuated) 2657; MS *haiene* 2299; *jovene* 1541; MS *leetre* 443, 1565, 1837; MS *ruee* 2333; MS *venuee* 2244.[38] On the other hand, the intercalated *e* in the future stem does have syllabic

---

[38] The spellings *aversaiere, faiere* and *haiene* may be scribal glances at the 'francien' reduction of the diphthong *ai* to *e*; *croiere* may have a similar explanation.

value (e.g. *renderoit* 584), and where the metre does not demand a syllable, the form without *e* is used (e.g. *rendroit* 377).[39]

There are forty cases in the text where the author appears to have permitted himself a measure of licence with hiatus for the sake of the syllable count. This affects only two words: *que* and *se*.[40] The four cases of *së* are all followed by the word *il*. In all its 142 appearances, *se* is written in full (rather than as *s'*) only four times before a vowel where elision is intended (525, 616, 644, 2322), and it is never used for elided *s'* before *il*, strongly suggesting that hiatus is intended in these four cases. *Quë* (*kë*) appears thirty-six times, twenty-seven times before the word *il*, seven before *on* and twice before *un*.[41] Both pronoun and conjunction are implicated. *Qu'il* and *qu'on* (always *c'on*, in fact) are much commoner, with 149 and fifteen examples respectively.

Roughly half the rhymes are masculine and half feminine, but with no patterned alternation. There are around 28% rich rhymes and a further 8% leonine ones (i.e. where the penultimate syllable of the line is also involved in the rhyme), again distributed at random, and not representing a deliberate striving for effect. About a third of the leonine rhymes are the result of a form having a prefix rhyming with a form that does not share it (e.g. *maintenir : tenir* 193, *vienent : avienent* 1045). The most noteworthy feature of the versification, however, is perhaps the author's extreme fondness for equivocal rhymes. These sometimes take the form of a noun rhyming with its related verb (*espie* = "(a) spy" : *espie* = "spies (on)", 659) but are often more inventive, e.g. *dure* = "hard" : *dure* = "lasts" 613, *fois* "faith" : *fois* "times" 1057. There are forty-five such rhymes in the text, not counting more elaborate rhymes such as *ostel* "house" : *ost tel* "such an army" 641, *mesdis* "lies, slander" : *mes dis* "my words" 1831, or *dit ai* "I have said" : *ditai* "I wrote about" 2785, making a total of 2.9% or so of all the rhymes, or nearly one equivocal rhyme every thirty lines.[42]

---

[39] For spellings such as *que ele* for *qu'ele*, see note 2 above.

[40] *Chë* appears four times as a stressed form after a preposition in competition with the form *chou* (ll. 1481, 1807, 2233, 2357); see also 1174*n*. In the sense 'nor', stressed *në* appears five times alongside *n'* (364, 855, 1309, 2081, 2403); see also 348*n*.

[41] See 866*n*.

[42] There are also three apparently identical rhymes in the text: 247*n*, 2210 and 2352.

BIBLIOGRAPHY

AND, see Rothwell below

Breymann, Hermann, *La Dime de penitance, altfranzösisches Gedicht verfasst im Jahre 1288 von Jehan von Journi und aus einer Handschrift des British Museum zum ersten Male herausgegeben von Dr Hermann Breymann für den litterarischen Verein in Stuttgart*, Bibliothek des litterarischen Vereins in Stuttgart 120 (Tübingen, 1874)

Bloomfield, Morton W., *The Seven Deadly Sins* ([East Lansing, Michigan], 1952)

FEW, see von Wartburg below

Foerster, Wendelin, Review of Breymann's edition in *Literarisches Centralblatt* (1876) pp. 20–22

Godefroy, Frédéric, *Dictionnaire de l'ancienne langue française*, 10 vols (Paris: Vieweg, 1880–1902, rpt. New York: Kraus, 1961). [**Gdf.**]

Gossen, Charles-Théodore, *Grammaire de l'ancien picard*, Bibliothèque française et romane, série A, n° 19, (Paris: Klinksieck, 1970)

Hasenohr, Geneviève, *Introduction à l'ancien français de Guy Raynaud de Lage, nouvelle édition* (Paris: SEDES, 1990)

Jacoby, David, 'La Littérature française dans les états latins de la Méditerranée orientale à l'époque des croisades : diffusion et création' in *Essor et fortune de la chanson de geste, Actes du 9e congrès de la Société Rencesvals, Padua, 1982* (Modena, 1984) pp. 617–46

Morawski, Joseph, *Proverbes français antérieurs au XVe siècle* (Paris: Champion, 1925)

Payen, Jean-Charles, *Le Motif du repentir dans la littérature française médiévale*, pp. 569–76 (Geneva: Droz, 1967)

Pope, Mildred K., *From Latin to Modern French, with especial consideration of Anglo-Norman* (Manchester: M.U.P., 1934, second (revised) edition, 1952)

Raymond of Peñafort [(St) Raimundus de Pennaforte], *Summa de Paenitentia*, ed. Xavier Ochoa and A. Diez (Rome, 1978)

Röhrs, Wilhelm, 'Sprachliche Untersuchung der Dime de Penitance (1288)' in *Romanische Forschungen* 8 (1896) pp. 283–351

Rothwell, William *et al.*, *Anglo-Norman Dictionary*, 7 fascicles (London: M.H.R.A., 1977–1992, second (revised) edition [A–E], 2005). [***AND***]

Segre, Cesare, 'Le forme e le tradizioni didattiche: Didattica morale, religiosa e liturgica' in Jauss, Hans-Robert (dir.), Jürgen Beyer (ed.), *Grundriß der romanischen Literaturen des Mittelalters* VI, 1 pp. 58–86, especially p. 72 (Heidelberg: Winter, 1968). [See also VI, 2, 1970, n° 2372.]

Sinclair, Keith V., 'The versified adaptation of the prone prayers by Jean de Journy' in *Romanische Forschungen* 92 (1980) pp. 247–50

Suchier, Hermann, Review of Breymann's edition in *Jenaer Literaturzeitung* 502 (1875) 550–52

Tobler, Adolf and Erhard Lommatzsch, *Altfranzösisches Wörterbuch*, 10 vols (Berlin: Weidmann, 1925–1936, Wiesbaden: Steiner, 1954–). [**T-L**]

von Wartburg, Walther, *Französisches etymologisches Wörterbuch*, 25 vols (Bonn: Schroeder *et al.*, 1922–). [***FEW***]

Wentzel, Siegfried, 'The Three Enemies of Man' in *Mediæval Studies* 29 (1967) pp. 47–66

LA DISME DE PENITANCHE

Ausi com chascuns crestïens
Si est tenus de tous ses biens
De rendre a Diu la droite dime,
4 Je — qui counois en moi meïme
Que j'ai de Diu maint bien eü
Et mainte grasse recheü
Dont j'ai paié poi de droiture,
8 Com chil qui poi ai mis ma cure
A faire chose qu'a Diu plaise,
De quoi je sui a grant mesaise —
Veul desormais a Dieu entendre
12 Et loiaument ma disme rendre.
Et pour che ke ma langue fole,
Qui a esté a fole escole,
A souvent dit mainte folie
16 Dont de Dieu est m'ame eslongie,
Especïaument en diter,
Si estuet il, pour aquiter
Moi des mesfais que ele a ja dis
20 Et pour gäaingnier Paradis,
Que je la bate et [la] laisdenge
Tant que ele a Dieu la disme renge
Des faus fabliaus que ele a trouvé.
24 Mais pour che qu'a droit fol prouvé
Doit l'en tenir tout crestïen
Qui raconter cuide nul bien,
Tant ait en lui grant counissanche,
28 Se Dieus ne li est en aidanche,
Jou, Jehans, sires de Journi,
Qui me counois a mal garni
D'engien soutill et de scïenche
32 D'usaige lonc ne de loquensce,
Requier a Dieu devotement,
Qui est et iert sans finement,
Qu'en chestui fait me veolle aidier,
36 Si que diter puisse et traitier
Cose qui me soit hounerable
Et quant a l'ame pourfitable
A moi et tous chiaus qui orront

40 Mes dis et entendre i vaurront.
Et a la benoite Marie
A jo[i]ntes mains requier et prie
Que ele pour moi son fil requiere   4r
44 Qu'en gré rechoive ma proiere.

Dieus, qui sor toute creature
Home ama tant qu'a sa figure
Et a s'ymage le forma
48 Pour che que li hom sa form[e] a,
Si veut que li hom si le serve
Qu'en bien servant le liu deserve
Que Lucifer perdi jadis —
52 C'est le siege de Paradis —
Et pour chelui fait proprement
Douna a l'oume entendement,
Et mist en lui sens pour connoistre
56 Le bien du mal por le bien croistre
Et pour le mal amenuisier;
Pour che doit a l'oume anoier,
Quant Dieus fourmé l'a a s'ymage,
60 Et il fait tant par son outrage
Qu'il pert le regne pardurable
Et laisse Dieu le merchïable
Pour rencheïr es mains chelui
64 Qui point de pité n'a de lui,   4v
Ains le heit de mortel haïne.
Pour che, li hom qu'a lui s'acline
Et en ses las se laist cheïr,
68 Sa vie doit forment haïr,
Car tout n'eüst li hom deserte
De Dieu servir, ne de sa perte
Ne son secours, si le deüst
72 Servir en tout quank'il peüst
De loial cuer sans changement
Pour ·iii· raisons: premierement
Pour chou ke ch'est grant honeranche
76 D'oume servir de grant poissanche,
Et qui sert Dieu, il sert tel houme
Qui trestout pueut et seit en soume,

Car plus de sens en lui abonde
80 K'en trestous chiaus qui sunt u monde,
Qu'il est fontaine de scïenche.
Nus hom, tant ait boine loquenche,
Ne porroit dire les deus pars
84 Du sens qui est en lui espars,   5r
Car nus hom ne pueut sens avoir
S'en la fontaine de savoir
Ne se voise tant abaissier
88 Qu'il puist a son puisor puchier
De la douche fontaine et clere
Qui nous doune sens et matere,
Puiske nos bien beü avons,
92 Conment deffendre nous savons
De l'Anemi ki nous veut faire
Par son engin maint grant malfaire.

Or est il drois ke je vous die
96 Que la fontaine senefie
Et li puisor et la cordele
Qui vait jusqu'a la fontenele,
Lau il s'estuet mout abaissier.
100 De la fontaine orrés premier:
Mainte vertu a la fontaine,
Car tous jours cueurt, tous jors est plaine;
Nus ne la pueut amenuisier
104 Pour sovent au ruissiel puchier.   5v
La fontaine si senefie
Le benoit fil sainte Marie
En cui tous sens ici s'ensache
108 Qu'il n'est persone ki riens sache
Qui de lui n'ait le sens eü
Et de sa grasse recheü.
Si dist sains Paus et le conferme
112 Que ses sens onques n'[en] amerme
Nient plus c'on ne voit amermer
Fu pour candelles alumer.
Encore i a sambla[n]che bele
116 De Dieu et de la fontenele,
Car la fontaine a tel nature

       Que sor gravele, qui est dure
       Et bien poignans, la si sort ele.
120 Or entendés par la gravele
       Le pechevor ki concheüs
       Est en pechié, et rencheüs
       Souventes fois par vanité,
124 Si recounoist s'iniquité
       Et prie Dieu qu'i[l] le sequeure,   6r
       Et gehist ses pechiés et pleure
       Si que moullie en est sa fache.
128 Lors vient la fontaine de grasse
       Qui moult aime tere moullie
       Pour che qu'ele est plus tost perchie,
       Si laisse arrier la tere roiste
132 Et si s'en cueurt parmi la moiste,
       Et si tres fort a li s'acoste
       Que de li tout le pantain oste,
       Et remain[t] la gravele nete
136 Qui est poignans, dure et asprete,
       Si que pantain ne souffreroit,
       Car l'iaugue aval l'emporteroit.
       Li pantain sunt males pensees
140 Et males euvres, qui lavees
       Sunt du ruissel de la fontaine
       Qui tant est douche, clere et saine.
       Li ruissaus est confessïons,
144 Li courres satiffassïons,
       Qu'ausi com li courres afine
       La fontaine, fait l'ame fine   6v
       Li satiffaires des mesfais
148 C'on a par negligenssse fais.
       Or estuet il que je vous conte
       Du sëel ki descent et monte.
       Li seeaus demoustre par raison
152 Les boines euvres que faison
       Qu'a Dieu nous mainent sans alonge,
       Mais que la corde soit bien longe
       Qu'avenir puist a la fontaine.
156 La corde ki le sëel maine
       Aval nous doune demoustranche

Qu'en bien aions perseveranche;
Car tout ausi com il avient
160 Quant li puisors aval s'en vient
Et la corde est ou courte ou route
Quë on n'en trait de l'iauge goute,
Ausi, sachiés, nus crestïens,
164 Combien qu'il puist faire de biens,
Ne peut avoir la Dieu aidanche,
S'en ses biens n'a perseveranche.
Mais chieus qui bien perseverra
168 Tout par loisir boire porra
De l'iauge assés et a grant aise,
Mais qu'au puchier ·i· peu s'abaise.
Que senefie l'abaissier?
172 Que chil se doit humilïer
Qui veut a Dieu avoir recours,
Ou autrement n'ara secours
Pour riens k'il faiche ne k'il die
176 S'il en son fait ne s'umelie.
De chou trouvons grant demoustranche:
Un sëel qui aval se lanche
Vuis, et revient plains contremont,
180 Che nous demoustre et nous semont
Qu'il nous estuet tout au premier
De tous nos cuers humelïer
Et puis puchier de la fontaine;
184 Et quant la cane sera plaine,
Ch'est quant nous bien beü arons
Du sens de Dieu, lors monterons
Encontremont trestout carkié
188 De l'iauge clere de pitié
Qui nous ensegnera la voie
Com chele qui les boins avoie
D'aler un Paradis de goie
192 La ou nus n'est qui ne se goie.
Pour che si fait moult boin tenir
Humelité et maintenir,
Car chil qui s'umelïera
196 Dieus dist kë il l'ensauchera
Et le mesra amont en gloire,

Qu'il li dourra de l'iauge a boire,
Dont est cele droite scïence
200 Qui doune a l'oume counissance
De garder soi de mauvais blasme
Et de suagir son cors et s'ame.
Je n'apele pas counissanche
204 De chest monde le soutillanche,
Car la scïenche si est vaine
Qui en infer son maistre maine,
Et cil qui l'apelent scïenche
208 Atendre puent grief sentence;
Car nous trouvons en Ysaïe   *8r*
Que chil qu'au mal dounent aïe
Et chil qui dïent du mal bien
212 Atendre pűent une rien,
Que, tout ausi come li fus
Art le restoble et art le fus
Par la calour de la grant flame,
216 Ausi ardra li cors et l'ame
De chiaus ki la male scïenche
Tesmoigneront a sapïenche.
Et lor scïenche, que fera?
220 Aval le vent s'envolera
Si com feroit ou chendre ou pourre.
Coment se porront donc rescourre
Chil avocat et chil legistre
224 Qui sont de l'Anemi menistre,
Pour che qu'il sont si menchongnier
Qu'a tous tesmoignent pour loier
Le mal a bien et le comferment?
228 Par lor faus tesmoins si aferment
Le dit saint Augustin a voir,
Que ainsi repreuve lor savoir,   *8v*
Qu'il dist que li niche gäangnent
232 Dieu et li sage se mehangnent,
Car par lor sens de Dieu s'eslongent
Tant qu'en infer aval se plongent.
Et li caitif maleüereus
236 Qui tant sont vaineglorïeus
Que par lor sens devienent faus,

Ne sevent il que dist sains Paus
Et qu'as Corrintiens commanda
240 En l'epistle qu'i[l] lor manda
Tout droit un tressime capitle?
Iluec si dist en celui title
Que chil qui sont au monde sage
244 Devant Dieu sont plain de folage,
Et que Dius les oublïera
Et lor scïenche perdera.
Ensi en ert il vraiement,
248 Pour coi je di tout vraiement
Que tous li sens de cheste vie
Nous vient de la Diu cortoisie,   9r
Et pour che di et rench sentensse
252 Qu'en Dieu est toute sapïence.

Du sens de Diu vous ai conté,
Et par le sens de sa bonté,
Car ches ·ii· coses sont ensamble;
256 Or est il drois, si com moi samble,
Que du pöoir je vous redie
Par qui Dieus souvent nous castie
Et si nous fait humelïer,
260 Pour che que le volons laissier
Par grant orguel qui nos cuert seure
Et qui a nous hounir labeure,
Dont nous devons avoir vergongne.
264 Sainte Escripture nos tesmoigne
Que Dieus est poissans en tous lius,
En tere, en mer, en air, es chieus,
Partout si est sa grans poissanche.
268 Du ciel avons nos demoustranche   9v
Par Lucifer, qu'il abati
Du ciel, pour chou qu'il s'enbati
En orguel, ou nus ne pueut estre
272 Qui veut sëoir a la Diu destre.
Encor le nous moustra il mieus
Quant venir fist le fu des cieus
Pour ardoir Sodome et Gomorre;
276 Et si le nous moustra encore

       Trop bien, se le volons entendre,
       Par la pluie qu'il fist descendre
       Du ciel pour le monde noier
280   Au tans Nöe, pour espurgier
       Les pechiés qui si grant estoient
       Qu'un ciel devant Diu tant puoient
       Qu'a Dieu si forment anoia
284   Que pour che tout le mont noia,
       Fors que Nöe et sa maignie
       Quë il en avoit espargnie.
       En la vies loy tout ce trouvons,
288   Mais par la neuve le prouvons
       Trop mieus en la nativité,
       Que Dieus rechut humilité,   *10r*
       Car adont li pasteur si virrent
292   Angles qui des cieus descendirent
       Et lor conterent la nouvele
       Que Dieus iert nés de la Pucele.
       Ausi cheste cose mëesme
296   Aparut le jor du bauptesme
       Ou Jesu Cris fu baptisiés,
       Dont li Diauble fu engingniés
       Et moult honteusement matés,
300   Si com tesmoigne sains Mathés:
       Si tost com fu baptisiés, Dieus
       Ouvri le porte des grans cieus
       Qui tres le tans Adan fu close;
304   Dont sor chest point si dist la glose
       Que puisque soumes baptisié
       Le ciel avons aparellié,
       Quar tous jors est la porte ouverte.
308   Cheste cose fu bien aperte
       Au jor que Guïs s'asamblerent
       Et saint Estievene lapiderent
       Si que des pierres fu couvers;   *10v*
312   Adont li fu li cieus ouvers
       Si qu'il vit Diu ens u ciel estre
       Et son fil sëoir a se destre.
       Aprés en avons demoustranche
316   Quant Dieus fu ferus de la lanche,

Car li solaus point de lumiere
Ne vaut douner d'une eure entiere,
Et la lune si en perdi
320 Clarté si que point n'en rendi.
Par la raison que j'ai moustree
Est la poissanche demoustree
Que Dieus si a dedens ses cieus;
324 Aprés orrés des autres lieus
Qui tout le vont obeïssant
Et a createur comnissant.

Li airs et quanqu'en li demeure
328 Obeïst Diu et si l'onneure
En tant que ses quemans ne passe.
Que cheste cose li airs faiche   *11r*
Essample avons de saint Elye,
332 Qu'a Dieu prïa par grand pitie
Qu'il fesist tant, s'i[l] li pleüst,
Que dedens ·iii· ans ne pleüst,
Et Jesus Cris li otrïa;
336 Et il aprés li reproia
Que la pluie venist arriere,
Et Dieus fist toute sa proiere.
Et cheste cose ausi parut
340 Quant l'estoile as rois aparut,
Car ele parmi l'air couroit,
Et en l'air ert et demouroit.
Donc est il bien cose certaine
344 Que l'airs de Dieu servir se paine.

Ausi fait l'iaige, sans doutanche;
De chou avons nous demoustranche
Par les Juïs qui mer passerent
348 C'onques lor piés molliés n'ierent,
Ains s'en passerent tout seür
Comme sour pont fait de boin mur,   *11v*
Mais Pharäons et sa manie
352 O tout son ost furent noïe
C'omques n'en eschapa nus d'eus.
Ausi nous conte sains Matheus

          Que li mers si obeïssoit
356   A Dieu, si que sor li passoit
          Com se che fust en tere ferme.
          Ausi sains Mars si nous conferme
          Que li vens a venter laissoit
360   Et que la mers si s'acoisoit
          Du tout a som quemandement.
          Dont pert il bien que entierement
          L'iaige ne fait fors che qu'il veut,
364   Në autre riens faire ne pueut;

          Con fait la tere sans doutanche:
          Ains porte a Dieu tel houneranche
          Que nule fois ne rendera
368   Fors tant com Dieus commandera.
          Car nous trouvons aparaument
          Un livre du vies testament
          Que chil qui bien a Dieu rendroient   *12r*
372   Lor dime, que de Dieu aroient
          Des biens assés et a fuison,
          Mais qui par fausse desraison
          Tauroit a Dieu sa droite dime,
376   Que Dieus de li ne feroit cure,
          Ains li rendroit tele saudee
          Qu'il li tauroit pluie et rousee
          Et sa tere seroit brehaigne.
380   Qui chifle Dieu ainsi gäagne,
          Car qui a Dieu taut les siens biens
          Dieus li retaut le plus des siens.
          Quant aucuns veut Dieu dechevo[i]r,
384   Il s'en set bien aprechevoir,
          Si l'en rent leus itel loier
          Que riens ne puet frutefier
          Que planter fache ne semer,
388   Nient plus com en sablon de mer.
          Ensi doit li hom gäaignier
          Qui Jhesu Crist quide engingnier.
          Encor de chou essample avons,
392   Se bien entendre le savons,   *12v*
          Quant Jhesus fu crucefïiés,

Car li temples en ·ii· moitiés
Fendi et les pierres fendirent,
396   Li monument si äouvrirent
Et s'en issirent pluiseur mort,
Ausi le tere craulla fort
Pour Dieu qui lors souffri martire
400   Pour la crüel mort desconfire.
Ainsi si servent fermement
A Dieu trestout li element
Et quanqu'i[l] est enclos en eus,
404   Fors que san plus li perecheus
Qui mieus li devroit obeïr.
Par ches raisons pöons veïr
Qu'en Dieu si est toute nobleche,
408   Et puisqu'il est de tel hauteche
Nus n'ara ja hounour gregnour
Com de servir si grant segnour,
Car li proverbes dist et conte
412   "Serjans de roi est pers a conte."
Et qui sert dont roi si poissant   *13r*
A qui tout est obeïssant
En pueut bien faire par raison
416   De lui droite comparison
A ches autres rois terrïens,
Car ja pour leur terrïens biens
A la table ne s'asesront
420   La ou li serjant Dieu seront
Assis moult hounerablement,
S'i[l] ne veulent premierement
Lors grans orgueus trestous laissier
424   Et envers Dieu humilïer
Et puis si serjant devenir.
Ensi porront il avenir
Par bien servir a la grant table
428   Qui as boins est moult delitable;
Et puisquë il estuet a force
Que cascuns princes si s'esforce
D'estre serjans au roi de gloire,
432   S'il veut u ciel mengier ne boire
De celui mengier glorïeus

    Qui si boins est et presïeus   *13v*
    Q[ue] nus qui pueut de li taster
436 Jamais ne veut d'autre gouster,
    Dont pert il bien apertement
    Que de servir Dieu seulement
    A on trop plus grant houneranche
440 Que d'estre rois de toute Franche.

    La seconde raisons est teus,
    Qu'en tout le mont n'est hom morteus,
    Qui bien en recordast la letre,
444 Qui ne deüst s'entente metre
    En servir Dieu tout son äage
    A son pöoir de ferm courage.
    Uns philosophes renoumés
448 Qui par non est Proclus noumés
    Si dist que cose qui se veut
    Movoir par soi par force me[u]t
    Ou par nature de croissance,
452 Ou par vie, ou par counissanche.
    Erbes par croissanche s'esmeuvent
    Au quemant Dieu quanqu'eles peu[v]ent, *14r*
    C'onques de sen quemant n'en issent,
456 Mais au quemant Dieu raverdissent,
    Et puis flourissent, et puis portent
    Les fruis, et puis aprés s'amortent
    Tant que lor saisons reconmenche,
460 Sans passer point l'obedïenche
    Qu'il ont de Jesu Crist eüe.
    Cheste vertu ont recheüe
    Par croissanche qui est en eles;
464 Et par vie s'esmeuvent celes
    Qui ont a la croissanche aïe
    De mouvoir par raison de vie,
    Si com poissons, oisaus et bestes
468 Qu'a Dieu servir sont toutes prestes,
    Car en chest monde si se passent
    Que le quemant Dieu ne trespassent.

    Premiers vous diray des poissons:

472	Quant li tans vient et la saisons,	
	Adont si fourssent lor semenche	
	Et font quamk'il afiert a eus,	14v
	Et se lor Sires glorïeus	
476	Lor fait aucun commandement,	
	Tantost le font sans targement.	
	Ce nous moustre Dieus par le cete	
	Qu'engoula Jonas le prophete,	
480	Et par les apostles qui misrent	
	Leur rois a destre, puis si prinrent	
	Tant de poissons qüe il enplirent	
	Lor vaissaus, et leur rois ronpirent.	

484	Que le gré Dieu li oisel faichent	
	Et que le sien quemant ne passent	
	Par le coulon pöons vëoir,	
	Qu'en tai ne se vaut assäoir,	
488	Mais prinst le rain de l'olivier	
	Et a l'arche s'en vint arrier	
	Dont il estoit partis anchois.	
	En la vie de saint Franchois	
492	Trouvons que, quant il sarmonnoit,	
	Que Dieus tel grasse li dounoit	
	Que li oiselet si venoient	15r
	A son sarmon si l'escoutoient,	
496	Et kant il l'avoient oï,	
	De la Dieu grasse resgoï	
	En lor langage Dieu löoient	
	Et efforchivement chantoient.	

500	Ausi vëons nous tous jours prestes	
	Au Dieu servir toutes lé bestes,	
	Car chascune vit en son liu	
	Seront l'ordounanche de Diu	
504	Ne n'en i a nule si ose	
	Qui aprés son kemant repose,	
	Mais toutes li font reverenche.	
	De chou avons nous demoustranche	
508	Par les lïons qui n'ade[se]rent	
	A Danïel, mais devourerent	

```
            Chiaus qui de mal l'eurent reté
            Tantost qu'il i furent jeté.
512         Ausi trouvons nous en la Vie
            Des Peres qu'en une abeïe                    15v
            Ot ·i· abé; Pol se noumoit.
            ·I· jour a[s] chans tere femoit;
516         O li avoit Jehan, sen moine,
            Qui estoit plains de grant sinpleche.
            "Jehan," dist Paus, "va si t'adreche
            Envers l'estable de nos beus
520         Et du fumier pren a nostre eus,
            Car nous en avons grant besoig."
            Jehans li dist par grant resoig:
            "Une lïones[se] demeure
524         En che liu qui la gent deveure."
            "Jehan," dist Paus, "se ele keurt seure
            A toi, si le me lie en l'eure
            Et si la maine o le fumier."
528         Jehans vint la sans delaier,
            Et quant le vit, la lïonesse
            Vers li courut par gran[t] apresse,
            Et il vers lui pour lui loier.
532         La lïonesse traist arrier
            Si s'en ala forment fuiant;
            Jehans aloit aprés crïant                    16r
            "A! lïonesse, fole beste,
536         Atent ·i· peu et si t'areste,
            Car il estueut que je te lie
            Pour toi mener en l'abeïe
            Pour presenter a dant abé,
540         Qu'il ne desist ke l'ai gabé."
            La lïonesse se tint coie;
            Chil le loia de sa coroie,
            Et puis l'en a a tant menee
544         Et a l'abé l'a presentee
            Qui en son cuer forment löoit
            L'obedïence qu'il vëoit.
            Et de parole l'eust löee,
548         Mais doute avoit en sa coree
            Vaineglore ne s'asesist
```

Se de ce fait nul bien desist,
Si li parla en entredeus:
552 "Ausi com t'es cose morteus
Qui as en toi peu de scïence
Ne de sens ne de sapïence,
As amenee beste nise;
556 Laisse l'aler que maus n'en isse
Si qu'ele voist tout a garant."
Par ches raisons est apparant
Que les bestes bien fermement
560 Tienent le Dieu commandement.

Li hom si a vie et poissanche
Et le vertu de comnissamche,
Et puisqu'en li sont ches ·iii· coses
564 Qu'en autre riens ne sont encloses
Trop mieus se doit il pourveïr
De Dieu fermement obeïr
Que les autres coses ne doivent
568 Qui n'ont ne sens ne n'aprechoivent
Fors que seulement de nature.
Li hom si doit metre sa cure
A Dieu servir sans mesproison,
572 Pour che qu'il a sens et raison,
Car ch'est bien cose couvenable,
[Car] rainable cose hom raisnable
Se doit pener toudis de faire,
576 Et de raisnableté la maire,
Si est de porter reverensse,
Honneur et grant obedïensse
A chelui dont on a eü
580 Pluiseurs biensfais et recheü,
Car il n'est hom si menuiers
Qu'il ne dounast moult volentiers
A chelui dont il cuideroit
584 Qu'a ·xx· doubles li renderoit;
Dont le doit le hom faire trop mieus
Et trop de melleur cueur a chieus
Dont il a ja eü le don,
588 Et rendre miudre gerredon

Qu'a chiaus que as dons font atendanche;
Dont devons plus d'obeïssanche
A Dieu qui nous daigna former
A sa samblanche et enfourmer
En la vertu de comnissanche,
Et puis fu ferus de la lanche
Ens en la crois, ou il rechut
La mort, dont l'Anemi dechut *17v*
Par son grant sens et son savoir,
Pour nous a son serviche avoir;
Et puisque tant de biens nous fist
Et nos serviches seul souffist
A lui, bien devons travellier
De lui bien rendre son loier,
C'est a savoir nostre serviche
Qu'il aime plus que nul delisse,
Car autre cose ne demande,
Dont devons metre paine grande
De lui en tel endroit servir
Que son gré puissons deservir.

Or entendés l'autre raison
Pour coi li hom fait mesproison
Qui ne sert Dieu de tout son cuer:
Li hom se jete bien en pueur
Qui a gerre crüel et dure
Et que toudis li croist et dure
Pour lui hounir et metre a mort,
Se a aucun houme ne s'amort
Qui ait pöoir de lui deffendre
Vers chiaus qui le veulent offendre. *18r*
Cascuns hom le devroit dont querre,
Car cascuns hom a mortel guerre
A l'Anemi crüel et fort
Qui tous jors met tout son effort,
Par sens et par soutilleté,
Coment il ait l'oume jecté
En sa prison maleüereuse
Qui si male est et perilleuse
Que nus ne met dedens le pié

628	Qui jamais ait le cuer haitié.	
	Li Anemis est li Dïaubles	
	Qui si faus est et dechevables	
	Que de guerre set tous les poins	
632	Quant aucun tien[t] dedens ses poins.	
	Et tout soit il poissans guerriers,	
	Si pourcache il moult volentiers	
	Grans aiues, pour mieus conquerre	
636	Chiaus envers qui il a sa guerre;	
	Et che pert bien, car pourcachié	
	A il ja tant et travellié	
	Qu'en nostre ostel si a sa gaite	
640	Qui nous espie et nous agaite;	*18v*
	Et quant venons dehors l'ostel,	
	Encontre nous a ·i· ost tel	
	Que ne pöons souffrir sa forche,	
644	Se aucuns puissans hom ne s'esforche	
	De nous encontre lui desfendre.	
	Et ch'est encor du tout le menrre,	
	Car tost nous soumes conbatu	
648	Qui tout l'ost avons confondu.	
	Aprés, li rois de l'ost s'en vient	
	A qui conbattre nous couvient,	
	Et il set tant gile et barat	
652	Qu'il n'est nus hom k'il ne barat,	
	Tant soit fors ne preus ne seürs,	
	S'il n'est si plains de boins eürs	
	Quë il pourcache tant et quere	
656	Qu'il ait aiue boine et fiere	
	Et qu'il puist bien l'estour atendre.	
	Or vous veul je dire et aprendre	
	Qui est chele crueus espie	
660	Qui en nostre ostel nous espie,	
	Et l'ost qui par dehors demeure	
	Qui nous atent pour courre seure.	*19r*
	L'espie qu'aveuc nous sejorne	
664	Et qui a nous hounir s'atourne	
	Est nostre chars a qui servons	
	Tant que nous nous en aservons.	

	Car quant no char bien nourrissons	
668	Double damaje nous faisons,	
	Car nous norrissons no contraire,	
	Si ne pöons nesun bien faire	
	Tant que sur nous ait segnourie.	
672	Trop est vix cose gloutenie,	
	Car despuis que li hom est ivres,	
	Il est de tous les biens delivres;	
	Il pert de Dieu toute l'aïde	
676	Et assés plus quë il ne cuide,	
	Car il en pert la connissanche,	
	Et puisqu'a li a fait fallanche	
	Il n'est nus maus qu'il ne desist	
680	Qu'il ne penssast et ne fesist.	
	Dont, ki se veut a droit garder,	
	Il se doit premiers resgarder	19v
	Que sa char si fort ne nourrisse	
684	Qu'au trespasser pour li perisse;	
	Car che nous dist Tulles li sages	
	Que nus ne fait plus grans damages	
	Com puet faire privés amis	
688	Quant on en li son quer a mis,	
	Ausi la chars qu'est bien peüe	
	L'oume tantost honnist et tue	
	Puisqu'ele est ·i· peu sejornee.	
692	Grans repos fait fole mellee,	
	Ausi la chars bien reposee	
	En orguel est tantost montee	
	Si qu'ele taut premierement	
696	A son segneur entendement,	
	Et puis aprés, comme vaincu	
	Qui n'a espee ni escu	
	Dont couvrir se puist n'asalir,	
700	Col estendu s'en va salir	
	En luxures et en pechiés	
	Tant que en infer est trebussiés,	
	Et qui est sires de la route	20r
704	Que cascuns hom si fort redoute.	
	Pour che, qui veut adroit conbatre,	
	Il doit sa char premiers abatre	

La Disme de Penitanche

   Desous ses piés, si qu'ele serve
708 Lui com segnour et soit sa serve,
   Car quant Maufés fait la batalle
   Encontre nous, si a sans falle
   La chars la batalle premiere.
712 Pour che qu'ele set no maniere
   Et qu'ele est de nous plus privee
   Si a la premiere melee,
   Si se conbat et nuit et jour
716 Encontre nous sans nul sejour,
   Et s'ainsi est qu'ele nous puet
   Desconfire, ja plus n'estuet
   Qu'autre cose nous queure seure,
720 Car leus tout maintenant en l'eure
   En tous pechiés nous laissons courre
   Sans ja penser de nous rescourre.
   Mais se la chars est desconfite,
724 Por che n'est pas la guere quite, *20v*
   Car ausi tost come nous soumes
   Hors de l'ostel, si encontroumes
   La batalle crüele et fiere
728 Du monde, ki en la frontiere
   Envie a mis, cui Dieus confonde,
   Ire [a] la batalle seconde,
   Et la tierche maine Avariche
732 Et se cousine Couvoitisse.
   Par ches batalles renoumees
   Qui crueus sont et redoutees
   Li mondes cascun jor nous tente
736 Et si nous doune tele entente
   Et jour et nuit sans definanche
   Que tout venons prins a grant route.
   Et s'il avient par aventure
740 Que no batalle soit si dure
   Que toutes chestes desconfisse
   Et que cascune camp gerpisse,
   Pour che n'est pas li hom delivres,
744 Car aprés vient li plus grans cuivres, *21r*
   Chou est li grans arrierebans
   La ou l'Orgueus et li Beubans

	Est assanllés, sachiés trestous.	
748	Li tirans qui moult est estous,	
	Qui de tout l'ost est gouvreneres,	
	De cheste eskiele est commanderres,	
	Lau il a moult de gent maudite	
752	Qu'il a tr̈iee et toute eslite	
	Pour faire as eskieles secours,	
	Qu'en la desraine est li recours	
	De toute l'ost et le fïanche.	
756	A tel orguel et tel beubanche	
	Que toute terre fait trambler	
	S'en vient il a nous asambler.	
	Orguel nous met un chief premier	
760	Et Negligensse au desraignier;	
	Par ches ·ii· visses sus nous cort,	
	Et si nous tient par aus si court	
	Et nous en va si arresnant	
764	Qu'a peu ne soumes recreant,	
	Car sa temptassïons ne chesse,	
	Mais toutes eures nous apresse	*21v*
	Com chil qui set nostre couvine	
768	Qui des chevaus jus nous souvine	
	Souventes fois, si k'il nous porte	
	Comme veincus jusqu'a la porte	
	De sa prison ou il nous lance,	
772	Ki a a non Desesperanche,	
	Et puisque la soumes venu,	
	Dont nous est il mal avenu.	
	Par che pert bien ke nous afaire	
776	Avons a crüel aversaire;	
	Et puisqu'il est fel et crueus,	
	Soutius, poissans et engigneus,	
	Si que ne nous pöons desfendre,	
780	A tout le mains nous devouns pendre	
	Devant nos ieus pour mirëoir	
	Che qu'ensement pöons vëoir.	
	Car quant aucuns povres a guerre	
784	A grant segnor, tantost va querre	
	Consel de aucun si grant segneur	*22r*

La cui poissanche soit gregneur
Que n'est cele de sen contraire,
788 Si li fait leus requeste faire
Qu'i[l] li otroit par courtoisie
De prend[r]e le de sa maisnie,
Sans che quë il li couste riens,
792 Si li fera honour et biens;
Et si grant pourfit en ara
Que, quant ses anemis sara
Qu'a tel segneur est chil venus
796 Et est ses vallés devenus,
Ja puis ne l'osera gerrier.
Ensi nous devons travellier
De servir Dieu a tout le mains
800 Pour nous garder dé males mains
De l'Anemi qui nous assaut
Et jour et nuit par maint assaut,
Desqueus tout delivre serons
804 Puisque Jesu Crist servirons.

Pour les raisons que j'ai chi dites, *22v*
Ja n'eust li hom nulles merites
De servir Dieu son creator,
808 Si devroit faire sans atour
Et metre son entendement
En Diu servir parfaitement;
Et puisque pour chestui serviche
812 Dieus si nous fait si grant frankise
Qu'il veut que nous aions la glore
Perpetüel, non transcitore,
De laquele dist l'Escriture,
816 Qui les doutanches asseüre,
Que cuers ne porroit deviser,
Tant se seüst bien aviser,
Në ius vëoir n'orelle oïr
820 Joie tant faiche resjoïr
Home mortel comme fait cele;
Car a nule ne s'aparelle
De repos, de deduit ne d'aise,
824 Ains est toute joie mesaise

En conparison de cheli,
Car sains Paus si nous dist de li 23r
Qu'ele est de si grant souatume
828 Que tous les cuers des boins alume,
Et [de] tel joie si les cuevre
Que tant quë un eus clot et oevre
Ne dourroit il de chele joie
832 Qu'il nous pramet et nous otroie
Pour avoir ·M· ans a devise
De la joie que li mons prise.
Dont nous devons bien travellier
836 De desconfire l'aversier
Qui de eure en eure se travelle
De nous outrer en la bataille,
Car se nous desconfit i soumes,
840 A tous jours en infer iroumes;
Pour chou si nous devons pener
Qu'en chu liu ne nous puist mener,
Car chil qui la herbegera
844 A nul jour mais n'en istera.

Pour chou veul jou a tous aprendre
Conment li hom se pueut desfendre 23v
En la bataille du Dïauble,
848 Que point ne li sera grëable,
Mais en ara grandes merites
S'escaper puet de l'estour quites.
Verités est que par nature
852 Hom est si feble creature
Et de tele complexion
Qu'en lui n'aroit desfencïon
·I· tout seul jour në ·i· demi
856 Contre l'asaut de l'Anemi
Sans l'esforch de la Dieu aidanche
Qui doune as siens perseveranche.
Pour chou est tost en mains pechiés
860 Li hom keüs et trebuschiés,
Quant en sa forche tant se fie
Qu'il ne requert la Dieu aïe
Qui est de si poissant afaire

864	Quë on ne peut sans li riens faire.	
	Et pour che, quant il tant meskiet	
	A l'oume quë en pechié kiet,	
	Li premiers fais, sans demourer,	*24r*
868	Si est qu'il doit de cuer ourer	
	A Jesu Crist qu'il li pardoigne;	
	Et qu'il jeünt; et pour Dieu doigne;	
	Car quant li hom est entekiés	
872	De pluisor[s] visse[s] de pecciés,	
	Ches ·iii· coses li font aidanche	
	Vers Dieu d'avoir tost repentanche,	
	Si croissent les biens temporeus,	
876	Et matent les travaus morteus.	
	Ausi dounent a l'oume usage	
	De faire bien tout son äage,	
	Et si en pecce li hons mains	
880	Quant a tel cose met ses mains,	
	Car ·i· pechiés ·i· autre acroist	
	Et li biensfaires mal descroist.	
	Et si oï douner sentensse	
884	·I· maistre plain de grant scïence	
	De droit et de thëologie,	
	Qui demoustra par sa clergie	
	Que chil qui ches coses feroient	
888	Et enaprés danpné seroient,	*24v*
	Que les paines du danpnement	
	Souferont plus legierement,	
	Et si seront trop mains lassés	
892	De soufrir les qu'autres d'assés,	
	Tout ne puissent li mal finer.	
	Ches[t] fait ne veul determiner	
	Pour che que sui chevaliers lais,	
896	Mais les raisons as clers en lais	
	A qui chis fais plus apartient.	
	A ches coses grans pourfis tient	
	Li biens que li pecchieres oevre,	
900	Et pour ches biens ses biens recuevre,	
	Mais quant au fait de sauvement	
	N'a il pourfit n'avancement	
	Pour riens qu'il die ne qu'il faiche,	

904	Duskes adont que la Dieu grasse —
	Qui a chascun aidier s'esmeut
	Qui le recuert et qui le veut —
	L'ait mis en tele repentanche
908	Qu'il faiche droite penitanche
	Des coses dont il a irie *25r*
	Nostre segnour par sa folie.
	Mais mainte gent ne sevent gaire
912	Conment on doit penanche faire
	Seront le Dieu ordounement
	Si k'ele vaille au sauvement.
	Pour che si veul aucuns aprendre,
916	Qui a mes dis vaurront entendre,
	Conment on peut par penitanche
	Avoir de ses pechiés quitanche,
	Et quantes coses il couvient
920	Faire a chelui qui i avient.
	Segnour, sachiés ke penitance
	Est d'oume tristre la venjance
	Qu'il prent de soi pour la folie
924	Que ses cors a u mont bastie.
	Cheste est la voie de justice
	En coi nostre Sires atise
	Les repentans de cheminer
928	A tous jours mais sans definer.
	Cheste est la droite medechine *25v*
	Qui en la tere s'enrachine,
	Par coi les plaies garisons
932	Que nous par faus delis faisons,
	Car tout ausi com nostre char
	Fait en chest mont de nous eschar,
	Estuet que nous eskernissons
936	La nostre char et punissons
	En chestui mont, ou autrement
	N'arons a Dieu acordement.
	Penitanche a grant segnourie,
940	Car ele doune treble vie
	A l'oume qui adroit le tient
	Et qui sans falir le maintient,

	Dont la premiere si est tele:	
944	Que ele acroist vie corporele,	
	Que nous trouvons d'Ezechïas	
	Que quant li dist Yzaÿas	
	Qu'a fin iroit prochainement,	
948	Li rois plora moult tenrrement	
	Et prïa Dieu par grant pitie	
	Qu'encor li alongast sa vie,	*26r*
	Et nostre Sire si li fist	
952	Moult volentiers che qu'il requist;	
	Pour che qu'il vit sa penitanche	
	Ne le mist pas en oblïanche,	
	Mais ·xv· anees li douna:	
956	Qui Dieu sert tel gerredon a.	

L'autre vie est esperitele,
Mais onkes hom si ne vit tele
Se de Dieu ne fu tant privés
960 Que de lui fust tous maus privés.
Cheste si vit sains Paus si bien
Qu'il dist: "Je vif et ne vif riens,
Mais dedens moi tout vraiement
964 Vit Jesu Cris presentement."

L'autre vie est la pardurable
Vers cui les ·ii· autres sont fable;
Ch'est la vie de Paradis
968 Qui est et fu et iert toudis
Crïee pour no sauvement,
Dont Jhesu Cris dist proprement
Qu'il ne veut pas que defenissent   *26v*
972 Pechëour, mais se convertissent,
Et puis aprés que cascuns vive
En vie qui les boins avive.
Dont pert il bien ke penitanche
976 Si a en li moult grant poissanche,
Si le devons donkes tenir
Et sans fallanche maintenir.
Qui penitanche faire veut
980 Trois coses faire li estuet:

La premiere est contricïons,
La seconde comfessïons,
Et qui a la tierche recuevre
984 Si a satisfacïon de evre.

Contricïons est le tristreche
Et le dolours ki l'oume apresse
Dedens le cuer pour les pechiés
988 Dont il connoist qu'il est carchiés.
Ceste tri[s]teurs est necessaire
A tout houme qui veut pais faire *27r*
A Jesu Crist, car autrement
992 Ne puet avoir acordement,
Mais cascuns hom si doit savoir
Que ·iii· coses i doit avoir.
Li premiere est amaritude:
996 Li hom qui met bien son estude
En resgarder premierement
Le dolereus approchement
Qu'il fait d'enfer pour ches pechiés,
1000 Et com de Deu est eslongiés
Par metre soi hors de sa garde,
Se ches ·ii· coses bien regarde,
Amertume de cuer ara
1004 Si grant que dire nel porra.
Et Dieus le nous senefïa
Trop bien quant u mont envoia
L'iaugue pour toute char noier,
1008 Car adonkes si fist voier
L'iaugue d'abisme contremont
Pour arouser trestout le mont,
Et l'iauge du ciel fist deschendre.
1012 Grans coses pöons chi entendre, *27v*
Car par l'iaugue qui vint dé chieus
Et d'abisme, nous moustra Dieus
·ii· coses, que doit resgarder
1016 Chil qui se veut de mal garder
A son pöoir. La premeraine
Est la grans joie souveraine
De Paradis, car chil qui pense

1020	Qu'il a perdu par negligense
	De Paradis chele grant joie,
	N'est mervelle s'i[l] li anoie.
	La seconde resgardeüre
1024	Est le paine crüele et dure,
	Perpetüele et sans pitié,
	Dont il se voit si aprochié,
	Chou est d'enfer, qui par coustume
1028	Si art toudis et point n'alume.
	Et quant li hom pour ses pecciés
	Voit et connoist ches ·ii· meschiés,
	Il n'ara ja si felon cuer
1032	Que son orguel ne jete en puer,
	Et que li cuers ne li aguise
	Mais que de cel pensé n'en isse;
	Et li doi oel li ploureront
1036	Pour l'aigreté kë il verront
	Et des pechiés pour la grant fole,
	Si com il font pour la cibole
	Quant i[l] la sentent ou la voient,
1040	Quë il pour l'agreté larmoient.
	Par l'iaugue qui vient de ·ii· lieus,
	D'enfer et autresi des chieus,
	Et qui toute la car noia,
1044	Nostre Sires senefia
	Les larmes qui a l'oume vienent
	Quant chist ·ii· pensé li avienent,
	Qui l'oume vont tout netoiant.
1048	Par la char qui aloit noiant
	Avons nous demoustractïon
	De le carnel affectïon
	Qui en ches larmes est noïe.
1052	Nöe le juste senefie
	Qui en tous biens se va noant,
	Non pas en folies noiant
	Et en pecciés son tans user —
1056	Dont ne se puet nus escuser
	En cui baptesmes maint et fois —
	Que, s'il resgarde aucunes fois
	Le chiel joiant, l'enfer qui fume,

28r

28v

1060	Qu'en li n'en ait tost amertume.
	Mais il sont mainte gent sans doute
	Qui ont ieus et ne voient goute;
	Che sont chil qui voient les biens
1064	Et les sevent si n'en font riens.
	L'autre branke est ferme esperanche
	D'avoir a Dieu boine atendanche,
	Mais qu'il en faiche droite amende
1068	Si com sainte Eglyse commande.
	Se pecciés fait ·i· houme esrrer,
	Il ne se doit desesperer,
	Mais ament soi et si s'acorde,
1072	Que en Dieu a grand misericorde.
	Du desespoir plus Dieus se deut
	Que des pecciés dont ele meut,
	Car desespoirs fait a Dieu honte,
1076	Et sains Jeromes nous raconte
	Que Judas [Dieu] plus offendi
	Quant par desespoir se pendi
	Que che qu'il l'ala envaïr
1080	Et le baisa pour mieus traïr.
	Desesperanche trop agree
	A l'Anemi, car definee
	Est maintenant la guerre toute
1084	Despuis que l'esperanche est route,
	Car che nous conte sains Grigoires:
	Mos de vaincu est ja despoires.
	Desesperanche nuist a l'oume,
1088	Car ele si li taut en soume
	Forche, viguer et la Dieu grasse;
	Faus est qui kiet en tele nasse,
	Car a paines peut retourner
1092	Pour soi a nul bien atourner.
	Chaÿm en desespoir kaÿ
	Dont si tres mal li enkaÿ,
	Tout eüst il contrictïon,
1096	Qu'il en rechut dampnacïon.
	Judas contrictïon rechut,
	Mais ·i· cose le dechut,

29r

29v

```
         Ch'est che qu'il eut desesperanche
1100     D'avoir de ses pecciés cuitanche.
         Pour che chist doi avoir ne peurent
         Confort de Dieu, quë il ne seurent
         Qu'il estuet en contrictïon
1104     C'on ait grant esperassïon.
         Mout est li hom faus de memoire
         Qui des biens Dieu se desespoire,
         Quant Dieus soffri la passïon
1108     Pour le nostre redempcïon.
         Ne cuidiés pas kë il en vain
         Morut pour les enfans Evain;
         Ja tant ne li aront mesfait
1112     En dit n'en penser ni en fait,
         Mais qu'il en aient repentamche
         Et d'avoir pais ferme esperanche,
         Quë il tantost ne lor pardoune          30r
1116     Et que sa grasse ne lor doune.

         La darraine est renonchemens
         A tous mauvais acordemens,
         Ch'est a dire quant il renoie
1120     Tous maus par quoi s'ame forvoie,
         Car chil qui est bien repentans
         A mal n'en iert ja consentans.
         Cheste seconde branche vient
1124     De l'amertume qui avient
         A l'onme quant du cuer larmoie
         Pour ses fautes dont li anoie,
         Si se vait lors abandounant
1128     Tant quë il va tout pardounant
         Che que on li a u mont mesfait,
         Et si restore tout affait
         Tout che qu'il a a tort eü.
1132     Maint houme voit on esmeü
         D'entre[r] en grant contrictïon,
         Mais tout est voir decepcïons            30v
         Së il de boin cuer ne pardoune
1136     Et a restorer s'abandoune
         Et ait sen cuer bien enfichié
```

De nient caïr mais en pechié.
Tous meffais pardouner estuet
1140 Qui a Dieu acorder se veut,
Car nous proions en l'orison
Que nous a no pere faison
Quë il nos dettes nous pardoinst
1144 Et en tel forme le nous doinst
Com nous lé pardounons a cheus
Qui vers nous sont fel et crueus.
Dont qui ne fait che qu'il pramet
1148 En grant condictïon se met,
Car il fait mal, et tel mal dist
Quë [il] soi meïsme en maudist.
Et puis a chiaus qui nous ont faites
1152 Pluisors folies et retraites,
Tous lors meffais devons quiter,
Dont nos devons mieus aquiter
Et rendre couvenaule pris *31r*
1156 A chaus dont a tourt avons pris,
Car nous trouvons en l'Escripture
Que, [se] nous n'amendons l'injure
Que faite avons ou pourcachie,
1160 Dieus n'ara ja de nous pit[i]e.
Aprés devons bien fermement
Avoir seür proposement
De nous de tous pecciés retraire,
1164 Car l'Evangille nous esclaire
Que chil qui veulent gäagnier
Le ciel et resgardent arrier
Vers les delisses du Dïauble,
1168 A Dieu ne sont pas couvenable.

Segnour, cheste premiere branche
Qu'estuet avoir en penitanche
Laquele j'ai ichi ditee
1172 Si est devant Dieu mout löee,
Car toute ordure jete en peur,
Che[ste] est contrictïon de cuer, *31v*
Qui a lescive est compare[e]
1176 De coi femmes font lor büee.

A femme estuet ·ii· coses faire
Qui veut laver, si k'il i paire,
Car il estuet qu'ele pourcache
1180 Chendre qui tel lescive faice
Qu'amere soit et bien tres forte;
Puis couvient aprés qu'ele aporte
Ses dras, et que dedans les rue,
1184 Et bien les frot et les remue,
Et quant il sont mout bien büé,
Qu'au soleil soient essüé.
Mout a droite comparison
1188 Lescive vers contrictïon,
Car les ·ii· coses sus noumees
Sont en contrictïon trouvees:
Forche premier et puis l'aigrure.
1192 Or entendés l'esclarchissure:
Contrictïons doit estre fors
Qui le cuer brise par effors,
Selonc s'inte[r]pretacïon   *32r*
1196 Brisans cuer est contrictïon,
Ausi dist Johel li proisiés:
"Segneur, vos cuers tous detrenchiés";
Dont affiert il qu'ele soit forte
1200 Si que de mal nos cuers amorte.
Ausi amere est la lescive
Et d'aigreté crüele et vive,
Que qui ·i· peu en buveroit
1204 Que vomir tantost le feroit,
Car contre cuer si li verroit
Quë il pour riens ne s'en terroit;
Ausi doit la contrictïons
1208 Si grans abhominacïons
Faire, que li cuers s'en aigrisse,
Si que par l'abome vomisse
Quanqu'il a fait dedens sa vie
1212 De mauvaisté et de folie.
Et, tout en peüst on plus dire
Et mieus contrictïon descrire
Que je ne l'ai ichi descrit,
1216 Puisque j'ai mis en mon escrit   *32v*

Les coses qui a chiaus couvienent
Qui a contrictïon avienent,
A tant ester je le lairai,
1220 Et de confessïon dirai.

Confessïons est salus d'ame
Et esrachinemens de blasme,
Des boines meurs cultiverresse,
1224 De nous a Dieu acorderresse,
Commenchemens de neteté,
Renonchemens de nicheté;
Toutes les coses sus noumees
1228 Sont en confessïon prouvees
Par Augustin et Ysidore,
Bede, Bernart et saint Grigore,
Pour che n'estuet que je le preve
1232 Ne qu'au prouver argument trueve,
Car che qu'il dïent sinplement
Nous devons croire fermement.
Mais tant di bien que mout est niches   *33r*
1236 Li hons qui est carkiés de visses
Qui point met de dilassïon
De faire se confessïon,
Car s'ensi fust qu'il avenist
1240 Que mors en tel point le prensist,
En enfer lors trebuscheroit —
La tourmente sans fin aroit.
Et d'autre part, chele atarjance
1244 Met les pecciés en oublïance,
Si que trop peu il en souvient
A l'oume qu'a confesse vient,
Dont seulement de l'oublïanche
1248 Estuet fornir grant penitanche.
Li hom qui volentiers delaie
Sa confesse, samble qu'il aie
Volenté grant de trouver place
1252 Ou fui[e]r puist de la Dieu face,
Com nous trouvons du premier home
Qui pour le mesfait de la pume
Si s'atapi et se chela,

1256	Mais nostre Sires l'apela	*33v*
	Et li conta sa mesproison,	
	Puis le jeta de sa maison —	
	Ausi jeté tout en seront	
1260	Qui atapir se cuideront.	
	Encore i a aucune gent	
	Qui sont si fol et negligent	
	Que toudis en peccié seront,	
1264	Ne ja ne se confesseront	
	Dusques adonc qu'il s'aprechoivent	
	Chertainement que morir doivent.	
	Tel gent sont plain de grant folie,	
1268	Car il requierent lor[s] aïe,	
	Et d'avoir le sont en escuel	
	Quant il ne püent le consel	
	Faire ke li prestres lor doune	
1272	Pour febleche de lor persoune.	
	Autele est, voir, cheste confesse	
	Que du larron quë on apresse	
	En la jehine pour li pendre:	
1276	Ausi pöons iche entendre,	*34r*
	Car se ne fust la maladie,	
	Sa comfesse ne fesist mie,	
	Mais la doutanche de la mort	
1280	A la comfessïon l'amort —	
	Cheste comfesse peu pourfite	
	Qu'assés peu porte de merite.	
	Mais nequedent, trop bien avient	
1284	A l'oume qu'en peccié se tient	
	Et que du maintenir ne chesse	
	Quant il a la fin s'en comfesse,	
	Mais qu'il ait grant contrictïon,	
1288	Car leus va a sauvassïon.	
	Mais mains cas peuent avenir	
	Par coi n'i puent avenir,	
	Si com defaute de scïensse	
1292	Par grant dehait et de loquensse,	
	Ou quant le hom est trop curïeus	
	D'ordouner ses biens temporeus.	
	Autre gent sont qui ont usage	

1296	Si sanble boins et si est rage,	
	Car il ont bien proposement	
	D'aus confesser devotement,	*34v*
	Mais demorant s'en vont es rasques	
1300	Disant qu'il le feront a Pasches.	
	Tes gens font conte de lor vie	
	Com s'ele fust en lor ballie	
	Et il seüsent a delivre	
1304	Cambien cascuns hom peüst vivre,	
	Et nequedent en l'Escripture	
	Ne trev[e] on lieu qui asseüre	
	L'oume de mort une seule eure.	
1308	Faus est qu'en tel delai demeure,	
	Car sens në oevre ne raison	
	Si ne vaut point en tel saison,	
	Car adonc est nostre eure morte	
1312	Et Dieus si est a nostre porte	
	Qui nous requiert et amouneste	
	Que entrer le laissons en no feste	
	Si qu'aveuc nous puisse megnier;	
1316	Mais nous avons ·i· lait portier	
	Qui est sor la maison tous seus —	
	"Corbiaus" a non, mout est hideus,	
	Ichis a haute vois li crie	*35r*
1320	"Cras, cras, mais che n'iert ore mie."	
	Ensi Jesu Crist ajournons	
	A l'endemain, et sejornons	
	Es faus delis, sour esperanche	
1324	De venir puis a repentanche;	
	Ensi ajournons a demain	
	Chelui qu'adés veut metre main	
	D'oster le mal qui si nous tient.	
1328	Mais chius "demains" onkes ne vient,	
	Et se Jhesus leur fait tel grasse	
	Et si leur doune tel espasse	
	Qu'a Pasches soient confessé,	
1332	Encore n'est che pas assés,	
	Car il samle que che soit gile	
	De faire feste ains que vegile.	
	Ausi font chil, selonc men esme,	

1336   Qui assés junent en quaresme
       Et puis a Pasches se confessent,
       Car les kemans de Dieu reverssent
       Quant il font chou au desrenier
1340   Que faire doivent au premier, *35v*
       Car chascuns hom qu'ensi veut faire
       Que sa penitamche li paire
       Premiers fait sa confessïon
1344   Et puis la satisfacïon.
       Salemons chou si nous conferme,
       Car es Proverbes nous aferme
       Que justes hom premierement
1348   Si fait de li acusement.
       Pour che si a la sainte Eglyse
       En ses cas fait bele devise,
       Car ordouné a le Septesme,
1352   ·xv· jours avant le Quaresme,
       Pour che que dedens la quinsaine
       Chascuns de confesser se paine
       Et en tous biens si bien s'achesme
1356   Que entrer puist nes dedens Quaresme
       Et faire lors tel penitanche
       Que au sauvement li faiche aidanche.
       Ensi le doit chascuns hom faire
1360   Qui veut a Dieu servir ne plaire, *36r*
       Mais li desus ramenteü
       Sont en confesse decheü
       Quant il i font dilacïon,
1364   Mais ch'est pour la contrictïon
       Qui n'est en aus pas bien conplie,
       Car il n'est hom en cheste vie
       Qui eust contrictïon bien ferme,
1368   Qu'en la confesse mesist terme.
       Faus est qui contre chou estrive,
       Car chil qui boit de la lescive
       A forche estuet qu'il le vomisse,
1372   Et que de lui par forche en isse.
       Ausi, aprés contrictïon
       Qui fait abhominacïon,
       Estuet que li contrius vomisse,

1376	Ch'est a dire qu'il regehisse
	De boin cuer par devocïon
	Ses mesfais en confessïon.
	Pour che, cascuns hastievement
1380	Qui contrius est bien fermement
	Ne doit atargier ne chescer
	Qu'i[l] ne se doive confesser *36v*
	A son parrochien, s'il le treuve,
1384	Car ainsi drois decrés le reve.
	Mais, s'ainsi fust qu'il couneüst
	Que ses curés si peu seüst
	Qu'adroit ne li seüst aidier,
1388	Leus li doit il dire et proier
	Qu'i[l] li doinst congié, qu'il se puisse
	Confesser ou boin prestre truise;
	Et se ses prestres li otroie
1392	Tout che qu'i[l] li recuert et proie,
	Il l'en doit mout regrassïer,
	Et maintenant sans delaier
	Au boin confessor se doit traire
1396	Et sa confessïon retraire.
	Mais se li prestres nel laissast
	Qu'il autre part se confessast,
	Prendre le peut tot maugré sien,
1400	Car tes [nel] forche que pour bien,
	Ou il a son souvrain s'enquere
	Pour che k'en ches cas le sequere
	Ou de consel ou de congié, *37r*
1404	Ou k'a li die son peccié.
	Mais il me samble grans savoir,
	Quant le congié ne peut avoir,
	Qu'a son parrochien se confesse
1408	Premierement, et puis s'adreche
	A chelui qui mieus le sara
	Consellier que chius fait n'ara,
	Car tant com a pluisors descuevre
1412	De ses pechiés trestoute l'evre,
	De Dieu en a gregnour merite
	Et Dieus plus tost si l'en aquite.
	Mais se li hom est en tel tere

1416	Qu'il ne puisse trouver ou querre	
	Prestre qui die sa confesse,	
	Et la nechessités l'apresse,	
	Sains Augustins si li ensegne	
1420	Quë il ·i· sien conpagnon pregne	
	A qui en liu de prestre die	
	La miseranche de sa vie,	
	Car li besoins qui si l'atise	
1424	Au conpaignon doune frankise	37v
	Que le contrit assaure peut	
	Du tout en tout; mais il estuet	
	Que li contris ki se confesse	
1428	Li fache maintenant pramesse	
	Que tantost se confessera	
	Que son droit prestre trouvera.	
	Et se chil fust en itel point	
1432	Que de conpagnon n'eüst point	
	Et il veut faire son devoir,	
	Dedens li doit ramentevoir	
	Tout ·i· a ·i· les siens pecciés,	
1436	Et estre en soi bien afikiés	
	Qu'il a nul tans n'i rentrera	
	Et au plus tost c'onques porra,	
	Se nostre Sire li fait grasse	
1440	Que venir puist n'en lieu n'en plache	
	Ou il puisse trouver le prestre,	
	Que de ses fais li dira le estre.	
	Cheste deerraine racordanche,	
1444	Tout soit li hom en sa poissanche,	
	Doit cascun jour en lui avoir,	38r
	Car ne sai nul de tel savoir	
	Qui cascun jour confesser veut,	
1448	Et s'i[l] le veut espoir ne peut;	
	Pour che, quant il en fait fallanche,	
	En li en faiche ramenbramche	
	Si com j'ai dit ichi devant,	
1452	Car David dist en endevant	
	"Si doit avoir sans definanche	
	Peccieres deul de sa fallanche."	
	Cascuns preudon qui a ensoinne	

1456	Doit ensi faire sa besoigne
	A joiant cuer sans nul refus
	Com jou l'ai dit ichi desus,
	Mais quant li hom peut en liu estre
1460	Que confesser se puisse au prestre,
	Je lo que sans delaiement
	Faiche selonc l'ensegnement
	Que chis miens livres li ensegne,
1464	Car n'est preudom qui l'en rep[r]egne.
	Or entendés, si orrés lire
	Che ke mes livres vous veut dire. *38v*

	Quant li dous Sires de pitié
1468	Ara douné et otrïé
	Au pechëour de sa fallanche
	Contrictïon et repentanche
	En cui il doit fonder son estre,
1472	Quant il venrra devant le prestre,
	Tantost se doit sans delaier
	Par devant lui agenoullier
	Et puis tenir le chief enclin,
1476	Car chieus a cui soume[s] aclin
	Ch'est Jesu Cris li fieus Marie.
	Quant il ala de mort a vie
	Ens en la crois ou il pendi,
1480	Le chief enclin l'ame rendi;
	En chë avons nous essamplaire
	Que nous du tout si devons faire
	Ensi com je l'ai dit ichi.
1484	Iche faisant que je di chi
	Li peccieres si li doit dire
	A dolant ceur et bien plain d'ire, *39r*
	Car la n'afiert ne ris ne ju:
1488	"Sire, je me confesse a Dieu
	Et a tous et a toutes saintes
	Des folies que j'ai fait maintes,
	Et autresi a vous, biaus pere,
1492	Car vie tres fole et amere
	Si ai en ch[e]stui mont menee
	En dit en fait et en pensee.

```
             Dont je me rench a vous coupaules,
1496         Et si renoie le Dïauble
             Et son pöoir et quank'il vient
             De lui et k'a lui apartient,
             Car laidement m'a envaï
1500         Par faus delis dont m'a traï,
             Si quë il m'a vif trebuschié
             Par son barat en maint peccié
             Desqués ne me souvient pas bien,
1504         Mais chieus qu'en memere [je] tieng
             Vous veol je dire plainement
             Sans metre nul escusement."
             Aprés li doit mot a mot dire                39v
1508         De ches pecciés toute la tire.
             Mais pour che que je voi u monde
             Que nichetés si i abunde,
             Et maintes gens i font les visses
1512         Qui au confesser sont si niches
             Qu'il ne sevent ou il ne veulent
             Dire le mal que faire seulent
             Se li prestres ne lor demande —
1516         Chertes chou est honte mout grande
             Quant j'atent tant quë on me die
             Et mete sus ma trecherie;
             Encore vaut mieus que la descuevre,
1520         Car droite confesse bouche oevre,
             Mais confesse qui clot la bouche
             A Jesu Crist gaires n'atouke —
             Pour les maus blasmer et reprendre
1524         Et pour les sinples gens aprendre
             Si veoul je chi dire et ditier
             Esqués endrois on peut peccier,
             Et pourkoi on s'en doit retraire,
1528         Et conment sa confesse faire.           40r
             Biau douch segneur, or entendés
             Se je di bien, si l'aprendés;
             Ne resgardés a ma persoune,
1532         Mais se je di parole boine,
             Pour vo pourfit le retenés
             Si que vous faire le devés.
```

De ma persoune ne vous challe
1536 S'ele petit ou gaires valle,
Mais que li dis a vous s'aproche,
Car chil qu'issir fist de la roche
L'iaue bruiant a grant fuison
1540 Peut faire issir sens et raison
D'aucun jovene houme mainte fois,
Et ·i· sage plain de boufois
Remetre peut en grant sinpleche;
1544 Or pri que Dieus vous doinst lëeche.

Li menistre de sainte Eglise
Ont demoustré par grant maistri[s]e
Que ·vii· peccié sont criminaus
1548 C'on apele pecciés mortaus: *40v*
Orguel premier, et puis envie,
Ire, avarisse, glouternie,
Pereche aprés et puis luxure —
1552 Uns lais pecciés et plains d'ordure.
D'orguel dirai u premier chief;
Dieus m'en laist bien venir a kief.
Par orguel peut li hons peccier
1556 En ·iiii· cas, dont li premier
Si est quant aucuns hom aësme
Que ses biens a de soi mëesme.
[Et] l'autre est quant il cuide avoir
1560 Vertus ou grasses ou avoir
De Jesu Crist par sa deserte;
Cheste est folie bien aperte.
Li tiers cas rest quant il n'a mie
1564 Le bien qu'avoir cuide en baillie.
Li quars cas est selonc la letre
Quant il se veut devant tous metre
En dit, en fait ou en pensee;
1568 Tes visses est vieutés prouvee.

Deus brankes a ausi envie   *41r*
Qui samblent droite d'iaublie.
La premiere quant on a joie
1572 Quant aucuns va a male voie.

        Du tierch visce vous veul jou dire;
        Trois brankes a, s[i] a non ire.
        La premiere est quant on desire
1576   Qu'ascuns de ses proimes enpire,
        La secunde quant on laidenge,
        Et la tierche quant on se venge
        Par l'ire, dont il est espris,
1580   De chaus qui ont vers lui mespris.

        Deus brankes principaus devise
        Sains Grigores en avarisce.
        Escarssetés est la premiere;
1584   Ch'est quant li hom a tel maniere
        Que, tout soit il manans et riche,
        Si est il si avers et niches
        Que du gäang que Dieus li doune
1588   N'ose bienfaire a sa persone
        Ne douner ent ·i· seul denier,   *41v*
        Tant resoigne l'amenuisier.
        Li secons rains est Couvoitise
1592   Qui son serjant ainsi atise
        Que, së il a pöoir assés,
        Pour che n'ert il ja si lassé
        Des biens som proisme couvoitier
1596   D'aquerre les et pourchachier,
        Ne ne l'en quaut com les aquiere,
        Mais qu'il les ait en sa ratiere.

        Couvoitise a ausi ·ii· rains
1600   Desus les autres souverains,
        Dont larrechins est li premiers:
        C'est quant avoir, tere ou deniers
        Aucuns conquert par tel berele
1604   Que li sires n'en set nouvele.

        En larrechin a ·iii· rainssiaus
        Qui ne sont ne boin ne loiaus.
        Li premiers est quant aucuns lerres
1608   Est de se propre main enblerres.

	L'autre est quant il a pourcachie	
------	Par douner ent a la maisnie	*42r*
	Sans chou que chil en sache riens
1612	De cui il a eü les biens,
	Car par son gré ne l[es] eust mie.
	Chis rains si a non symonie,
	Mais sains Grigores nous devise
1616	Que chis rains est trop bien d'Eglise,
	Car es autres biens temporeus
	Devienent chi[st] doi raim ·i· seus.

        Li autres rains a non rapine
1620 Qui a en li double rachine.
        La premier[e] est quant on desreube
        De son avoir ou de sa reube
        Aucun a droite force faite,
1624 Soit qu'i[l] li grieve ou qu'i[l] li haite;
        Conte n'en font que d'une beste.
        L'autre branke est quant li hom preste
        A son voisin de son avoir
1628 Par couvenenche de ravoir
        Le gerredon de la prestanche;
        En tel bonté a grant vieutanche
        Qu'ele est contre droite nature —   *42v*
1632 Ceste branke a a non usure.

        Li quins visce[s] est gloutounie,
        ·I· pecciés plains de vilounie
        Qui en ·ii· brankes se depart
1636 Qui sont as leur de male part,
        Car trop hounissent lor maniere,
        En trop mengier est la premiere,
        Et en trop boire est la seconde —
1640 Ceste si taut sens et faconde.

        Li sistes visses est pereche
        Qui est du mont la pire teche,
        Car par cestui si vont a honte
1644 Tout chil qui d'aus ne font nul conte.
        Par chu peccié tout chil se perdent

Qui au bienfaire ne s'aërdent
Et le laissent par negligensse;
1648 Faus est li hom qu'a Dieu ne pensse.

Aprés pereche vient luxure, *43r*
·I· lais pechiés dont Dieus n'a cure.
Chis visse chi si est carchiés
1652 De ·v· manieres de pecciés,
Dont il n'est nus que l'un d'aus use,
S'i[l] a son prestre ne l'acuse
Et il ens un peccié remaint,
1656 Qu'en abisme droit ne le maint
S'il trespasse sans repentanche.
Sachiés que la premiere branke
Fornicacïon est nomee
1660 Qui est de gent non marïe[e].
La seconde ne rest pas bele:
Quant li hom femme despuchele.
Li tiers visses peu m'atalente:
1664 Quant li hom gist a sa parente.
Li quars pecciés est avoutire,
C'est chil qui marïaje enpire,
Et chou avient quant li ·i· d'eus
1668 Soit marïés ou tous les deus.
La quinte branke rest trouvee
En persone d'ordre sacree. *43v*
Les ·iiii· brankes desrenieres
1672 Sont trop plus griés que les premieres,
Car eles sont contre nature.
Pour che ne veol metre ma cure
En deviser les lor manieres,
1676 Car trop par sont laides et fieres,
Et je ne cuit que nus tant hache
Son cors ne s'ame qu'il les faiche;
Pour che si n'en veol je plus dire,
1680 Ains poursivrrai l'autre matire.

Conté vous ai et mis en rime
Tous les pecciés qui sont de crime,
Et com li uns de l'autre meut;

1684	Autres pecciés avoir i peut
	Mais chiaus qui sont plus renoumés,
	Et chil a chaus sont ramenés.
	Mais pluseur cas souvent avienent
1688	Dont chist peccié plus grant devienent
	Qu'il ne soient de lor nature,
	Che nous raconte l'Escriture; *44r*
	Pour che vous veol lé cas retraire
1692	Qui le peccié font gregnour faire,
	Car chil qui se confessera
	S'il ne les dist, riens ne fera.

Li hons qui gehist ses pecciés,
1696 S'il en veut estre descarkiés,
Quantes coses li ont mestier
En sa persone d'encherkier?
Premiers rikeche, puis äages,
1700 Et ordre aprés, et s'il est sages.
Li hons poissans assés plus pecce
Que ne fait chil qu'est en povreche,
Car essamplaire chiaus i prenent
1704 Qui ses fais voient et aprenent.
Ausi li vieus trop plus mesprent,
Quant luxure l'art et esprent
Et il du tout s'i abandoune,
1708 Que ne feroit jovene persone;
Et ausi est plus crueus visse *44v*
U cors du v[i]ell grant avarisse,
Car selonc che ke les gens croissent,
1712 Li peccié montent et descroissent.
Ausi li hom qu'est ordonnés
De peccié est plus sourmenés,
Et en lui est pecciés plus lais
1716 Quë il ne soit assés es lais.
Es mariés mout plus abonde
Pecciés qu'es autres gens du monde,
Et plus est grans es chevaliers
1720 Qu'es gens qui sont d'autres mestiers.
Aprés doit faire resgardanche
Li hom ques est sa conissanche,

```
             Car trop fait grande mespresure
1724         Li hom qui a sens et mesure
             Quant as pecciés ne contralie
             Que ne fait hom de sinple vie,
             Car sages hom se doit mener
1728         Tous jours si k'il puist amener
             Par le sien boin demainement
             La sinple gent a sauvement.                45r
             Com li miroirs si est li sages,
1732         Car en lui mirent li volage
             Lors fais et tout lor portement,
             Dont s'en lui a boin esrrement
             Par son essample si l'airont,
1736         Et s'il fait mal ja ne saront
             Le mal laissier, ains le feront
             Et par son fait [l']escuseront,
             Disant c'on ne les doit reprendre
1740         Puisk'as sages vont garde prendre.
             Li hom ches poins, selonc mon esme,
             Resgarder doit en soi mëesme.

             Aprés ne doit li hom tarder,
1744         Ains doit ·iii· coses resgarder
             Sour le peccié tout erraument:
             L'un, s'i[l] pecca apairaument,
             Car ki ensi s'i abandoune
1748         A tous mauvais essample doune;
             L'autre, s'il est pecciés morteus;
             Li tiers, se li visses est teus            45v
             Que pluiseurs visses s'i asamblent,
1752         Com il avient de çaus qui emblent
             Par larrechin iceles coses
             Qui sont en sainte Eglise encloses,
             Car furt si est pecciés morteus,
1756         Et sacrileges si n'est preus.

             Aprés doit il espelukier
             Le cause qui le fist peccier,
             S'ele longuement l'envaï
1760         Ou se de legier i kaï,
```

Car chil qui pecce de legier
Si doit souffrir plus d'enconbrier;
Et, s'il la cause pourcacha
1764 Qui a che faire l'encaucha,
Si come font aucun caitif
Qui a tous biens sont li restif,
Qui font souvent grans sorcheries
1768 Et grans mengiers et bueveries,
Et de tout chou sont curïeus
Pour estre plus luxurïeus. 46r

Aprés doit li hom reconnoistre
1772 Sans point amenuisier n'acroistre
Conment il fist le mesproison,
Car enfers qui quiert garison
Au mire doit conter a trie
1776 Conment il prinst la maladie
Se volonté a de garir,
Ou autrement porroit morir;
Ausi quant aucuns hom a l'ame
1780 Plain[e] de pecciés de grant blasme,
A son confessor si doit dire
Conment il mist s'ame a martire
Et s'il, quant le peccié faisoit,
1784 Son cors plus u peccié laissoit
Et i faisoit plus demouree
Qu'em tel peccié n'en est usee
Pour le delit qu'en lui avoit
1788 Ou pour l'ire qu'en lui manoit.
Il doit ses coses si retraire
Que riens ne cuevre de l'affaire, 46v
Et qu'il n'i mete tele alonge
1792 Pour sambler voir que soit menchoigne,
Car sachiés bien ke qui se cuevre
En confesse, Dieus le descuevre —
L'oume qui se vait accusant
1796 Tantost le vait Dieus descusant.

Aprés doit resgarder le nombre
Li hom du peccié ki l'emcombre,

	Car quant plus fait de mespresure,
1800	Besoig i a de melleur cure;
	Et [s']il de chë est en doutamche,
	En soi en doit faire l'esmanche
	A bien tres grande diligenche
1804	Par boine pure conscïenche,
	Et aprés se confessera
	Selonc l'esmamche qu'il fera.

Ses coses faites, si entans 47r
1808 Qu'il doive resgarder le tans
En coi il fist a Dieu moleste,
C'est s'il le fist en jour de feste
Ou en vegile ou en jeüne,
1812 Car il n'est folie nesune
Qui en chest terme plus ne grieve
A tout houme qui les alieve
Qu'ele ne fait en autres termes,
1816 Si come sains Bernars l'aferme.

Li lius doit estre puis veüs
Ou li pecciés fu concheüs,
Car a Dieu fait plus grant injure
1820 Qu'en liu sacré fait mespresure
Qu'il ne feroit en autre lieu,
Car chis lieus propres est de Dieu,
Dont chil ki fait mal en tel plache
1824 Plus grant pecció fait et pourcache,
Selonc raison, k'il ne feroit
En lieu ki sacrés ne seroit.

Les ·vii· pecciés et les croissanches 47v
1828 Rimé vous ai atout lor branches.
Encor vous di que nus pecciés
Si n'iert ja fais ne pourcachiés,
Ou soit en fais ou [en] mesdis,
1832 Quë on ne truist dedens mes dis,
Qui les list et i met bien cure,
Car sachiés bien, la mespresure
Des ·v· sens, des ·vii· sacremens

1836	Et des ·x· grans commandemens
	Puet chil trouver dedens la letre
	Qui bien i veut s'entente metre.
	Pour che, quant a confesse vient
1840	Aucuns a qui il n'en souvient
	De ses pecciés, je si l'avise
	Que chest livret resgart et lise,
	Car chil qui au lire entendra
1844	Si grans pourfis l'en avesra,
	S'il de boin cuer i estudie,
	Qu'a paines ara fait folie
	A cui penitanche apartiegne *48r*
1848	Que maintenant ne l'en souviegne.
	Quant li hom s'est aprecheüs
	Des maus en coi iert encheüs,
	Tantost les die sans delaie,
1852	Mais bien se gart k'en lui n'en aie
	Coustume tel qui soit maniere
	[D]es fais de cheler la maniere,
	Car Dieus het mout itel usage;
1856	Et chil qui veut sambler au sage
	Au curé die plainement
	Tous ches pecciés nouméement,
	Conment li uns de l'autre meut;
1860	Car cascuns qui ensi remuet
	Les siens pecciés, plainement samble
	Qu'a la lavendiere resamble
	Qui ses dras pour blanchir atourne
1864	Et si les tourne et les retourne
	Et du batoir les bat souvent
	Et puis les met sechier au vent.
	Li tourners doit senefïer
1868	En confesse l'espeluquier *48v*
	Que li hom fait en conscïenche
	De ses pecciés quant s'en apense,
	Et li batoirs si senefie
1872	Quant il regehist son pecie,
	Car adont la honte le prent
	Qui bien le bat et le reprent.

	Dit ai che k'as pecciés couvient,
1876	Desoremais voloirs me vient
	Des coses dire sans targier
	Qui ont en comfesse mestier,
	Quar chil qui l'un oblïeroit
1880	Toute sa paine perderoit.
	En confesse sont pourfitables,
	Nechessaire[s] et agrëables
	·vii· articles; or les öés,
1884	Se je di bien si m'en creés.

	Confessïons premiers doit estre
	De bouke a bouke dite au prestre,
	Car sains Paus dist: "Les vos pecciés
1888	L'uns a l'autre regehissiés",
	Dont ne doit l'on tenir a sage
	Qui par escrit ou par message
	Veut faire sa confessïon,
1892	Car la grande confusïon
	Que li hom a et la grant honte,
	Quant ches pecciés dist et raconte,
	Li tourne plus a aleganche
1896	C'une bien grande penitanche.
	Aprés doit estre la confesse
	Faite de gré, non par destreche,
	Car tot ausi comme li fais
1900	Du peccié fu tout de gré fais,
	Ausi doit estre voluntaire
	La confesse, non nechessaire.

	Ausi couvient k'ele soit sage,
1904	Non pas faite de cuer volage,
	Car Dieus veut estre fermement
	Servis par grant apensement.
	Aprés doit estre veritable
1908	Confessïons, non dechevable,
	Car aucuns plains d'iniquité,
	Pour sambler plains d'umilité,
	Au prestre dïent maint peccié

49r

49v

1912	Dont ains ne furent entechié;
	Sains Augustins nous en castie
	Et dist que ch'est mout grans folie
	De che fui[e]r par sa menchongne
1916	C'on puet ataindre sans alonge.
	Sachiés ke la quinte maniere
	Si est qu'ele doit estre entiere,
	Car cascuns hom doit tout son estre
1920	Dire et moustrer a ·i· seul prestre,
	Car qui a ·ii· en fait partie
	De Dieu est s'ame departie.
	Et chil qui dist tous ses pecciés
1924	Fors quë ·i· seul, est plus carchiés
	Quë il ne fu au descarchier,
	Pour che k'il veut Dieu engignier.
	Li septismes kas de comfesse *50r*
1928	Si est que chil qui se confesse
	Ses propres pecciés doit conter,
	Non pas les autrui raconter,
	Ne si ne doit noumer le non —
1932	Qu'ensi taurroit l'autrui renon —
	Se che ne fust ou pere ou mere
	Ou f[ieus ou] niés ou seur ou frere
	Ou persone qu'ainsi atiengne
1936	Au confessant quë il couviegne
	A force k'il ensi le noume,
	Car par ches nons connoist on le oume.
	Les ·vii· coses que j'ai noumees
1940	Si doivent estre resgardees
	Du peccë[o]ur qui se confesse
	Qu'eles soient en sa confesse,
	Et quant il les ara noumees
1944	Et les folies confessees
	Desqueles il li souverra,
	Aprés dire li couvenrra: *50v*
	"Sire, je vous ai conneüs
1948	Les maus en coi je sui keüs

Dont il me peut souvenir ore.
Autres pecciés ai fait encore
Lesqués n'ai pas en ramenbranche
1952 Par ma fole mescounissanche,
Soient venïel ou morteus,
J'en sui repentans et hounteus,
Et d'uns et d'autres enssement
1956 Pramet a Dieu amendement,
Si li requier sans plus d'alonge
Que tous mes pecciés me pardoigne,
Et a tous sains et a vous, sire,
1960 Que li prïés qu'il pardoi[n]st s'ire,
A moi qui counois ma folie
Et pramet d'amender ma vie."

Li prestres le doit maintenant
1964 Assaure, par tel couvenant
Que fermement li prametra
Que tout le sien pöoir metra
En soi desfendre de peccier;   *51r*
1968 Et aprés li doit encarquier
Tel penitamche qu'il verra
Que li preudom soffrir porra;
Et chil le doit de boin cuer prendre,
1972 Non pas estriver ne contemdre,
Car chil qui vont ensi faisant
Il vont contrictïon laissant,
Sans qui confesse ne vaut gaire.
1976 Desoremais me veul je taire
De confesse, car j'en ai dit
Grans sentensses en poi de dit.

Satisfacïons est la paine
1980 Qu'en chestui monde li ons maine,
Pour che qu'il perdi par peccié
La grasse Dieu et l'amistié,
S'il se veut a Dieu amender
1984 Par sa charoigne vergonder;
Car il est drois que chil si porte
La paine ke le mal aporte,

	Et cheste paine est nechessaire	
1988	Aucune fois, et voluntaire.	*51v*

       Nechessaire est tele noumee
       Qui est en confesse dounee,
       Car il estuet que chil le faiche
1992 Qui pramis l'a, maugré sa faiche,
       Së il ne veut reconmenchier
       Tout quamk'il ara fait arrier;
       Car assaus fu par tel devise
1996 Quë il fessist chele amendise,
       Dont estuet il, s'il en defalle,
       Que l'assolicïons ne vaille,
       Ains couverra reconmenchier
2000 Penitanche des le premier.

       Satisfacïons voluntaire
       Si est de trop gentil affaire,
       Car ele meut et naist en l'oume
2004 Quant ses peccïés conte et assoume,
       Et puis aprés la penitanche
       Qu'il doit faire pour chele esrranche,
       Si treve adont en son aconte

	Que ses peccïés a trop plus monte	
2008	Que ne peut faire s'amendise	*52r*

       Qu'il a rechut de sainte Eglise;
       Ainsi met il toute sa cure
2012 En soi garder de mespresure,
       Et puis au bienfaire s'esmeut
       Et en fait quamke faire en peut,
       Car de deseure chele amende
2016 A sainte Eglise le conmande.
       Ceste vertu trop en gré prent
       Dieus de chelui qu'a droit le rent,
       Car pour che qu'il le fait de gré
2020 Et porte en lui tel digneté
       Tel bien et tel prosperité,
       Si com sains Grigores conferme,
       Que du tout Dieu[s] plus en amerme
2024 Les grans tourmens d'Espurgatore
       Et aproche du ciel la glore.

Li hom qui a affectïon
De cheste satisfacïon
2028 Apoursivir, je lo k'il lise
Ches[t] mien livret, car il devise
Conment on doit l'amende faire
Des maus qu'avés oï retraire. *52v*

2032 Segnour, conté vous ai arriers
Des anemis crueus et fiers —
C'est de le car et ch'est du monde
Et des maufés, que Dieus confonde —
2036 Qui tous les boins vont gerroiant
Tant qu'i[l] les metent a noiant.
Or est ainsi que sainte Eglise
Au crestïen fait conmandise
2040 Qu'il ait acorde ferme et monde
Vers Dieu, vers soi et vers le monde.
Pour che, cist ·iii· gerrier se partent
En ·iii· et les pecciés departent,
2044 Que cascuns en a grant partie
Pour faire nous perdre la vie,
Et cascuns d'aus si s'entremet
Par soi et grande paine i met
2048 De nous grever et travellier,
Tant que par forche fait brisier
La pais que Dieus a conmandee,
Car puisque la pais est faussee *53r*
2052 Desconfite est nostre batalle,
Le grain perdons, s'avons le palle.
Li Anemis, plains de vieuteche,
Par grant orguel et par pereche
2056 Se travelle de faire fraindre
Cele concorde qui est graindre,
Et qui nous tient le plus grant lieu
De la pais de nous et de Dieu,
2060 Laquele chist ·ii· raim nous tolent,
Dont en tolant nous en afolent.
Pour che, quant nous avons perdue
La pais de Dieu, sans atendue
2064 Metre devons sens et savoir

Conment la pais puissons ravoir.
Ceste pais pöons recouvrer
Se sagement volons ouvrer,
2068 Car si veut Dieus que nous faisons
L'amende a lui par orisons.
Orisons est la droite corde
Par coi li hom a Dieu s'acorde,
2072 Car ele perche d'outre en outre 53v
Le ciel, com la terre le coutre,
Et a Dieu moustre le besoig
Par coi on s'amende selonc.
2076 Dont pert il bien que trop profite
L'orisons qui est a droit dite,
Mais mainte gent en verité
Si sont si plain de nicheté
2080 Qu'il ne sevent qu'est orison
Në a coi vaut n'en quel saison.
Pour che veul jë ichi retraire
Conment on doit s'orison faire,
2084 Et quel cose nous a mestier
Que nous doions a Dieu proier.

Li hom ki veut s'orison faire,
Il doit premierement retraire
2088 Son cuer et soi en tel maniere
Que l'orisons soit si entiere
Que, quamques la lamgue dira,
Que li cuers s'i ascentira
2092 Sans autre part avoir pensee
Tant que l'orisons soit finee, 54r
Car l'orisons a Dieu atouke
Quant li cuers s'acorde a la bouke.
2096 Aprés si doit en soi enquere
Que[l] cose vaut a Dieu requerre.
·ii· coses sont certainement
C'on doit requerre vivement:
2100 La premiere est, bien le sachiés,
D'avoir pardon de ses pecciés,
La seconde est d'avoir le grasse
De Dieu et puis vëoir sa face,

2104	Car ches coses outrëement
	Apartienent a sauvement.
	Autre cose peut on proier
	A Diu quant on en a mestier,
2108	Com de faire requeste tele
	Qu'il ost la paine temporele;
	L'autre qu'il prit Dieu qu'i[l] li plaise
	Qu'il n'ait temptacïon mauvaise;
2112	La tierche rest de Dieu requerre
	Quë il nous prest des biens de tere.
	Mais sachiés bien que toutes cestes
	Sont sous condictïon requestes, *54v*
2116	Q[ua]r devons metre tele alonge
	Qu'il les nous prest com nos besoigne.
	Aprés, sans atardanche faire,
	S'orison doit a Dieu retraire
2120	Ouvertement et humlement,
	Entierement, devotement;
	Et ne li quaut gaires du lieu,
	Car toutes places sont de Deu,
2124	Et nekedent a l'orison
	Est li moustiers droite maisons,
	Mais qui ne peut trouver moustier
	Pour che ne laist Dieu a proier —
2128	Qui ensi s'orison fera,
	Saciés, a Dieu s'acordera.
	La chars, qui est nostre anemie,
	Par luxure, par gloutrenie,
2132	Qui sont ·ii· visses de grant blasme,
	Si fait entre le cors et l'ame
	Brisier le pais qui i doit estre
	Et bien souvent la gerre metre.
2136	Pour ce, quant cele pais est route,
	Li hom si doit faire sans doute *55r*
	Qu'ele soit si raconfortee
	Qu'avoir puisse longue duree,
2140	Et che peut estre vraiement
	Par jeüner devotement;
	Et qui devotement jeüne,

Il fait la volenté tout une
2144 De cors et d'ame, si apaise
La guerre qui estoit mauvaise.
Or est il drois que vous esclaire
Quele june li hom doit faire:
2148 Cascuns preudoum qui juner veut
De ·iii· coses faire le peut,
Car ·iii· rain si sont de juner,
Et ches trois en ·i· aüner
2152 Cascuns preudom se penera
Qui droite jeüne fera.

La premeraine june est tele:
D'esqui[v]er joie tenporele.
2156 Li hom qui tele joie esquive,
Il fait jeüne boine et vive,
Car chil qui fuit passable joie
Pour le traval va droite voie,   *55v*
2160 Car trop vaut mieus peu d'iretage
Que tere grande par louage,
Et nequedent petis n'est mie
Mais grans et plains de segnourie,
2164 Si dure perpetuaument,
Dont n'evre pas cil vassaument
Que le mains prent et le plus laisse —
Ensi fait li hom qui s'abaisse
2168 En prenant cheste joie vaine
Et laist la joie premeraine.

L'autre june est de tel afaire
C'au sauvement est nechessaire,
2172 Car chascuns hom si l'a de veu
Quant au bauptesme fait le veu
D'esqui[v]er tout mortel peccié;
Li hom qui n'a cuer affichié
2176 De tous pecciés morteus laissier,
Sa jeüne doit on brisier,
Car moult peu vaut grans astenanche
Ou li cors est plains de beubanche,
2180 Mais li juners du cors est riches   *56r*

Quant li cuers jeüne de visses.
Ceste june tout vraiement
Nechessaire est au sauvement,
2184 Car en la Loi est conmandee,
Mais l'autre n'est fors que löee;
Pour che, fait pis chil qui la brise
Que chil qui le consel mesprise,
2188 Car cheste est de plus grant renon,
Si est enjointe, l'autre non.
Mais nekedent, li hom qui veut
A droit juner, a forche estuet
2192 Que la premiere june faiche,
Qu'il n'est nus hom si plains de grasse,
Tant soit ore de haut affaire,
Qui cheste june ne puist faire,
2196 Car li cors peut sans nul resoig
Prendre des biens a son besoig
Tant com il set qu'il en pourfite,
Mais que li cuers ne s'i delite,
2200 Car li cuers ne doit allors tendre
Fors qu'au serviche Dieu entendre.

Li tiers jeüners, sans fallamce,   56v
Si est d'umaine sostenamce.
2204 Chis si vaut mout avec les ·ii·,
Et nequedent, s'il est tous seus
Pour che ne doit estre laissiés,
Car së il li fu enkerquiés
2208 Et il pour chou n'en fesist mie,
Il feroit voir mortel peccie,
Car desobedïens seroit.
Mais chil a cui il ne seroit
2212 Point encarkié en penitamche
Le devroit faire sans doutamche
Et metre se car a mesquief
Pour mieus venir de li a kief,
2216 Car toute cose bien punie
Si fait tous jours mains de folie
Que chele qui on ne castie.
Cheste vertus est departie

2220	En ·iii· bramkes par les pensees
	Qui sont es jeünans trouvees.

	La premiere si est de cheaus	57r
	Qui jeünent tout maugré aus,	
2224	Si com li povre et li malade	
	Et chil qui sont en autrui garde.	
	Tes jeüne a Dieu trop peu haite	
	Pour che qu'ele est a forche faite,	
2228	Se che ne soit par tel devise	
	Qu'en grant passcïenche soit prinse;	
	Chele le fait de grant merite —	
	Tel june s'est destrainte dite.	

2232	**L**'autre june est mult desrainable,	
	Pour chë a non abominable,	
	Que ch'est encontre sainte Eglise,	
	Si est de tous les boins reprinse.	
2236	Tel june font, bien le voit on,	
	Aver, ypocrite et glouton.	
	Des avers vous dirai premier	
	Qui jeünent pour espargnier:	
2240	June d'aver si est trop fole,	
	Car le cors son segnour afole	
	Et si fait l'ame mal de Dieu.	
	Si ne vient li avers en lieu	57v
2244	Ou on soit lié de sa venue,	
	Mais en derrier cascuns le hue,	
	Car nus n'a sa venue chiere;	
	Se devant lui fait bele chiere	
2248	Aucuns, ch'est voir pour li mokier.	
	Nus ne s'en doit esmervellier,	
	Car nus hom ne doit demander	
	Ami dont ne puist amender,	
2252	Et de l'aver n'amende nus.	
	Pour che si est il mal venus,	
	Car il veut adés les mains tendre	
	Si ne veut point douner ne rendre;	
2256	Ains c'on eüst de lui denier,	
	Fors par doute ou manechier,	

On li trairoit ains la coraille.
Il resanlle l'espargne-malle
2260 De quoi riens n'ist qui i soit mise
Dusques adont quë on le brise;
Ensi d'aver riens n'istera
Dusques adonc [que] mors sera.
2264 Conment peut nus avoir fiance
D'avoir confort ne sostenamce   *58r*
D'oume qui cuer a si lanier,
Qui pour son cors propre äaisier
2268 N'ose despendre sa mounoie?
Pour ches raisons, se Dieus me voie,
Si est sa june mout blasmee
Du mont, et en la Loy vëe[e],
2272 Car sains Jeromes dist — aucune
Gent parolent sur cheste june —
Il dist: "Amis, je te requier
Que ne junes pour espargnier,
2276 Mais pour garder te car de blasme,
Car drois juners encraisse l'ame;
Pour che te pri par courtoisie
Que t'ame en soit bien encraissie."

2280 Puisque vous ai les junes dites
Que font aver, des ypocrites
Est il raisons que je vous die.
Tel gent si mainent fole vie,
2284 Car cors et ame tout ensamble
En perdent il, si que moi samble
Tout par raison, assés souvent;   *58v*
Or entendés raison conment.
2288 Li ypocrites tout premier
Par jeüner et par vellier
Et par souffrir assés de paine
Si met son cors a courte alaine;
2292 Ensi le cors a honte cache
Sans avoir ent ne gré ne grasse
De Dieu; mais encor boin seroit
Se son maugré n'en aqueroit,
2296 Mais pour che qu[e] la gent cunkie

Si fait il voir mortel peccie,
Et au peccié nus ne s'acline
Qui n'ait tantost la Dieu haïne.
2300 Pour ches paroles que recors
Pert il souvent l'ame et le cors,
Si n'en doit nus avoir doutanche,
Se li cors meurt sans repentanche.
2304 Mais tout fust il qu'il n'aquisist
Nul mal de cose qu'il fesist,
Pour che qu'il a entendement
Doit il ouvrer resnablement,
2308 Et il n'est hom si vuis de sens,   *59r*
Si com je croi et que je sench,
Qu'il ne puist bien aprechevoir
Qu'estre vaut mieus que d'aparoir,
2312 Car mieus vaut assés que painture
Et bontés plus que couvreture;
S'il dist qu'il le fait pour la gent
De che le tieng a negligent,
2316 Car toutes gens si aiment mieus
Les boins que les samblans a eus.
Et partout va seürement
Qui toudis oevre boinement,
2320 Mais ypocrites si se doute
C'om ne le voie ou ne l'escoute,
Si que se oevre soit descouverte.
Certes, chou est mervelle aperte,
2324 Qu'ipocrites set tous biens faire,
Si a le cuer si deputaire
Que si bien, pour s'entensc ïon
Qui plaine est de decepcïon,
2328 Si li tournent tout a damage,
Dont il feroit son avantage
S'il eust pensee nete et monde
Premiers a Dieu et puis au monde;
2332 Mais sa pensee corrompue   *59v*
Tous les biens en[s] u tai [si] rue —
Li tais par raison segnefie
Le lait peccié d'ypocrisie.
2336 Pour ches raisons est deffendu

D[e] Dieu tel june corrompue,
Car en l'Evangile nous dit
Nostre Sires ·i· mout bel dit:
2340 "Segneur qui junés, je vos prie
Que vous gardés d'ypocrisie."

La tierche june font glouton:
Chist sont plus niche ke mouton,
2344 Car de fain seuffrent la haskie
Pour che que, quant fains [les] aigrie,
Plus se delitent au mengier.
Tel gent font trop a mesprisier,
2348 Car par lor grande gloutenie
Perdent de Dieu grasse et aïe,
Car sains Grigores nos tesmoigne
Ou Pastoral que mal besoigne
2352 Li hom qui a juner se met
Et sa vïande en garde met
Pour mengier puis a plus grant aise —   60r
Tel jeüne est certes mauvaise.

2356 L'autre june est mout honerable,
Pour chë a non june loiable;
C'est quant li hom fait astinanche
Pour Dieu vengier et sa beubanche,
2360 Et che quë il souffraint de soi
Ont chil qui ont et fain et soi.
·iiii· coses si ont mestier
A cheste june acompaignier,
2364 Dont la premiere a non lëeche,
De coi Dieus dist par vois e[s]presce:
"Quant tu junes, si oing ton chief",
Et la glose dist derechief
2368 Que chil encraisse bien sa teste
Qui s'esjoïst de vie honeste.
L'autre cose doit estre l'eure,
Car il estuet quë il demeure,
2372 S'il veut faire june honeree
Dusques a l'eure commandee.
L'eure si est a droite none,

	Et qui avant s'i abandoune,	
2376	Sachiés pour voir que ch'est pecciés —	
	Jonatas fu a mort jugiés	*60v*
	Pour che qu'il prinst ·i· disnee	
	Avant l'eure qu'iert ordenee.	
2380	La tierche cose a non mesure,	
	Car Dieus si n'a d'outraje cure,	
	Et aucun sont si outragier	
	Que, quant il junent, au mengier	
2384	Mengüent plus qu'il ne feroient	
	A ·iii· mengiers s'il ne junoient.	
	Aumosne a non la quarte cose,	
	Dont Augustins nos dist en glose	
2388	Qu'autant vaut sans eoule lumiere	
	Com june qui n'est aumosniere.	

	Li tiers guerriers qui nous guerroie	
	Pour nos oster de droite voie	
2392	Par ·iii· batalles mout grevables,	
	C'est li faus mondes desrainables	
	Qui si nos destruit et argüe	
	Que nos cournons la recreüe	
2396	Souventes [fois] par la fallamche	
	Que nos avons de comnissanche;	
	Car s'entre nos sage fuissiemes	
	Et [si] queme sage ovrissiemes,	*61r*
2400	Par ·i· seule cose faire	
	Metriens a nient nostre aversaiere,	
	Si qu'avarisse ni envie	
	Në ire aveukes, le hounie —	
2404	Puisque venrroit au batellier —	
	Ne nos porroient damagier.	
	Et nequedent, s'il avenist	
	Que li mondes si nous tenist	
2408	Que de nous fust toute brisie	
	Et de nos proismes l'amistie,	
	Par le cose que vous devise	
	Revenrions nous a no frankise:	
2412	C'est par asmone, qui esscache	
	Pecciés com li solaus la glache.	

Aumosne apel, tant qu'en ches[t] liu,
Che que li hom doune pour Dieu.
2416 En amosne donke besoigne,
Quant on le fait, que l'om i doigne
Don [qu]i couvient, car par le don
A on d'amosne guerredon.
2420 Le don estuet par estovoir
Toudis de largueche mouvoir,
Dont estuet par necessité
Qu'amosne soit de largueté;
2424 Pour che vos veul chi ensegnier
Quanbien largueche puet aidier
A chelui qui le veut user
Si com il doit, sans refuser.
2428 Li hom qui par largueche done,
Largueche si li guerredoune,
Ou en avoir ou en amis,
Quamqu'en la gent pour li a mis —
2432 Par usage le puis prouver,
Car gent assés puet on trouver
Cui par largueche est avenu
Qu'il en sont rike devenu,
2436 Mais ains par droite largueté
Ne keï hom en povreté.
J'ai bien veü et bien avient
Que par fol don povretés vient,
2440 Car gast est mere de povreche,
Mais je n'apel pas gast largueche,
Car gast n'a de mesure cure,
2443 Et largueche requiert mesure
2445 Pour che que toudis puist durer.
Cil qui se veut amesurer
Tous jors puet douner par nature,
2448 Pour che dist on: "Mesure dure."
Dont pert il bien que par largueche
Puet chil venir a grant rikeche
Qui a droit douner s'abandoune,
2452 Car au boin dounë[o]ur Dieus doune,
Com u proverbe se contient,
Et ensi estre li couvient,

61v

62r

```
           Car largueche est com la fontaine
2456       Qui tous jors cuert, tous jors est plaine.
           Nus ne le peut amenuisier
           Pour souvent au ruissau puchier
           Despuis qu'i[l] de corre ne fine;
2460       Ausi est de largueche fine,
           Car a nul tans n'amenrrira
           Avoirs qui de largue sera
           Pour don qu'a droit en sache faire.
2464       Pour che si doit largueche plaire,
           Mais mieus encore, m'est avis,
           Pour chou, c'on en aquiert amis
           En qui plus grans pourfis abonde
2468       Qu'en nul avoir qui soit u monde,           62v
           Car amis peut sovent aidier
           Ou li avoirs n'aroit mestier;
           Et si n'est il si douche cose
2472       Com boins amis a qui on ose
           Descouvrir toute sa penssee
           En liu ou ele iert bien chelee.
           Aprés en aquiert on usage
2476       De metre en tous biens son corage,
           Car en maint liu a on retrait
           Que l'une vertus l'autre atrait.
           Encor doit estre desiree
2480       C'on en aquiert grant renoumee;
           Plus aquiert los par sa largueche
           Mains chevaliers que par pröeche,
           Car chil qui j'ai douné le mien
2484       Doit par droit dire de moi bien,
           S'il est en moi, et du contraire
           Se doit il bien par raison taire,
           Car qui mesdist de bienfaiteur
2488       Je le tieng voir a traïteur,
           Car de desloiauté li vient.
           Pour che voit on bien k'il avient
           Que nus n'iert ja si entechiés           63r
2492       De grans blasmes ne de pecciés,
           Mais que largueche le renoume,
           Qu'il ne soit tenus pour preudoume;
```

Par che pert bien qu'il n'a en tere
2496 Cose millor pour los aquerre
Com d'estre larguement donans
Et doublement guerredounans.
Puisque largueche a tel pöoir,
2500 Cascuns peut clerement vöoir
Qu'amosne de largueche meut,
Que cascuns hom aquerre en puet
Les biens que chi desus dis ore.
2504 Mais vraiement vous [di] encore
Que quamk'ai dit si samble blasme
Vers che quë on aquiert a l'ame,
Car amosne, bien le sachiés,
2508 Estaint autresi les peccïés —
Ja d'aus ne sera si destrois
Et especïaument des trois —
Com l'iaugue jetee a fuison
2512 Estaint ·i· enbramé tison.
Avec l'estainte de peccié
Aquerons par li amistié   63v
De Dieu, laquele par raison
2516 Vers autre n'a comparison,
Car Dieus pour che[ste] amor nos done
U ciel pardurable couroune,
Mais qu'au douner l'entenssïon
2520 Soit pour avoir sauvassïon.
Et puis c'om puet par li aquiere
Pourfit, honor, boin los en terre,
Cascuns doit douner volentiers
2524 Pour Dieu, quant il en est mestiers.
Mais mainte gent si se dechoivent,
Car il dounent chou qu'il ne doivent,
Et autrement c'on ne doit faire.
2528 Pour che m'estuet ichi retraire
Desqués coses li preudon puet,
A cui, et quant, douner, s'il veut,
Et ques doit estre la maniere
2532 De la boine gent amosniere
Qui dounent par devocïon.
Or oiés la secussïon:

2536	**A**mosner puet tous crestïens Selonc son gré de tous ses biens Qu'il a gäagnié justement, Se n'est de rente seulement,	*64r*
2540	Car au segneur fait tort mult grief Qui amosne sans lui son fief, Et as oirs n'en fait mie mains S'il ne lor laist a tout le mains	
2544	Lor part qu'il ont par le lingnage. A che doit on veïr l'usage C'on a u liu dont li fiés meut, Mais de tous meubles li hom puet	
2548	Douner du tout a sa devise, Fors seulement en sa devise, Car il ja cose moitïie Qui doit as oirs estre laissie —	
2552	Es lois si en treuv[e] on la somme Selonc l'ordounement de Roume — Mais le sou[r]plus douner si puet Li hom en quele part qu'il veut.	
2556	Mais de la cose mal aquise Doit on ovrer par autre guise, Car d'aucuns biens puet li hom faire Amosne qui puet a Dieu plaire;	*64v*
2560	Pour che m'estuet distinctïon Faire de l'aquisicïon. Li hom en cose mal aquise A le fois n'a point de frankise,	
2564	Ch'est a dire de segnourie, Com en furt ou en reuberie; Et puisque pöoir n'en aquiert En tel don, amosne n'afiert,	
2568	Car il l'estuet a forche rendre — Pour che dist on: "Ou rendre ou pendre." Encore i a une devise En segnourie mal aquise,	
2572	Car une i a qu'il couvient rendre C'on ne le puet douner ne vendre, Com est simonie ou usure,	

Car Dieus n'a de si fait don cure;
L'autre poissanche mal aquise
2576 Si est en la frankise mise
Du conquerant, ch'est a entendre
Qui la puet retenir ou rendre,
Com est gäang de puterie,
2580 De hyraus ou de jouglerie;
Li hom qui fait tele conqueste,   *65r*
Tout ait il peccié en l'aqueste,
Du pourfit puet il bien ballier
2584 As povres qui en ont mestier.

Or soit ensi qu'il avenist
Qu'aucuns preudom avant venist
Si me desist: "Biaus amis chiers,
2588 Tous jors ai jüé volentiers
As jus plaisans et delitables,
Si com as eschiés et as tables,
Et a hazart souvent m'envoise
2592 A plus de poins, a la grigoise,
S'en ai ·iii· dés per ou nonper,
Souvent ai amenri mon per,
A escakons et as mereles
2596 Ai conquis sercos et coteles.
Se dé me falent soulagier,
M'e[n]vois[e] au point de l'eskekier,
Ou au toupet enmi la voie,
2600 Ou au ju de boute en coroie.
A rauller met souvent ma chiere,
Et si jete en la plache pierre;
Denier conquier souvent de billes,
2604 D'un court baston et [de] ·ix· quilles.   *65v*
De tous ches geus en verité
Ai souvent mon escot quité
Et gäagnié tel remanant
2608 Dont je me truis riche et manant;
Or veul du conquest de men geu
Faire aucun bien, s'i[l] plaist a Dieu,
Mais je ne sai s'i[l] li ahaite
2612 Qu'amosne soit de tel don faite;

>
> Pour che, sire, je vous requier
> Que vous me veulliés consellier."
> A ces[t] cas li responderoie:
2616 "Biaus dous ami, se Dieus me voie,
> Je ne sai pas tant de clergie,
> Ne ne sui de si haute vie
> Que requerre me deüssiés
2620 Consel ou vous ataquissiés;
> Nekedent, puisqu'il vous agree
> Je vous en dirai ma pensee.
> Sachiés, amis, se vous juastes
2624 Et vo conpagnon apelastes
> Pour jüer, ou l'en destrainsistes,
> Sachiés pour voir, vos mespresi[s]tes
> Se pour desir d'avoir le sien   66r
2628 Le traisistes a chele rien;
> Pour che couvient que li rendés.
> Mais se vous a jüer tendés
> Pour vos deduire et soulagier,
2632 Non pour desir de gäagnier,
> Et vostre ami n'en semounés,
> Tout le pourfit pour Dieu donés,
> Se volés faire, sans mesprendre.
2636 Au perdant ne le devés rendre,
> S'il n'est tes hom qui ne puist faire
> Sans son tutor le sien contraire."
> Or puet chascuns, s'il bien s'avise,
2640 Par la desus dite devise
> Savoir de ses biens sans atente
> Se li dons d'aus a Dieu talente.
> Or öés sans arestison
2644 Qui amosner puet par raison.

> Amosner puet, selonc mon esme,
> Cascuns sires de soi mëeme,
> Mais chil qui est sous autrui pié
2648 Ne puet doner sans son congié,
> Si com sont femmes marïe[e]s   66v
> Ou persones a Dieu vöe[e]s,
> Car il ont mis lor sauvement

2652	Tout en autri commandement,
	Pour che ne puent faire don
	Dont de Dieu aient gueredon,
	Fors en especïalité —
2656	Or en öés la verité:
	Femme puet don, s'i[l] li plaist, faire
	Des biens qui sont de son douaire
	Et des coses dont par usage
2660	Les femmes ont le segnourage,
	Si com sont pain, char, vin, vïandes,
	De che puent bien faire offrandes
	As povres gens, par tel droiture
2664	Qu'en lors dons ait toudis mesure,
	Se lor mari ne lor desfendent
	Qu'en povre gent plus ne despendent.
	Ausi ne doit relegïeus
2668	Douner pour Dieu sans son prïeus
	Ou son souvrain, s'il n'est de ceus
	Qui gardent les biens temporeus.
	Encor i a ·i· autre point
2672	En coi la desfensse n'est point,
	C'est quant il est ens u voiage
	D'escole ou de pelerimage,
	Car puisqu'il s'en part par congié,
2676	Si pert c'on li ait otrïé
	De son voloir faire e[n]terrin
	En che que font boin pelerin
	En lor chemin, ou escolier,
2680	Qui sont tenu d'estre amosnier.
	Mais tant vous di ge bien en somme
	Que toutes femmes et tout houme,
	Contre le gré de lor souvrain,
2684	Sont tenu au morant de fain
	A doner lui de lor vïande,
	Car nostre Sires le quemande
	Qui servir devons par nature
2688	Plus que nule autre creature.
	Or avés vous en chest ditier
	Qui amosne puet otrïier;
	Or est raisons que je vous die

67r

| 2692 | Cui ele doit estre ballie. |

	Amosne puet on otrïer
	A toute gent k'en ont mestier.
	Que che soit voirs, je le vous preuve	67v
2696	Par Thobie, liqués nous reuve
	Que nus ne soit si desdegneus
	Qu'i[l] pour nul povre besoigneus
	Doive sa chiere destourner,
2700	Qu'a peccié li doit on tourner.
	Mais or soit a[i]nsi de Thobie
	Qu'il ne sache quel cose il die,
	Jhesu Crist en devons nous croire,
2704	La qui raisons est toudis voire,
	Liqueus tout ensi nous kemande:
	"Doune a toute gent qui demande."
	Mais s'aucuns hom, pour demoustrer
2708	Mon dit a faus, vausist moustrer
	Que chil qu'au pechavour aïe
	Si le soustient en son peccie —
	Car u proverbe se contient
2712	Qu'assés escorche qui pié tient,
	Et, tout fait mal qui mal maintient,
	Peu en fait mains qui le soustient —
	A ches[t] fait sans dilactïon
2716	Feroiie tel condictïon:
	Aidiés peut estre li peccieres
	De l'amosnier en ·ii· manieres,	68r
	L'un pour soustenir sa nature
2720	Pour che qu'il a d'oume faiture,
	Et chil qui ensi le soustient
	Si fait che qu'a li apartient;
	L'autre pour croistre s'ordurie,
2724	Tes dons si est mortel pecchie.
	Or me porroit uns preudom dire:
	"Aumosne voel faire, biaus sire,
	Mais ne sui pas de tel rikeche
2728	Qu'a tous puisse faire largueche.
	A cui devrai dont commenchier
	Pour faire com droit aumosnier?"

A si petit d'apenssement
2732 Com j'ai, me samble vraiement
Que par raison et par usage
Si ont le premier avantage
Es dons d'aumosne li povre honme,
2736 Et aprés chiaus l'ont li preudoume,
Et puis li viel souräagié,
Et aprés les gens dehaitié,
Aprés sont li parent el conte,
2740 Puis chaus qui ont de prïer honte,
Aprés si sont li encheü   68v
En povreté qui mescheü
Ne s[on]t par leur outrecuidanche,
2744 Mais par diverse meschëance.
Ensi estuet a l'amosnier
Pour aumosner estudïer,
Car tout soit il que tout pourfite
2748 A l'amosnier, plus a merite
Por che, selonc m'entencïon,
Li dons fais par discrectïon
Que nus autres dons ne feroit
2752 Qui sans discrectïon seroit.
Or avés vous par ches vers miens
A cui pöés douner vos biens;
Aprés vous dirai la maniere
2756 De l'aumosne que Dieus a chiere.
Aumosne estuet aconpagnier
De ·v· menbres qui moult sont chier.
Li premiers est plains de bonté,
2760 C'est dons de boine volenté
Fais et dounés au rechevant,
Non pas de cuer vain dechevant,
Car Dieus ne garde pas l'ofrande   69r
2764 Mais le cuer qui a lui le mande,
Car carités n'est mie en fuer
A Dieu qui n'est faite de cuer,
Mais carités de Dieu löee
2768 Est aumosne de cuer dounee.

Li secons menbres proprement

	Est aumosne faite humlement,	
	Car chis dons est de carité	
2772	Qui est garnis d'umilité,	
	Car chil qui drois humles sera	
	S'umelités le gardera	
	De ·iii· coses dont la persone	
2776	Se doit garder qui pour Dieu done,	
	S'il veut que Dieus l'ait en memore,	
	Dont la premiere est vaineglore.	
	C'est a dire quant aumosniers	
2780	Veut de ses dons los seculiers,	
	Dont, puisque du monde se paie,	
	De Dieu n'ara ja autre paie,	
	Car Dieus ne veut que nus qui tende	
2784	A sa paie d'autrui l'atende.	
	Por che di jë, ou je dit ai,	69v
	Les biens d'aumosne que ditai,	
	Qu'ele complist proposement	
2788	Et che couvient au sauvement.	
	De che devons saint Mathieu croiere	
	Et son dit avoir en memoire	
	Qui dist: "Amis, ja ta senestre"	
2792	Ne sache che que fait ta destre."	
	L'autre visce dont ele est quite	
	Si est que cheli ne despite	
	Qui a volu son don rechoivre,	
2796	Car mieus ne s'en porroit dechoivre,	
	Car Yzaïes si nous livre	
	·I· tel deffens dedens son livre	
	U title ·lviii·tisme:	
2800	"Car ne despis ta char meïsme."	
	La desraine desfensciön	
	Si est d'avoir presonssïon	
	D'estre par s'aumosne quités	
2804	De toutes les iniquités,	
	Sans estre des pecciés confés.	
	Ensi n'alege il pas son fes,	
	Car la carités que j'ai dite	
2808	Autre cose ne li pourfite	70r
	Fors tant com font en verité	

Li bien fait hors de carité.

Li tiers menbres, che m'est samblant,
2812 Si est qu'il faiche lié samblant.
De che Salemons nous ensegne,
Si gart cascuns que bien l'enpregne,
U ·xxxv·ime traitié:
2816 "En tous tes dons te fai haitié."

Li quars menbres tot home escole
Qu'en son don ait douche parole,
Car plaisans dis est la viele
2820 Qui les cuers en amour apele,
Dont hom qui parlle plaisaument
Est amés de tous coreument.
Ausi ne tien ge l'onme a sage
2824 Qui laidenge le Dieu message,
Car chil qui li mesfait en dis,
Se Dieus veut, iert ausi mendis,
Et u proverbe se contient:
2828 "Bele parole boin lieu tient."
Cele puet mieus tenir boin lieu   *70v*
Qui est dite au message Dieu
Que nus autres dis ne porroit
2832 C'ascuns alleurs dire vaurroit,
Dont lo je bien a l'amosnier
Que, s'aucuns hom li vient proier,
Qu'i[l] li otroit courtoisement
2836 Ou escondisse simplement.
Et si nel faiche trop atendre;
En Salemon, qui veut entendre,
Porra trouver qui i veut lire:
2840 "Fin cuer de mendïant n'aflire."

Li quins menbres d'aumosne droite
Si veut que chascuns hom esploite
En aumosner si sagement
2844 Que s'aumosne durt longement,
Car chele c'un petit ne dure
Samble moustres contre nature,

	Car li moustres a la suistanche	
2848	Mais il i faut droite ordounamche;	
	Ausi est drois ordounemens	
	D'aumosne lons complissemens,	
	Car il n'est drois qu'aumosne faille	71r
2852	Tant com u cors l'ame travalle,	
	Car vertus n'est pas de vaillanche	
	S'il n'a en li perseveranche.	
	Or sont aucun qui s'abandounent	
2856	As grans dons faire, qui si dounent	
	Qu'a forche estuet lors dons remaindre,	
	Et seut pour tant l'aumosne fraindre.	
	Pour che li quins menbres [commande]	
2860	Que chil qui fait pour Dieu offrande	
	Faiche ses dons selonc sa rente,	
	Car si fais dons Dieu atalente.	
	De che trouvons nous ou traitie	
2864	Ou quart capitle de Thobie,	
	Que chil qui a des biens assés	
	De moult douner ne soit lassés,	
	Et chil qui peu a en ballie	
2868	Si doinst petit a cuer haitie.	
	Ensi estuet que chil le fache	
	Que veut aquerre le Dieu grasse,	
	Car boins paintëours qui veut faire	
2872	Bele painture doit pourtraire	
	O le ploumet premierement,	
	Puis metra plus seürement	71v
	Ses coleurs ou il les veut metre;	
2876	Tout ausi se doit entremetre	
	Aumosniers ententivement	
	De douner apensëement,	
	Car chil qui par apens ne doune	
2880	S'aumosne gaires ne fuisone,	
	Et sages hom amesurer	
	Se doit, si ke puisse durer	
	S'aumosne tant qu'il iert en vie,	
2884	Si k'a la mort li faiche aïe	
	De li mener de Purgatoire	
	Pour lui poser net en la gloire	

Qui fu et est et si sera
2888 Tous jours que ja ne finera,
Car fins i est si definee
Et joie ausi si afinee
Que chele joie dur[e]ra
2892 Tant qu'en nul tans ne cessera,
Mais samblera millors toutdis.
A tant faut d'aumosne li dis.

Segnour, dit vous ai en mon livre,
2896 Selonc le sens que Dix me livre,   *72r*
Che qui apartient au mestier
Du junant et de l'aumosnier
Et de chelui qui par raison
2900 Veut a Dieu faire s'orison,
Car par les coses que j'ai dites
De ches mesfais sont les gens quites
Dont Anemis par traïson
2904 Getés les a en sa prison,
Car penitanche bien conplie
A la porte mout tost brisie;
Et puisque chele porte est route,
2908 Des prisoniers s'en ist grans route,
Ch'est a entendre sans doutanche
De chiaus qui ont fait penitanche;
Car penitanche, qui le porte
2912 Brisa, tous ses amis enporte,
Si qu'Anemis si n'a poissanche
De faire leur point de grevanche
Tant com penitanche feront,
2916 Car tant com en tel point seront —
Mais qu'en Dieu croient fermement,
Et aient afermëement
En lui toute lor esperanche,
2920 Et puis metent leur counissanche   *72v*
En faire oevre de carité
Et les ·iii· biens k'ai rechité —
Li Anemis n'ara poissanche
2924 De faire leur point de grevanche.
Mais s'a la fin, sans desvoier,

	Puëent aler tout che sentier,
	Li angles qui ara gardee
2928	La sainte ame boineüree
	Lasus u chiel l'enportera
	Et devant Dieu le posera.
	Lors maintenant sera douee
2932	De Dieu, qui mout l'ara amee,
	D'avoir joie perpetüel
	Et clarté esperitüel,
	A laquel joie parvenir
2936	Nous laist, quant nos devro[n]s fenir,
	Ichil qui fu, est, et sera
	Regnans, ne ja ne finera.
	Amen, amen, cascuns en die,
2940	Que Dieus en celi liu nous guie.

    Chi fait Jehans a tant finanche   *73r*
De "le Disme de Penitanche",
Mais aprés vient une proiere
2944 Que tous preudons doit avoir chiere,
Car cascuns est tenus de faire
Si que sains Paus le nos esclaire;
Jehans aprés son dit l'avise,
2948 Or faites che qu'ele devise.

    Segnour, en la fin du ditié
Que je vous ai ichi traitié,
Faites pour moi une proiere
2952 A Dieu de volenté pleniere.
Prïons Jhesu Crist sans faintise
Premierement pour sainte Yglise,
Qu'il li otroit toudis a faire
2956 Tel cose qui li puisse plaire,
Noumëement pour l'Aposto[i]le
Qui doit estre come l'estoile
En cui maronier ont recuevre,
2960 Car li Papes par sa boine oevre
Si doit le monde enluminer
Et ses subjeus endotriner.

Aprés pour tous les cardonaus 73v
2964 Qui tout sont devenu venaus,
Car orendroit si ne fait Romme,
Si queme on dist, a nesun honme
Grasse nule pour boine vie,
2968 Pour gentilleche ne clergie,
Mais qui d'avoir doune grant masse,
Chil trouvera leus tantost grasse,
Mais chil qui est plains de poverte
2972 Ne trouvera le porte ouverte.
Et tout soit il qu'a Dieu desplaise
Tel usage vill et mauvaise,
On ne s'en doit esmervellier,
2976 Car la furent fait li denier
Premierement; dont couvoitise
Si s'est des lors en Romme mise;
Dont il a ja des ans deus mile
2980 Que herbegier vint en la vile,
Dont samble il bien par teneüre
Qu'ele ait en la chité droiture.
Pour che n'i voi consel ne voie
2984 Fors k'a chelui qui tout avoie
Prïons de cuer qu'il s'entremete
Du fait de Roume, si qu'il mete 74r
Couvoitise, qui trop s'avanche,
2988 Fors de toute l'apartenanche
De Roume, que tant on diffame
Que je ne voi houme ne feme
Qui vient de la, quë il ne die
2992 Que couvoitise la maistrie.

Prïons encor Dieu en pitie
Que Roume ne soit engingnie
Es sentenses qu'el a a rendre,
2996 Mais les rende si sans mesprendre
Que de Dieu et de gent senee
Tous jors en puist estre löee,
Et que toutes fauses parties
3000 I soient de leur tort punies.

Aprés prïons qu'as jugemens
Doinst Dieus tes acomplisemens
Que la sentensse soit tenue
3004 Que sainte Yglise ara rendue.

Aprés les desus dis capitres
Prïons pour trestous les menistres
Qui ont en Eglise ballie, 74v
3008 Que cascuns puist mener sa vie
Si que chaus qu'il doivent aprendre
I puissent tel essample prendre,
En leur ovres premierement
3012 Et puis en lor prëechement,
Qu'il en puissent encore aquerre
Repos sans fin, honeur en tere,
Et li souvrain si se conduisent
3016 Qu'a che meïsme venir puissent.

Aprés prïons Dieu humlement
Pour tous prinches noumëement,
Que chil qui sont obeïssant
3020 Au siege saint, en acroissant
Tiegnent toudis l'obedïenche;
Et chil qui par sinple scïence
D'obeïr i ont volenté
3024 Soient des or entalenté
D'obeïr com gent droituriere
Tous jors au vicaire saint Piere,
Et qu'il puissent si maintenir
3028 Raison et justiche tenir
Que li pueples puist a delivre 75r
En boine pais desous aus vivre,
Et que li peuples si les serve
3032 Que d'aus et de Dieu en deserve
Boin gerredon et tele amour
Que Dieus n'en oie ja clamour.

Aprés prïons devotement
3036 A Dieu qui est sans finement
Qu'il doinst honor, joie et gäagne

　　　　　Au tres poissant roi d'Alemagne,
　　　　　Qui preudom est, vallans et sages,
3040　　 Et a toudis mis ses usages
　　　　　En honerer chevalerie.
　　　　　Prïons a Dieu par sa pitie
　　　　　K'il li envoit prochainement
3044　　 Pöoir qu'il puist hastivement
　　　　　De l'enpire estre courounés,
　　　　　Car Dieus en seroit houneŕes,
　　　　　Sainte Eglise et chevalerie,
3048　　 Et toute gent de boine vie,
　　　　　Car preudons est et droituriers —
　　　　　Diex li envoit ses desiriers!

　　　　　Aprés prïons sans delaianche　　　　　*75v*
3052　　 Pour le roy Phelipe de Franche
　　　　　A cui Dieus par largueche pure
　　　　　A doné bel don de nature,
　　　　　Ch'est che qu'il est plains de biauté
3056　　 Qui li vaut une roiauté;
　　　　　Et s'il a de biaté plenté,
　　　　　Si li doinst Dieus sens et bonté
　　　　　Dont maintenir sache ses gens,
3060　　 Si iert en tout et biaus et gens.

　　　　　Aprés faisons requeste bele
　　　　　Pour le noble roy de Castele,
　　　　　Qui toudis a mout mortel gerre
3064　　 As Sarrasins pres de sa terre,
　　　　　Que Dieus si l'ait si en memore
　　　　　Qu'avoir puisse toudis victore
　　　　　Des mescreans, et en saudee,
3068　　 Quant s'ame iert de son cors sevree,
　　　　　En ait la joie souveraine
　　　　　Pour son traval et pour sa paine.

　　　　　Aprés pour le roy d'Engletere,
3072　　 Millor de lui n'estuet il querre,
　　　　　Que Dieus li envoit longe vie,
　　　　　Voloir, savoir et tele aïe　　　　　*76r*

111

>   Que decha mer puisse venir
> 3076 Pour la guerre Dieu maintenir,
>   Dont il s'est ja si avanchiés
>   Que pour che fait s'est il croisiés;
>   Si prïons Dieu qu'il l'en otroie
> 3080 Victore, honor, boin los et joie.
>
>   Aprés faisons une proiere
>   Pour les enfans du noble pere
>   Qui d'Arragon fu jadis roys,
> 3084 Que Dieus leur doinst, si com ch'est drois,
>   Que cascuns d'aus ensi s'apensse
>   Qu'il viegnent a l'obedïensse
>   De saint Pierre et de son vicaire,
> 3088 Lequel truisent si deboinaire
>   Qu'a lui aient boine acordanche,
>   Et ferme pais a cheus de Franche.
>
>   Aprés, si prïons en ches[t] livre
> 3092 A nostre Segneur qu'il delivre,
>   S'i[l] li plaist, sans arestison,
>   Le prinche qui est en prison,
>   Car a preudome le tesmoignent
> 3096 Toutes les gens qu'a li besoignent,
>   Et d'autre part s'oneste vie
>   Li enporte grant garantie.
>
>   Prïons pour le conte d'Artois,
> 3100 Qui est sages, pieus et courtois
>   Et conpains a tous chevaliers
>   De son cors et de ses deniers,
>   Que Dieus li laist si bien tenir
> 3104 Tout che qu'il a a maintenir
>   Qu'encore l'ait et si ami;
>   Et chil qui se sont arrami
>   Ou arramissent par beubanche
> 3108 De faire a lui n'a siens grevanche,
>   Dieus si leur veulle consentir
>   Qu'encor s'en puissent repentir,
>   Car tout che qu'il font au preudome

76v

3112	Il font a l'Eglise de Roume	
	Qu'il a establi[e] en chest liu	
	Pour maintenir les drois de Diu.	

       Segnour, encor je vous requier
3116   Que vous doiés a Dieu proier
       Pour le frere du tres boin roy
       D'Engletere, qui grant conroi
       A mis piecha de cuer entier
3120   Et met pour lui apparellier   *77r*
       A sa venue decha mer.
       Tel prinche doit on mout amer,
       Car courtois est, sages, loiaus
3124   Et as povres drois appoiaus.
       Mesire Edmons est il noumés
       Et de grans grasses renoumés,
       Si est garnis de tel largeche
3128   Dont grant renon prent sa nobleche,
       Car "non" ne seut il onques dire,
       Mais "prendés." Sa riquech[e] enpire
       Et si amende sa value;
3132   Prïons a Dieu sans atendue
       Qu'il li envoit joie et santé
       Et pöoir, que la volenté
       Qu'il a de venir en Surie
3136   Puisse bien tost estre acomplie,
       Car la tere en amenderoit,
       Et Dieus honerés en seroit.

       Aprés prïons, se ferons bien,
3140   Que tout li prinche terrïen,
       Qui dela mer sont demourant
       Dieu et sainte Eglise honerant,
       Puissent tous jors si maintenir   *77v*
3144   Raison et justiche tenir
       Que li pueples puist a delivre
       En boine pais desous aus vivre,
       Et que li pueples si les serve
3148   Que d'aus et de Dieu en deserve
       Boin gerredon et tel amour

Que Dieus n'en oie ja clamour.

Aprés devons Dieu reclamer
3152 Pour les segneurs de decha mer,
Et premiers pour le Patrïarche
Qui est gouvrener[e]s de l'arche
De sainte Eglise qui i maint;
3156 Prïons a Dieu qu'il se demaint
En tel maniere et en tel sens
Qu'il et li clergiés, par son sens,
Puissent mener si sainte vie
3160 Que par l'essample du clergie
Li lai puissent tel cose faire
Tous jours k'a Jhesu Crist puist plaire.

Aprés requerons humlement
3164 A Dieu qu'il maint acroissement
De gens, d'ounour et de tous biens
Celestïens et terrïens 78r
A monsegneur le roi Henri
3168 Que Sarrasin ont amenri
De toute la gregneur partie
Qui affiert a sa segnourie,
Ch'est a savoir et a entendre
3172 De la tere ou Dieu[s] vaut estendre
Ses bras pour tous chaus enbrachier
Qui veulent aler droit sentier;
Car Jerusalem ont comquise
3176 Et trestoute le tere prinse
Qui a son roiaume apartient,
Fors Acre qui encor se tient,
Saiete et Castiau Pelerin,
3180 Sur et Barur dont enterin
Ne sont li mur que par frankise;
En ches[t] conté est Cayfas mise.
Et ches cités que j'ai noumees
3184 Si sont si griefment apressees
Qu'eles n'ont tere pour semer
Ne dont vivre, fors que de mer,
Dont est il bien cose certaine

LA DISME DE PENITANCHE

3188	Que grant despens et moult grant paine	
	Couvient a ces cités deffendre;	78v
	Pour che couvient au roi despendre —	
	Et il le fait mout volentiers —	
3192	Quamqu'amasser puet de deniers	
	En Chipre dont est rois et sire,	
	Et a paines puet che souffire.	
	Or prïons dont Dieu finement	
3196	Qu'il maint au roi delivrement	
	Si com il set qu'il est mestiers,	
	Secours de gens et de deniers,	
	Par cui Jherusalem soit mise	
3200	Ens ou pöoir de sainte Eglise;	
	Car grant honte est as crestïens	
	Et plus as prinches terrïens	
	Qui se metent pour pris en paine	
3204	Quant autre tienent la fontaine	
	Dont des ruissaus crestïen boivent.	
	Li anemi bien les dechoivent	
	Quant entr'aus les font gerroier	
3208	Tant qu'il ne püent Dieu vengier,	
	Mais Anemis si les encombre	
	Qui la veüe leur äombre;	
	On en voit hui bien l'essamplaire.	
3212	Mais je m'en veul a itant taire —	79r
	Sourparllers nuist et est vergoigne —	
	Mais prïons Jhesu Crist qu'il doigne	
	Au roi dont je fais mensïon	
3216	Pöoir, voloir, discressïon	
	De maintenir si bien justice	
	Vers la gent qui li est sousmise,	
	Que toute gent mainent lor vie	
3220	En pais desous sa segnourie.	
	Aprés pour le roi d'Ermenie	
	Prïons Dieu et sainte Marie,	
	Que de son fait si lor remembre	
3224	Que son roiaume puist deffendre	
	Contre Tartars et Sarrasins	
	Et Turquemans et Haussasi[n]s	

	Qui moult li font grant encombrier	
3228	De son roiaume gerroier;	
	Si prïons Dieu qu'il ne consente	
	Que li rois plus damage en sente,	
	Car il acuelle volentiers	
3232	Courtoisement les estrangiers	
	Qu'en sa tere vont sodoier,	
	Si com j'ai oï tesmoignier.	
	Or repairons au noble prince	*79v*
3236	D'Antïoche qui on espi[n]ce	
	De Triple mout vilainement,	
	Et si houme noumëement	
	Qui contre lui sa vile ont close	
3240	Sans che qu'il dïent nule cose	
	Ou on puisse noter raison.	
	Chi a vilaine mesproison	
	Quant, sans moustrer raison nisune,	
3244	Contre le prince font conmune,	
	Et departent sa segnourie,	
	Et afferment par äatie	
	Que la princhesse asegeront	
3248	Et en la fin le prenderunt.	
	Certes il font grande mervelle,	
	Et mervelle ai qu'on lor conselle,	
	Et plus quant il le consel croient,	
3252	Que si laidement se desvoient,	
	Car a tout le mains pour le blasme	
	De lor fois, dont on les diffame,	
	Devroient il ches[t] fait laissier.	
3256	Pour che devons a Dieu proier	
	Qu'a chaus de Triple meche en cuer	
	De jeter chest orguel en puer	*80r*
	Qui les a volut dechevoir,	
3260	Si que leur dame rechevoir	
	Veullent a joie et a lëeche,	
	Et que madame la princhesse	
	Lor pardoinst deboinairement	
3264	Trestout leur divers errement.	

           Pour le segneur de Sur faison
           Ausi a Dieu nostre orison
           Qu'e[n] che qu'il a encomencié
3268   Li envoit Dieus par sa pitié
           El mieus toudis perseveranche,
           Car comencement, sans fallanche,
           A il et bel et boin et sage;
3272   Et il li meut bien de lignage,
           Car ses peres iert pourvëans,
           Sages, courtois et cler vëans,
           Si est bien drois et raisons gente
3276   Que de son bien li fiex se sente,
           Car ou proverbe se contient
           Que "de boin arbre boins fruis vient",
           Et il s'en sent si bien sans falle
3280   Que moult pris[e] on sa comenchalle.
           Pour che prïons nostre Segnour   *80v*
           Que sens, pöoir, valoir gregnour
           Li veulle otrïer et mander,
3284   Et que toudis puist amender
           Et Sur ausi puist maintenir
           Qu'a grant honour puisse venir.
           En l'an de l'incarnatïon
3288   De Dieu qui soffri passïon
           ·M· et ·iii^c·, se ·xii· anees
           Estoient de ches[t] conte ostees,
           Si conmencha et parfurni
3292   Che livre Jehans de Journi
           En Chipre, droit a Nicossie,
           Lau il gisoit en maladie;
           Et qui du non veut counissanche,
3296   Ch'est "la Disme de Penitanche".

NOTES TO THE TEXT

Above line 1 in the same hand: *adsit principio sancta maria meo.*

16 *eslongie*: a Picard feminine past participle, see Introduction p. 9.

19 *ele* here refers to *langue*, and *dis* is the past participle of *dire*.

32 The scribe writes *loquence* as a separate word on all three of its appearances (cf. 82, 1292).

40 *vaurront* = *voudront*; see Introduction pp. 11 and 16.

45 The reference is to Genesis 1:26–27, 'et ait [Deus] "faciamus hominem ad imaginem et similitudinem nostram" [...] et creavit Deus hominem ad imaginem suam, ad imaginem Dei creavit illum.' (Cf. 2:7, 'formavit igitur Dominus Deus hominem de limo terrae.')

53 T-L has "ebenso (similarly)" as a possible sense for *proprement*, which would fit well here.

64 *pité*: except for the obvious scribal slip at 1160, this is the only occurrence of the form *pité*. It is doubtless due to the scribe, the author favouring the form *pitié*.

69ff. The general sense is clear ("even if man received no recompense for serving God [...] he ought still to serve him for three reasons"), but the word *perte* is perhaps surprising in context. The sense of *deserte* appears to be "something earnt/deserved" (whether reward or punishment), and so we should understand *ne de sa perte ne son secours* as "neither to his detriment nor his benefit", though *de* is not the preposition one might expect. T-L has no other examples of the two terms being contrasted like this. The theme is taken up again in lines 805ff.

88 *puisor* = "bucket". This is the spelling on all three appearances (cf. 97, 160), and *-ore* for *-oire* in learned words is common in this manuscript (see Introduction p. 11). However, *puisor* is the only word where *-or* might be thought to stand for *-oir*, with the exception of *dechevor* (: *aprechevoir* 383); elsewhere *-or* is always interchangeable with *-eur*. Ours is the only text quoted in T-L s.v. *puisëoir, puchëoir*.

90 *matere* in the well attested sense "Art, Wesen, Natur".

99 Other examples of monosyllabic *lau* are known to the dictionaries; the word appears again at 751 and 3294, and cf. also *la ou* at 192, 420, 746. Röhrs (p. 288) suggests that this is a northern or north-eastern form. It appears alongside the form *lou* in Anglo-Norman (e.g. in *Liber Donati* ed. B. Merrilees and B. Sitarz-Fitzpatrick, ANTS, Plain Texts Series no. 9 (1993), p. 24, 1. 249).

107 *ici*: This is the only appearance of *(i)ci* in the text (elsewhere only *ichi* and *chi* are found, though *ce*, *ces*, etc. occur sporadically — see Introduction p. 13), and it is possible that it is intended for *issi*, a form which the scribe never uses, but which might also be behind the *ichi* of 1276. *Ensacher* is problematic; the manuscript has *sensauche*. The basic meaning of *ensacher* is "to put something in a bag, put away". Ours is the only example of a reflexive form known to the dictionaries. We might understand: "in whom all wisdom is stored up, so that there is nobody...".

111 The reference here is not apparent. The first three chapters of I Corinthians are about wisdom, but there is no clear parallel to these lines.

112–14 The scribe has *amenrrie(r)* in both lines, inventing a form *alumier* to engineer a rhyme.

119 *sort*: pres.ind.3 of *sordre*.

121 *pechevor*: the manuscript also has the form *pechavour* at 2709, alongside *pechëour* at 972, 1469 and *peccëour* at 1941. See Introduction p. 15.

134 *pantain* = "mud, mire"; our text furnishes the only example in T-L, there is one other in Gdf.

136 T-L has two further examples of *aspret*.

144, 147 The manuscript quite clearly reads *satiff*-, a form unknown to the dictionaries; perhaps the learned forms have been crossed with the popular *satifiier/satefiier*. Elsewhere only the form *satisfacïon(s)* appears (984, 1344, 1979, 2001, 2027).

150–51 *Seeaus* appears to be monosyllabic here, pretonic *e* in hiatus having fallen (cf. Gossen §30). T-L has one other example of monosyllabic *sel* (*: consel*) from another north-eastern author Philippe Mousket, otherwise one might have emended to *moustre*. The scribe is given to spellings with inorganic *e*; see Introduction p. 26.

152 *faison*: the author allows himself the same licence (*-on* for *-ons* in rhyme with *raison, orison*) twice more (1142, 3264) all three times with the same verb *faire*. The form is predominantly western (see Hasenohr §147).

153–54 For this rhyme, see Introduction p. 17.

169–70 This is probably not an impure rhyme in Picard dialect; see Introduction p. 13.

171–72 On this rhyme, see Introduction p. 8.

191 *un*: a contraction of *en* + *le*, this rare form (our text provides all of T-L's examples) appears again at 241, 282, 370, 759 and 1655, while the commoner *u* appears twenty-two times (e.g. 80, 313, 432), and *ou* five times (e.g. 2351, 2863).

196 The idea is quite commonplace, but the source of the lines may be 'et exaltabit humiles' of the Magnificat, or Matthew 23:12 'qui autem se exaltaverit humiliabitur et qui se humiliaverit exaltabitur', or Luke 14:11 or 18:14, both of which read: 'quia omnis qui se exaltat humiliabitur et qui se humiliat exaltabitur.'

197 *mesra*: future of *mener*; see Introduction p. 15.

199 *dont* for *donc*, as often in this text, cf. 413, 681, etc.

202 *suagir*: The scribe originally wrote *sauoir*, then made the *o* into a *g*, giving *saugir*. Suchier (see Bibliography) suggests reading *d'esaugir* with the same sense as *ensauchier* of 196, which presents semantic difficulties (though the reduction of *ier* to *ir* is common enough in the North of France, see Pope §1320 vii), or alternatively *de sauver*, which would apply more happily to *ame* than to *cors*. T-L reads *d'esangier* in the sense "wash, purify". The emendation adopted here assumes that we are dealing with a form of Central O.F. *soagier* with the meaning "relieve, ease", etc.

204 *soutillanche*: T-L lists our example of this word and two further ones, both from Brunetto Latini. Gdf. cites the *Assises de Jérusalem* of 1240–50 as first attestation. The sense is "I do not call the cunning/cleverness of this world (true) wisdom".

209 The likely source here is Isaiah 5:20–24 'vae qui dicitis malum bonum et bonum malum [...] propter hoc sicut devorat stipulam lingua ignis et calor flammae exuret sic radix eorum', though the *fus* of 214 (= "wood") may be a recollection of 'ligna, faenum, stipulam' of I Corinthians 3:12.

213 *Que* in the sense "for, because". (The manuscript reads *Qui*.)

214 *restoble*: Gdf. lists half a dozen examples of this word, though they are all rather late; *FEW* 12, 273a, however, suggests that it may have been quite widespread. The manuscript has *li fus* here, presumably repeated from the previous line, since this is the only time in the text where the article *li* is used for *le*.

216 See 747*n*.

220 T-L has two further examples of the expression *aval le vent*.

223 A comparable attitude to lawyers is shown by *La Petite Philosophie*, ed W. H. Trethewey, ANTS 1 (Oxford, 1939) 205–08: 'Dunt la terre est mult afeblie E la gent tantost devie Par les pledurs, par les legistres Ke tuz sunt Antecrist ministres.'

228 *tesmoins*: here in the sense "testimony".

229 The source here has not been identified.

236 *vaineglorïeus*: T-L has three other examples of the word, two of which are from Brunetto Latini, and one of which is rather earlier.

237 *faus* = *fous*. See Introduction p. 11.

241 *un*: see 191*n*.

246–48 *perdera* may be transitive here, in the sense "destroy" (with *Dieus* as subject), or it may be intransitive, in the slightly commoner sense "perish, be lost" (with the subject *scïenche*). The problem is not resolved by reference to the source, which is not the well known I Corinthians 13, as *tressime* might suggest, but rather I Corinthians 3 (*tressime* being an example of the relatively rare synthetic ordinal, showing typical Picard variation between -*s*- and -*ss*-, cf. Gossen §49), verses 19–20: 'sapientia enim huius mundi stultitia est apud Deum; scriptum est enim: "conprehendam sapientes in astutia eorum", et iterum: "Dominus novit cogitationes sapientium quoniam vanae sunt".' The author is fond of equivocal rhymes (see Introduction p. 27), but this is one of only three cases where he appears to use an identical rhyme (or one with such a trifling nuance of sense), and it is possible that the text is corrupt.

251 *rench*: see Introduction p. 22.

267 The scribe writes *grans* as a feminine singular four more times in our text, cf. 1018, 1914, 2178, 2908.

269–78 The references here are: 269 Isaiah 14:12 (cf. Revelations 9:1); 275 Genesis chapters 18–19; 278 *ib.* 6–8.

282 *un*: see 191*n*.

287 According to Gossen (p. 79 n. 33), 'l'ancien picard préférait *vies* < VETUS, fém. *viese*. La forme *vieus, viex, vix* n'est que rarement attestée.' *Vies* appears again at line 370. However, *vieus* does appear in our text at 1705, as does *viel(l)* at lines 1710 and 2737. More significantly, *vies* is feminine here, true to its Latin third-declension origins.

291 See Luke 2:8.

297 Matthew 3:13–17. Nominative *J(h)esu(s) Cris* and oblique *J(h)esu Crist* are always written as one word in the manuscript.

298 *Diauble* here appears to count for two syllables; elsewhere (629, 847, 1167, 1496) it is always trisyllabic (*Dïauble*), cf. *dïaublie*, 1570. One might suppress *li*, though the article accompanies the noun on all its other appearances; one might even suspect a Picardism *Diaule/Diale* (see Gossen §52).

300 Matthew 3:16: 'baptizatus autem confestim ascendit de aqua et ecce aperti sunt ei caeli.'

309 It would be easy to emend to *[les] Guis*, here and to read *Juis qui [la] mer passerent* at 347, but the two lines taken together suggest that emendation would be otiose. Cf. Acts 7:55–57.

310 *Estievene*: on the silent *v*, see Introduction p. 15.

316 The lance appears in John 19:34; the darkness at noon is mentioned in Matthew 27:45 and in Luke 23:44, though in both accounts it lasts for three hours and no reference is made to the moon, which may be a reminiscence of Matthew 24:29.

318 *vaut* = *vout*, see Introduction p. 11.

329 *passe*: T-L has two further examples of *passer* used with *comant/commandement* in the sense "exceed, break", a sense which recurs in our text at 460 and 485.

331 See I Kings (III Kings) 17:1, and cf. 18:1.

333 The emendation may at first sight seem unnecessary, but *si* is used in the sense of "if" on only ten occasions in the whole manuscript (out of some 350 appearances), all but one of these

before a consonant, and all before a verb in the third person. Given the frequency with which final -*l* is lost elsewhere (e.g. 125, 1039), it seems likely that the scribe intended *s'il* rather than *si* on all ten occasions, particularly since he writes *s'il* in full thirty-four times.

340 See Matthew chapter 2.

345 *iaige*: the word appears again in this form at 363, but on both occasions the scribe originally wrote *iauge*, then the second minim of the *u* has been erased; elsewhere only *iauge* appears, except at 1539, which has *iaue*. See Gossen §43.

347 See 309*n*. Cf. Exodus chapter 14.

348 The manuscript has *ne erent*, but this would be the only case in the text where *ne* < NON did not elide, hence our emendation.

350 *mur*: is used extremely frequently without an article, but T-L has no example where "stonework/masonry" is unmistakably intended. There may be some influence here from the word *murus* in Exodus 14:22 or 29: 'et ingressi sunt filii Israhel per medium maris sicci, erat enim aqua quasi murus a dextra eorum et leva [...] filii autem Israhel perrexerunt per medium sicci maris, et aquae eis erant quasi pro muro a dextris et a sinistris.'

351–52 *manie*: countertonic *ai* is sporadically reduced to *a* in our text; see Introduction p. 8.

355 *Mer* appears with an article only here and in line 360. The word is very occasionally masculine in Old French (a Latinism), though here we may be dealing with a Picard form: just as *le* is common as a feminine article alongside Central O.F. *la*, so *li* is sometimes used analogically in subject function (see Gossen §63). Cf. Matthew 14:25, Mark 4:39.

365 Although in middle of a sentence, the coloured initial shows that a new element is introduced in this line.

366–68 The subject of *porte* is *tere*: "[the earth] will never (*nule fois*) yield [anything] but what God commands". While *tant* in the sense *ce* is not uncommon (see T-L 10, 82), *que* would be more idiomatic than *com*. The abbreviations for *com* and *que* may have been confused here.

370 *Un*: see 191*n*. Cf. Malachi 3:10–11.

372 *que* repeats the *Que* of line 371 ("we find that"), as is normal in Old French when a subordinate clause is interrupted by a relative or similar expression (cf. Hasenohr §301 and lines 1060, 1204, 2091, 2835).

375–76 Suchier cleverly suggests emending these lines to *Sa droite dime a Dieu tauroit Dieus de li cure ne feroit*. However, if this really was in the exemplar, it is not clear what might have led the scribe to make his mistake, and it is not implausible that he has instead simply omitted two lines.

380 *chifle*: the verb appears in this form (and also as *chuffler*) even in non-Picard texts.

385 Probably an allusion to the story of Cain and Abel which was often used as an illustration in the context of giving tithes; see Genesis 4:3–12.

393 Matthew 27:50–52: 'Iesus autem iterum clamans voce magna emisit spiritum, et ecce velum templi scissum est in duas partes a summo usque deorsum, et terra mota est, et petrae scissae sunt, et monumenta aperta sunt, et multa corpora sanctorum qui dormierant surrexerunt.' (This intransitive use of *fendre* is very common.)

403 *quanqu'i[l]*: for the emendation, cf. lines 474 and 1497, though the expressions are rather unexpected. *Quanque* appears again as subject pronoun in 327 without *il*.

404 *perecheus*: the manuscript has the abbreviation for *pro* then *ceuns* or *ceuus*; the exemplar may have read *perec(h)eus*. Our emendation is slightly uncomfortable, but has the merit of not departing too far from the manuscript. It is not impossible that two lines are missing. The idea is that everything in the universe serves God (an idea which will be expanded upon later), except for man. Cf. *La Lumere as Lais* 1113–42 (see 883n.) or the *Sermo de Sapientia* (see *Li Dialogue Gregoire lo Pape*, ed. W. Foerster, Niemeyer/Champion: Halle/Paris, 1876, repr. Rodopi: Amsterdam, 1965, vol. 1, pp. 286–87). Both of these passages are based on the *Elucidarium* of pseudo-Honorius (Migne *P.L.* 172), which does not contain the reference to man. Indeed much of the material here about how the elements respond to God's command (cf. 452ff.) may ultimately be inspired by *Elucidarium* I.5.

412 The proverb appears as Morawski n° 2255 in the form 'Sergent a roi per est a conte', and appears (in an identical form to

that of our text) in *Poésies de Gilles li Muisis* (ed. K. de Lettenhove, Louvain, 1882), II.21.

419 *asesront* for *asserront*, see Introduction p. 15.

423 An early example of the inflected form *lors* (cf. 1153, 1733, 2664, 2857), though perhaps not a very convincing one, since it is hard to see why *orgueus* should be plural.

443 *Qui* here has the sense "if anyone". The manuscript reads *leetre* here, as it does on the other two appearances of the word at lines 1565, 1837; cf. 150*n*.

448 The fifth-century Neoplatonist philosopher Proclus had some influence in the faculties in the later Middle Ages, but it is surprising to find him mentioned in a broadly popular work such as ours. He does not appear in other, much more encyclopaedic manuals such as the *Lumere as Lais*, the *Tresor* of Brunetto Latini, the *Breviari d'Amors* of Matfre Ermengau, or *Placides et Timéo*.

450 The manuscript reads *quar force met*. In the context, the expression *par force* in the emended version must mean "perforce, necessarily", rather than "by force", the awkward juxtaposition perhaps having given rise to the error. The three types of movement are taken up at lines 453 (*croissance*), 464 (*vie*) and 562 (*counissanche*). Cf. also *Mirour de Seinte Eglyse*, ed. A. D. Wilshere, ANTS 40 (London, 1982), 6.18:

> Sun savoir poez vus ver si vus pernez garde cument il ad doné a checune creature: [as uns] estre sanz plus, cum as peres; e as autres, estre e vivre, cum as arbres; as autres estre vivre e sentir, cum as bestes; as autres estre, vivre e sentir e resuner, cum a homme e a angle.

454 Pres.ind.6 of *pöoir* appears as *pueent* four times (212, 1270, 2926, 3208) and *puent* three (208, 2653, 2662); here the manuscript has *peuent* as it does again in 1289. However, this is the only place where the word appears at the rhyme, and, since *esmeuvent* seems incontrovertible, we must be dealing with an alternative present-tense form of *pöoir*; the case at line 1289 is less clear.

469 T-L has two other examples of *se passer* (both from North Eastern texts) in the sense "behave".

473 A line (probably only one) is missing here, perhaps caused by the scribe's beginning a new page. The range of possible rhymes is very wide; perhaps something with *saison* and *commence* before

our line 473, or possibly something with *obedience* after 473. *Forser* ("to spawn") is little attested, and is not known to the dictionaries in this transitive use.

477 *targement*: T-L does not pick up our example of this rare word, but it has one other from the Picard Le Renclus de Moiliens.

478 See the Book of Jonah, especially 1:17.

481 *rois* = "nets". A conflation of two different miraculous draughts of fish: John 21, which has 'mittite in dexteram navigii rete' but continues 'cum tanti [fish] essent, non est scissum rete', and Luke 5, which contains 'rumpebatur autem rete', and 'impleverunt ambas naviculas' but where no reference is made to the right-hand side of the ship.

486 See Genesis 8:8–12 (though there is no reflex in the Bible of our author's *tai*).

491 The *Legenda Maior* (in *Analecta Franciscana* X, 1926–41, pp. 555–652) reads (VIII, 9):

> Alio tempore ambulans cum quodam fratre per paludes Venetiarum, invenit maximam avium multitudinem residentium et cantantium in virgultis. Quibus visis, dixit ad socium: 'Sorores aves laudant Creatorem suum; nos itaque in medium ipsarum euntes, laudes et horas canonicas Domino decantemus.' Cumque in medium earum intrassent, non sunt aves motae de loco; et quia propter garritum ipsarum in dicendis horis se mutuo audire non poterant, conversus vir sanctus dixit ad aves: 'Sorores aves, a cantu cessate, donec laudes Deo debitas persolvamus!'. At illae continuo tacuerunt, tamdiu in silentio persistentes, quamdiu, dictis horis spatiose et laudibus persolutis, a sancto Dei cantandi licentiam receperunt. Dante autem eis viro Dei licentiam, statim cantum suum more solito resumpserunt.

495 The manuscript has *Et* instead of *A* of the edition; one might instead have suppressed the *l'*.

499 *Efforchivement*: T-L suggests that the *v* is intrusive (as it is in *pechavour* 2709 *jovene* 1541, *Estievene* 310 — see Introduction p. 15). The dictionary has no other examples of *esforcivement*, (though it has plenty of *esforciement*); however, like *FEW* (3, 727b) it lists both *forcif* and *esforcif*.

501 The manuscript reading *Au* has been retained on the assumption that *servir* is being used as a noun "ready for the service of God/for serving God". It would be easy to read *A* instead

(assuming that the *u* has been taken up from *Ausi* at the start of the line above), making the sense "ready to serve God".

503 *Seront*: this rather confusing form is not unknown for *selon(c)*, and appears again at 913 (alongside fifteen examples of *selonc*).

508 See Daniel 6:6–24.

514 *Ot*: this is the only appearance of this form in the text; all other preterites and past subjunctives of *avoir* use the stem *eu–*, much more characteristic of Picard. In the manuscript the letter *O* is aligned normally in the column ruled off for initial letters, but the *t* is written in the gap between this column and the column ruled for the rest of the line. It is likely that the scribe wrote *O* expecting it to mean "with" (cf. 516) and had to add the *t* subsequently.

515 A line is missing after 515. Suchier suggests a possible rhyming word *avoine*, but this form is largely unknown in Picard, where *avaine* would be expected (see Gossen §19); alternatively the rhyme might be between the very common palatalized form *moigne* and a *cheville* such as *sans nule aloigne*. Migne's edition (*P.L.* 73) of the *Vitae Patrum* reproduces Rosweyd's printed version of 1628. In it we read (III, 27):

> Dicebant sancti seniores de discipulo abbatis Pauli, nomine Joanne, quoniam magnam haberet humilitatem et virtutem obedientiae, ut etiam difficiles causas imperante ei abbate, in nullo penitus contradiceret, sed nec leviter in aliquo murmuraret. Cum autem necessarius esset in monasterii utensilibus fimus boum, misit eum abbas in proximum vicum, ut requireret ibi fimum boum, et cum celeritate afferret ad monasterium. Erat autom in loco illo mala bestia leaena. Statim ergo egressus discipulus ejus Joannes, ibat secundum praeceptum abbatis; cumque pergeret, dixit abbati suo: Domine pater, audivi quamplurimos dicentes quia in illo loco mala bestia leaena sit. Tunc senior, quasi joculariter dicit ei: Si venerit super te, tene et alliga eam, et adduces eam tecum. Cum autem venisset ad locum jam vespere, statim egressa leaena irruit super eum, et ille comprehendens tenere eam voluit, illa vero excutiens se, de manibus ejus aufugit. Sequebatur autem ille, dicens: Quia abbas meus praecepit ut alligatam te perducam ad eum. Continuo autem stetit bestia, et tenens eam, revertebatur ad monasterium. Dum autem retardaret in itinere, abbas nimis sollicitus pro eo, tristabatur graviter; et ecce subito supervenit discipulus ejus tenens ligatam leaenam. Quod cum vidisset senior, admiratus valde, gratias agebat Salvatori nostro Domino. Dicit autem discipulus ejus: Ecce, domine, sicut praecepisti, adduxi leaeanam ligatam. Volens autem

> humiliare sensum ejus senior, ne extolleret se in cogitationibus suis discipulus suus, ait ei: Sicut tu insensibilis es, ita etiam et istam insensibilem bestiam adduxisti; solve ergo, et dimitte eam, ut pergat ad locum suum.

Our author's economy of treatment will be immediately apparent. It is noteworthy that the original seems to be much more about John's obedience than that of the lioness.

522 *resoig*: the only other (rather earlier) example in T-L is from Philippe Mousket (see 150*n*). The word reappears at 2196.

526 *en l'eure*: the expression is attested in the sense "straightaway", and reappears at line 720.

530 *apresse*: the noun is not listed in T-L, let alone the prepositional phrase (though Gdf. lists the word, glossing it as "action de presser, d'accabler"); it is not clear whether our example is derived from *presser* or from *pres*.

531 *lui* = *li* both times, the stressed form of *ele*; *loier* of course = "to tie up", cf. 542.

547–48 *löee* is feminine to agree with *l'* (i.e. *obedience* of 546). The manuscript erroneously has *son courage* in 548. *Coree* is attested in the sense "heart, mind". and, if this were the reading of the exemplar, the word's relative rarity might account for the scribe's mistake. One might instead emend to *sa pensee*. For the monosyllabic past subjunctive form *eust*, see Introduction p. 25.

549 As the text stands, it must mean "[the abbot] feared lest vaingloriousness should establish itself/take root in his (i.e. Jehan's) heart". T-L seems to read the lines thus, and offers one further example of a comparable use from *Eracle* ('l'ire Deu sour li s'assiet'), though the preposition *sour* makes this interpretation more likely in *Eracle* than in our text. One is tempted to emend to *l'asesist*, i.e. "[the abbot] feared in his (own) heart lest vaingloriousness should lay siege to/beset him (Jehan)".

551 *entredeus*: T-L glosses this as "auf dem Mittelweg (steering a middle course)", and here the abbot's words must be a compromise between praising Jehan and saying nothing.

552 *t'es* shows Picard *te* for *tu*.

557 *a garant* = "in safety".

576 *maire*: probably for *mere* in a metaphorical sense; compare, for example, 'largesce est meire d'amour Et de proesce et de valour' quoted in T-L. The spelling is not uncommon in Picard (see Gossen §6).

586 The word order here is unorthodox; one might emend to *Et de trop melleur cueur*.

594 Cf. John 19:34.

624 *coment* used as a conjunction with the subjunctive normally means "in such a way that"; here there seems to be an idea of "until".

625–28 Cf. line 771, where the prison is explicitly called *Desesperanche*; cf. also line 2904.

639ff. This is the first introduction in our text of the topos of the 'Three Enemies of Man', which will be taken up again in more detail in lines 2032ff. The spy in our midst (663) is the Flesh, linked with the deadly sins of gluttony (672) and lust (701); the army encamped outside the gate (728) is the World, linked with envy (729), wrath (730) and avarice (731); finally the leader bringing up the rear (744) is the Devil, linked with pride (746), and sloth (here represented by *Negligence* at 760). As Wenzel shows, the topos of the Three Enemies engaged in a battle with man was quite commonplace by the end of the thirteenth century. The allocation of the deadly sins to the different enemies was less so, and not standardized (other allocations than ours are found; cf. also Bloomfield chapter V, especially section 3). Cf. 845*n*.

647 *tost*: the manuscript has *tout*, perhaps in anticipation of the following line. As edited the lines must mean: "we who have beaten this whole army have had an easy fight" (i.e. so far, because next we have the leader of the army to contend with).

649 *rois de l'ost*: T-L has a few examples of *roi* in the sense "Vorsteher von Körperschaften (head of a group of people)" (e.g. *roi des hirauz, des ribauz, des bergiers*, and *roi d'armes*), but does not list *roi de l'ost*.

657 The expression *atendre le coup* is attested, and means "not to run away, stand one's ground"; *atendre l'estour* ("the [noise of] battle, attack") seems to have the same sense here. (T-L has another example of the collocation, but the sense is not evident.)

671 As Röhrs points out (p. 306), *sur* is anomalous; the normal form is *sour*, appearing five times in the text, as preposition or prefix — one might emend to *s[o]ur*, but *sur* appears once more at line 2273. (Röhrs's example of *pur* for *pour* is a misreading of the manuscript.)

672 *vix* < VILIS; see Introduction p. 10.

685 The source of this quotation has not been traced; it is not to be found in the *De Amicitia*.

692 This expression is evidently intended as a proverb, but a search for other examples of its use has drawn a blank.

694 T-L has one example of *tantost* glossed as "manchmal, leichtlich, oft (frequently, readily)", a sense that would fit well here. The expression *montee en orguel* is perhaps ill-chosen here: the poet is not suggesting that pride is one of the deadly sins particularly associated with the flesh (he attaches it to the Devil in lines 746 and 759), merely that when it is underemployed the flesh will rebel against man's will.

703 The term *sire de la rote* appears twice in T-L in the sense "head of a troop (of fighters)". If, as seems likely, this refers to the Devil, then presumably a couplet is missing here; it is hard to find an antecedent for *qui* otherwise.

726 The ending *-o(u)mes* on pres.ind.4 and fut.4 is characteristic of Picard (Gossen §78, Pope §895); it appears once more in our text, again to provide a rhyme for *soumes*, on *iroumes* (840).

737 If *Et* here means "both", the rhyme needs correcting. However, it is more likely that it means "and", and it is probable that two lines are missing here, the first rhyming with *definanche* and the second with *route*. If this were the case, the sense of the missing lines might be something like "...[the world] attacks us, so that if we do not resist...". Various equivocal rhymes are possible with *rote*, and it might be that one of these has led to the omission. This use of *venir*, apparently as a passive auxiliary, is extremely rare in Old French, and the word could belong to the missing section.

741 *chestes*: refers to envy, wrath and avarice/covetousness, as does *cascune* of line 742.

747 The agreement here is with the closer of the two subjects, *li Beubans*, as sometimes happens in Old French (Hasenohr §259), hence the singular verb and participle. Cf. 216.

749 The manuscript reads *Qui de lost est tous gouvreneres*, which finds no parallel in the dictionaries s.v. *tout*. It may be that *estous* of line 748 has caused some confusion.

759 *nous* here seems to be ethic dative. (The *nous* of line 758, on the other hand, is object of the expression *asambler a*, "to join battle with".) For *un* (= *en* + *le*), see 191*n*.

771 *prison*: cf. line 625.

778 *Soutius*: this development of -ILIS is typically Picard — see Introduction p. 10.

790 The line is ambiguous: the request may be for the powerful overlord to overcome the adversary with his followers, or for him to take the man making the request into his household. The latter interpretation is more likely, as the preposition *de* is very common with *maisnie(e)* in the sense "as part of the household/among the followers".

797 *gerrier*: T-L accepts this apparently disyllabic form, but the word is a hapax, and it certainly looks rather doubtful. (A form *gerrer* has a tenuous existence, but it would not rhyme with *travellier* for our author.) Elsewhere in our text only *gerroier* is used. One could read *Ja ne l'osera gerr[o]ier*, or *Ja puis n'osera gerr[o]ier*.

806 *eust* is subjunctive (see Introduction p. 25), "even if man had no reward from serving God"; cf. 69ff.

808 *atour*: the word has a range of meanings, including "preparation" and "decoration"; here *sans atour* seems to mean "without delay/hesitation" or "without fuss".

817 See I Corinthians 2:9, 'oculus non vidit nec auris audivit nec in cor hominis ascendit quae praeparavit Deus his qui diligunt illum.'

820 The relative pronoun is often omitted in Old French after an indefinite antecedent, especially in a negative context (cf. Hasenohr §127).

821 *cele*: Although dental *l* occasionally rhymes with palatal *l* in Picard (Gossen §59), our author uses this rhyme nowhere else in the text. T-L does have two examples of a palatalized form *cille* (: *fille*), but none of *ceille*, and in all probability the rhyme here is a licence.

826 The reference remains unidentified, but does not appear to be Pauline.

842 *chu*: this rare form recurs at 1654; it appears sporadically in other Picard texts, and occasionally in Norman ones. Röhrs likens the alternation between *chou* and *chu* to that between *dou* and *du* or between *ou* and *u* (*en* + *le*); see also Gossen §64 note 2.

843 *herbegera*: T-L has two further examples of the form without the second *r*, (both from Picard texts, though this may just be coincidental). The same form appears again in our text at 2980.

845ff. Having introduced the topos of the Three Enemies, and their accompanying deadly sins at 639ff. (to be developed in lines 2032ff.), Jehan now introduces his second trio of prayer (868), fasting and almsgiving (870), which will be treated more fully in lines 2069 to 2940 (see 1979*n*). These are the three acts of satisfaction, normally performed after confession; curiously in lines 845ff. they are presented as also preceding confession, disposing the sinner to penance, and emphasis is placed on their efficacy even in the absence of confession (see 883*n*). The tone at 883ff., it should be noted, is quite technical, with allusions to scholastic theology.

857 *esforch*: for *esforz*, cf. *douch* (1529), *tierch* (1573).

862 *requert*: the form is anomalous for the expected *requiert*. The vowel is probably remodelled on that of the infinitive (unless it is a hypersophistication in a dialect where *apiel*, *tiere*, etc. exist alongside Central *apele*, *tere*) and appears again at 906, 1392 and 1603. Lines 655–56 suggest that the form is scribal, and the opposite remodelling appears in line 2521. The expected forms are much more numerous.

866 *quë*: hiatus appears elsewhere only before *il*, *on* and *un* (see Introduction p. 27); it is possible that one should read *qu'il* here.

873 *Ches ·iii· coses*: i.e. the three things just mentioned, prayer, fasting and almsgiving.

876 *travaus* is unknown in the sense "sin"; the line must mean that good works done during one's lifetime overcome sufferings/torments after death. Cf. 887ff.

883ff. This question is treated in the *Sentences* of Peter Lombard (Migne *P.L.* 192) IV.xv.7, though Jehan's source must have elaborated on Peter's simple formulation ('ostenditur bona, quae sine caritate fiunt, prodesse quidem ad tolerabiliorem poenam sentiendam, sed non ad vitam obtinendam'). *La Lumere as Lais* (by Peter of Fetcham, ANTS 56–58, 1996–2000) seems to follow the same source as Jehan, when the pupil asks: 'Si bienfez ke fet peccheur Rien li vaudrunt a chief de tur', and receives the reply:

> E des bienfez ke demandez
> Ke fet sunt en morteus pecchez
> Saciez ke iceus ke lé funt
> Meindre peine aillurs averunt,
> U meillur grace en poen[t] aver
> Par ceo lur pecchiez de lesser,
> U il averunt veraiment
> De temporaus biens enoitement. 10,571–78

891 *lassés*: is nominative plural, the form influenced by the rhyme.

894 *Ches[t] fait*: one could read *ches fait[s]*, but *chis fais* of 897 suggests that a singular is intended here. Cf. 2029n.

896 *lais* = "I leave".

898ff. The dictionaries have the expressions *tenir pro/bien/profit a* "to benefit, help" (and also *tenir mal a* "to harm"). The meaning is that the good that the sinner does helps against the pains of hell, (and for his good deeds he gets his reward), but is insufficient for salvation unless God's grace leads the sinner to repentance and doing appropriate penance.

913 *Seront*: see 503n.

922 *tristre*: the form is attested, cf. *tristreche* 985, and the relatively common *legistre* 223.

929 *medechine*: appears to mean "a medicinal plant", a sense unknown to the dictionaries.

935 *eskernissons* = Central O.F. *escharnissons*, continuing the idea of *faire eschar de* in 934. (On the confusion of *ar* and *er* before a consonant, see Gossen §3).

939 Jehan continues in his 'scholarly' vein, subdividing the effects of penance, and supporting his argument with Biblical references.

945 See II Kings (IV Kings) 20:1–6 or Isaiah 38:1–5.

960 We must be dealing here with an early appearance of the verb *priver* in the sense "remove": "so close to God that all evil would have been removed from him", that he would be free of all wickedness.

961 *Cheste*: sc. *vie*. See Galatians 2:19–20, 'ego enim per legem legi mortuus sum ut Deo vivam Christo confixus sum cruci; vivo autem iam non ego, vivit vero in me Christus, quod autem nunc vivo in carne, in fide vivo Filii Dei.'

971 'Nolo mortem peccatoris sed magis, ut convertatur et vivat'; cf. Ezekiel 18:23, 33:11 — the form in our text is liturgical. *Defenir* is attested in the (rare) sense "die".

979 Jehan continues with his description of penance. The standard theological formula can be found in, for example, 'In perfectione autem poenitentiae tria observanda sunt, scilicet compunctio cordis, confessio oris, satisfactio operis' the opening of *Sentences* IV.xvi.1. The section on confession begins at line 1221 and that on satisfaction at line 1979. First, we learn here about contrition, and the table below shows the 'scholarly' system of division and subdivision, presumably taken over from Jehan's source, that underpins the exposition, with its appeal to Biblical and patristic authorities. There is, nonetheless, a clear effort to popularize the technical material here, with the reference to the onion, the moralizing comments etc., and the example of the lye, which follows the description of contrition proper.

Three things are necessary for penance:				979
A	contrition, which itself requires three things:			985
	1	sorrow		995
		a	at going to hell	996
		b	at not going to heaven	1000
	2	hope for salvation (not despair)		1065
	3	renouncing sin by:		1117
		a	not sinning oneself	1120
		b	being reconciled with other people	1123
			i forgiving those who sin against us	1127
			ii making amends for our sins	1130

See further 1221*n*.

983 *recuevre*: although one might read this as a verb (in the sense "reach, attain", with *a* as a preposition), it is more probably a noun (cf. 2959) meaning something like "help, remedy, relief, comfort" (with *a* as a verb).

984 *de evre* is to be read as *d'evre*; for *evre*, see Introduction p. 11.

995 *amaritude*: T-L has only our example of this Latinism (which doubtless points to a Latin original), though Gdf. has a few fourteenth- and fifteenth-century specimens.

1002 The ·*ii*· *coses* are (1) going to hell, and (2) not going to heaven (they are elaborated on in what follows), consequently it is very probable that manuscript *ne garde*, although it just about makes sense ("does not observe/keep in mind"), is a slip for *regarde* of the edition (always spelt *resgarde* by the scribe).

1008 The manuscript has *plouvoir* instead of *voier*. There could be two lines missing here, but the sense seems complete as it stands. No easy correction suggests itself, particularly since the author does not rhyme -*er* with -*ier*. The Vulgate is of no assistance (Genesis 7:11–12, 'rupti sunt omnes fontes abyssi magnae et cataractae caeli apertae sunt, Et facta est pluvia super terram'). The suggested emendation is, of course, mere conjecture, though the relative rarity of the verb (compared with its compound *envoier*), coupled with a superficial similarity to the second syllable of *plouvoir*, could account for a scribe's desire to correct it.

1022 *s'i[l]*: see 333*n*.

1023 *resgardëure*: this is one of only two examples in T-L; the parallel *resgardanche* at 1721 is hapax.

1031 This and the following lines appear to mean: "he will not have such a wicked heart that he does not repudiate his pride, and that his heart does not prick him as long as he does not leave (i.e. persists in) this attitude".

1037 I take this line to be the equivalent of the prose *Et pour la grant fole des pechiés*, hence the emendation of manuscript *lor* to *la*, though other (more radical) changes would be possible.

1039 The manuscript reads *Quant ilasentent ou ileuoient*; it would equally have been possible to emend to *ou le voient*, assuming a Picardism.

1049 There are two more examples of the learned *demostracïon* in T-L, one from Brunetto Latini of roughly the same date as our text, and one much earlier from Le Renclus de Moiliens.

1053–54 *noant* of 1053 means "swimming", and *noiant* of 1054 probably means "drowning", both doubtless punning on the name *Noë*.

1060 For reduplication of *que*, cf. 372n.

1061 For this impersonal *il*, cf. Gérard Moignet *Grammaire de l'ancien français* (Paris: Klincksieck, 1984) pp. 263–65.

1071 *acorde*: for the analogical *-e* on the subjunctive, influenced by the rhyme, see Introduction p. 23. The reflexive use of *acorder* is well attested in the sense "make peace", etc., e.g. T-L's 'Ki de toz (pechiez) ne s'acorde, perduz est'. *Que* of 1074 means "for".

1074 *ele* might conceivably refer to *misericorde* (i.e. God's mercy is prompted by man's sin), but this seems very far fetched; perhaps the feminine *desperatio* (or even *des(es)perance*) was in the author's mind.

1076 Cf. Matthew 27:3–5, and see 1085n.

1077–79 *Envaïr* with a person as object is quite well attested in the sense "seize, lay hands on, attack" (cf. 1499). The *l'* of line 1079 would refer more precisely to Jesus than to God, and Breymann emends the line to *Que qu'il ala Jesu veïr*, though the licence of the original might be thought acceptable. (One might supply *mout* instead of *Dieu* in 1077.) For the construction with *que ce que* see Hasenohr §293.

1085–86 The fact that this reference to Gregory comes so close on the heels of the reference to Jerome in 1076 strongly suggests that both are taken from some scholarly work that cites copious authorities. T-L knows only three examples of *despoir*, and none of *despoire* (nor yet *desespoire*); perhaps the form is simply designed to provide an eye-rhyme.

1090 *Faus = fous*; *nasse* is a kind of net or trap for catching fish, and *retourner* of 1091 means to turn around and swim out of the net, free oneself.

1093 Cf. Genesis 4:13–14. Cain and Judas (see Matthew 27:5) are ubiquitously used as examples of *desperatio*.

1094 Ours is the only example in T-L of this impersonal construction with *encheoir*. The sense is "it befell him so ill, even though he might have had contrition, that he received damnation for it (i.e. his despair)".

1104 *esperassïon* appears to be a hapax legomenon; ours is the only example in T-L, and Gdf. does not list the word at all.

1105 *faus de memoire*: "foolish in his mind/way of thinking", etc.

1112 The schoolmen found this threefold distinction in Jerome (*Super Ezechielem* 43, 23): 'Tria generalia delicta sunt quibus humana subiacet genus: aut enim cogitatione, aut sermone, aut opere peccamus.'

1120 The manuscript seems to read *fornoie* rather than *foruoie*, but the sense ("deny") would seem to rule out this very rare verb. As edited, *s'ame* could be object of *forvoie*, in the sense "lead astray", or it could be subject in the sense "go astray".

1123 The expression *seconde branche* points to an omission in the manuscript. The prerequisite for contrition currently under discussion (after sorrow and hope for forgiveness) is the third one, the renouncing of sin. The following lines suggest that this was perhaps divided into sub-branches, one dealing with the penitent (not sinning oneself, the gist of lines 1119–22) and another with other people (forgiving those who sin against us, and making restitution where we have wronged them), and that it is to this second sub-branch that line 1123 refers. The three aspects are summed up in lines 1135–38; the omission is thus unlikely to be a long one.

1126 *fautes*: the manuscript has *faites*, Suchier suggests emending to *mesfaits* (though the scribe spells this word *meffais*, indeed, he never writes final *-ts*).

1144 *en tel forme* appears to translate *sicut* of the Lord's Prayer: 'dimitte nobis debita nostra sicut et nos dimittimus debitoribus nostris.'

1148 *condictïon*: T-L gives this example, glossed as "Dienstverhältnis, Abhängigkeit (service/servitude, dependency)", with one further example (which does seem more clearly to have this sense). In Latin CONDICIO can mean "situation", particularly an unfavourable situation, and the word in our text may be either an unconscious Latinism, or a calque on some Latin original.

1152 *retraite*: there is a noun *retraite* meaning "reproach, blame, slander", which might fit better here than the feminine past participle of *retraire*.

1155 On the Picard ending *-aule* for *-able*, see Introduction p. 15. It is not clear whether the *u* of the manuscript represents a *u*- or a *v*-sound.

1164 Cf. Luke 9:62, 'ait ad illum Iesus: nemo mittens manum suam in aratrum et aspiciens retro aptus est regno Dei.'

1165 Manuscript *or* has been suppressed for the syllable count, since *gäa*– appears to be disyllabic for our author.

1169 I.e. the first major branch, dealing with contrition, with its three subdivisions.

1174 *Che[ste]*: scribal *che* is a haplography; cf. 925, 929, 1562.

1178 *si k'il i paire* is a set phrase, "as it may appear".

1179 The manuscript reading (*il estuet ·ii· coses faire*) looks like a dittography taken up from line 1177. The rhyming word is *faice*, an isolated spelling, which suggests that the scribe might have expected to write *faire* again, when he noticed that his exemplar actually contained *fac(h)e*.

1194–97 These lines seem to point to an etymology in a Latin source in which *contritio* is derived from *conterere*, "to wear down". *Contritio cordis* is a standard collocation in theological literature of the period, and the quotation from Joel 2:13 'scindite corda vestra et non vestimenta vestra' is typically used as an exhortation to contrition.

1196 One might be tempted to emend *brisans* to *brisiés*, but the present participle does appear with a passive sense in Old French, where one would expect a past participle in Modern French, e.g. 'Sor sa poitrine tenoit ses mains croisans' (*Aliscans*, ed. F. Guessard and A. de Montaiglon, Paris 1870, l. 725); cf. the well-known Modern French fossils *une couleur voyante*, *de la musique chantante*, etc. (See Hasenohr §217.)

1205–06 In the future stem $n + r$ generally becomes *rr* in our text (e.g. *couverra* 1999, *dourra* 198), see Introduction p. 16. The lines must mean "for it would be so unpleasant to him that he would not hold off/stop himself [vomiting] for anything".

1210 *l'abome*: the manuscript clearly reads *la boine*. The noun *abome* ("horror, loathing, abomination") is not common (T-L gives only two sources; ours is not among them), and it is possible that the scribe was unacquainted with it.

1213 "And, even though one could say more about it..."

1221 Here Jehan starts his description of confession. Unlike the foregoing section on contrition, this section seems much less clearly articulated into divisions and subdivisions, it is more anecdotal and sermonizing, and scarcely refers to authorities after the first few lines. One is rather inclined to suppose that it has a different source from the preceding and following passages. By line 1545, we seem to be back on more scholarly ground, and the clearly organized treatment is continued with the checklist of deadly sins, the discussion of circumstances, etc. See further 1545*n*.

1223–24 T-L has one further example of *cultiverresse*, but in the sense "inhabitant" (a translation of *incola* from the *Oxford Psalter*); *acorderresse* appears to be a hapax legomenon.

1229 The proliferation of authorities here strongly suggests a compilation as source, which the author may be condensing still further. See Introduction p. 7.

1242 The feminine form *tourmente* is not uncommon.

1250 The pres.sbv.3 *aie* also appears at 1852, though the expected *ait* is commoner, with twenty-six appearances.

1252 The line is originally one syllable short, as is line 1915, the only other place where *fuir* appears in the text; it seems likely that the author used the alternative form *fuier* in both cases. The reference is to Genesis 3:8 and 3:23–24.

1269 *escuel*: the manuscript seems to have *eschll*, with the top of the first *l* erased. Gdf. has a few entries under *escueil* that parallel this one, e.g.: 'Tant l'amerez qu'en droit escueil serez de mort' (*Livre des cent ballades*); 'Avoirs t'a mis en mal escuel' (Le Renclus de Moiliens, *Miserere*). The entry in T-L is not very clearly articulated, but contains, for example: 'ele le met en tel escuel [...] Que petit a petit l'attrait a s'amour.' The sense appears to be "difficulty, awkward situation, danger". As is shown by *consel* of 1270, our scribe writes *l* for final palatal *l* (*orguel* 261, *traval* 2159), hence the form adopted here. (*Le* is a Picardism for *la* = *aïe*.)

1274–75 *apresser* is not recorded with the specific sense "torture" (though *opresser* is); however, it would seem that either this is its sense here, or, if it has its customary sense of "press", then *jehine* must mean a specific instrument of torture rather than torture in general. *Pour li pendre* is presumably elliptical, meaning "in order to (get a confession that would allow one to) hang him"; it seems unnecessary to emend to *prendre* as T-L suggests.

1284–85 *qu'* of 1284 is for *qui*, as, we must assume, is *que* of 1285.

1290 *puent*: the verb apparently agrees with the logical subject (all people who put off making confession) rather than the grammatical one (the *oume* of 1284). This is one of the author's equivocal rhymes: the first *avenir* means "happen, occur", the second "achieve, carry out".

1291–92 The lines seem to refer to the loss of one's faculties of thought (?consciousness) or speech through serious illness, though "thought" is not one of the senses of *science* listed in T-L.

1293–94 The lines describe failure to make a deathbed confession because one is preoccupied with making a will or organizing one's worldly/financial affairs.

1299 *demorant* appears to be used adverbially, "while delaying".

1300 *Pasches* is, of course, not just a *cheville*; Christians were obliged by Canon 21 of the fourth Lateran council to confess at least once a year at Easter. Cf. line 1331, and see Introduction p. 6.

1301 *Tes* = *tels/teus*. The form appears seven times in the text (e.g. 1400, 1568) as against two examples of *teus*, both at the rhyme; cf. *ques* (1526, 1722, 2531).

1304 *Cambien*: cf. *quanbien* at 2425, the forms probably influenced by *quant* (or even QUAM). The only other appearance of the word is at line 464 in the conventional form *combien*.

1315 *magnier*: for this Picard form of *manger* (with palatalized *n*) cf. Gossen §62.

1320 The raven's cry of 'cras' is, of course, the Latin word for "tomorrow", and points to a Latin source for these lines. Though ultimately, perhaps, derived from Suetonius (*Vita Domitiani*, 11), Jehan seems to have them from William Perrault's *Summa de vitiis* (perhaps via a compilation) on acedia, II, 5: 'Secundum (i.e. the second thing) quod impedit ne Dominus intret ad peccatorem est procrastinatio. Et ista procrastinatio est velut "corvus in superliminari", (Zephaniah 2:14) dicens Domino pulsanti ad ostium, "Cras, cras."' (*Summa virtutum ac vitiorum*, Paris, 1629).

1323 *AND1* (266a) has an example of this expression: 'Ne promittez nulle rien sur esperance (= "expectation") d'autruy.'

1334 The expression looks like a fixed collocation, but I can find no other example.

1338 For this rhyme, see Introduction p. 15.

1342 *Parer* is a little unexpected here. It is used figuratively (usually in the passive) when someone is improved by the presence of some good quality or accomplishment (*paré de vertus*), and the sense here may be "everyone who wants his penance to be a credit to him". *Li* could be a stressed pronoun but one might emend to *le*.

1346 A reference to Proverbs 18:17, which in the Vulgate version reads: 'iustus prior est accusator sui.'

1350 *ses*: for *c(h)es*.

1351 There is no miscalculation here: the fortnight is that between Septuagesima Sunday and Quinquagesima (Shrove) Sunday; *Quaresme* means "Lent", and not "Quadragesima Sunday". *Septesme* is a hapax legomenon.

1356 *nes* = masc. nom. sing. of *net*.

1375 *contrius*: this bizarre form appears again at 1380, while the text has *contrit* and *contris* at 1425 and 1427. Röhrs asks whether this might be a change of suffix from -ITUS to -IVUS (which, like -ILIS, might give *-ius* in Picard, cf. Gossen §21), though the fact that *contrit* is restricted to more or less learned registers would make this rather less likely.

1383 *parrochien*: this word normally means "parishioner"; the two examples from our text (cf. 1407) are the only ones in T-L with the sense "parish priest". Gdf. has three more, one from Douai dated 1273 and two fifteenth-century examples. Though it may not be our author's immediate source at this point, Raymond of Peñafort's *Summa de Paenitentia* III.xxxiv.15 (see Bibliography) reads:

> Tenetur ergo paenitens confiteri proprio sacerdoti [...] Fallit regula supra dicta in quinque casibis, in quibus potest, cui est data potestas imponendi paenitentias in aliqua parochia ab episcopo, audire confessionem alterius parochiani, videlicet: [...] si petiit et obtinuit licentiam a sacerdote suo quem videbat imperitum et insufficientem, volens ire ad alium discretum.

1397 The *l* of *nel*, strictly speaking redundant, anticipates the following clause (cf. Hasenohr §296).

1399ff. I take this passage to mean "[the priest] can take the penitent against [the penitent's] will, for such [a priest] is only forcing him for good reasons, or he [presumably the priest?] should ask his superior for help in the form of advice or permission [to let the penitent go elsewhere?], or even [ask that] he should confess to [the superior]". Since the sense "apply moral (rather than physical) force" is so rare for *forcer*, one might equally adopt Suchier's more radical suggestion: *Car che n'est fors que pour son bien.*

1417 *Qui* for *cui*, as again at 1421, etc.

1419 The ultimate source of this idea is *De vera et falsa poenitentia* 10, 25 (Migne *P.L.* 40, 1122), though Jehan de Journi may well have had it at second hand.

> Qui vult confiteri peccata [...] quaerat sacerdotem qui sciat ligare et solvere [...] Tantaque vis confessionis est, ut, si deest sacerdos, confiteatur proximo: saepe enim contigit, quod poenitens non potest verecundari coram sacerdote, quem desideranti nec tempus nec locus offert. Etsi ille cui confitebitur potestatem solvendi non habeat, fit tamen dignus venia ex sacerdotis desiderio, qui confitetur socio crimen.

1422 *miseranche*: the word appears only in T-L and this is the only example given. *Miserantia* is picked up by the *Novum Glossarium Mediae Latinitatis* (ed. Franz Blatt, Copenhagen, 1959–1969), though *miserance* need not be a Latinism.

1427 The manuscript has *si* for our *ki*, which might stand in the sense "if", except that *si* is not typically used in that sense in our text (cf. 333*n*).

1442 *estre* here = "existence".

1444 *en sa poissanche*: the phrase does not appear in T-L meaning "in good health, in his prime", but the intention seems clear, and the expression *en sa poesté* is attested in this sense (e.g. 'bien garie et en sa poësté'; 'di moi [...] se il est en sa poësté | Delivres et heitiez et sains').

1446 "For I know of no one so wise..."

1452 This and the next two lines are very puzzling. For *en endevant*, the manuscript has *enondevant*. The verb *ende(s)ver* is well enough attested in the sense "rave, be mad", and David, it will be remembered, feigns madness in I Samuel (I Kings) 21:13. However, there is no reflex of our lines 1453–54 in the Bible at this point. One might have assumed that some lines were missing after 1452 giving David's actual words, with 1453–54 being an authorial comment, except that David does not actually say anything at all during his madness, hence it is not clear what *dist* could refer to even if one were to edit the manuscript in a different way. In fact, I can find no Biblical parallel whatever to this couplet, attributable to David or to anyone else.

1455 *ensoinne*: The manuscript actually looks more like *ensoume*, a possible misreading of *ensoinne* in the exemplar, since this is the only place where the scribe spells palatal *n* as *inn*.

1471 Figurative uses of *fonder* seem to be rare; one of its most basic senses is "to lay the foundations of a building", and the noun *estre* can, of course, mean "house". Nonetheless, it is likely that we have a play on words here with a non-literal sense "on which he must base his behaviour".

1479 Cf. John 19:30, 'inclinato capite tradidit spiritum'.

1492–93 The manuscript reads *Que iai en chstui mont menee*; the emendation assumes that an *S* has been misread as the abbreviation for *Que*.

1508 *ches* for *ses*?

1511 The skeleton of this rambling sentence seems to be constituted by lines 1509–10, 1523 and 1525ff. with *veoul* as the main verb (i.e. *Pour che que nichetés abunde, pour les maus blasmer si veoul je dire es ques endrois...*). This would make manuscript *qui* of line 1511 out of place, hence the emendation to *i*; another possibility might be to read *si*.

1518 *mete sus*: "accuse of, charge with".

1525 Manuscript *retraire* (for *ditier* of the edition) must be a result of the scribe's eye slipping two lines in his exemplar; cf. 2689, 2949. However, one cannot rule out the possibility that there are some lines missing or inverted here.

1526 *Esqués*: "in which".

1534 In this sense, the expression *si que* is unusual in our text, with only four examples, as compared to twenty-one examples of *si com*. (Cf. 1178, 2285, 2946.)

1536–37 "[do not be worried] whether [my person] is worth little or hardly anything, so long as what I say concerns you". Breymann sets *S'ele [est] petit* (*sic*) which seems unnecessary.

1539 Cf. Exodus 17:5–6.

1541 *jovene*: this Latinising spelling (typically Picard, cf. Gossen §26) must have been pronounced as one syllable. In all likelihood the *v* is merely decorative; cf. Röhrs p. 321 and see Introduction p. 15.

1545 The table below may help to clarify the author's treatment of the deadly sins here.

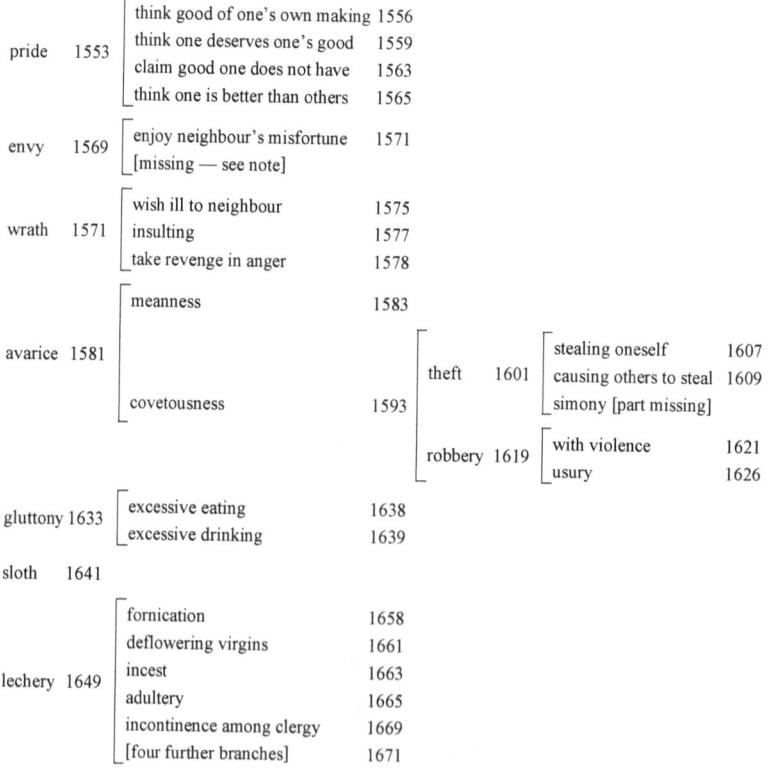

See further 1681*n*.

1556 This fourfold distinction is derived ultimately from Gregory's *Moralia* (Migne *P.L.* 75–76) XXIII.vi ('Quatuor quippe sunt species quibus omnis tumor arrogantium demonstratur, cum bonum aut a semetipsis habere se aestimant, aut si sibi datum desuper credunt, pro suis se hoc accepisse meritis putant; aut certe cum jactant se habere quod non habent; aut, despectis caeteris, singulariter videri appetunt habere quod habent'), though quite possibly by way of a compendium.

1559 One should perhaps rather emend to *Li autres est quant cuide avoir*, though the author allows himself two further liberties with *l'autre* at 1609 and 2793.

1568 *Tes* = *tel* + *s*; for *vieutés* see Introduction p. 10.

1572 Clearly lines are missing here, though perhaps only a couplet. In *Moralia* XXXI.xlv.88 (cf. 1556*n*) we read 'De invidia [...] exsultatio in adversus proximi, afflictio autem in prosperis nascitur'. It is doubtless some reflex of this second category that is missing from our text.

1581 The next eighteen lines may ultimately be inspired by *Moralia* XV.xxv.30, but the treatment here is so very different (and so much more detailed) as to suggest a predigested compilation as the source, in which Gregory was perhaps cited as only one of the authorities.

1594 *si* is rather unexpected; perhaps we should read *n'en ert il ja lassé[s]*?

1603–04 *berele*: has a range of meanings, including "game" and "battle, attack". The *sires* of 1604 is reminiscent of the use of *dominus* in the canon (P. E. Huschke, *Institutionum Libri Quattuor*, Leipzig: Teubner, 1899, IV.i.6): 'Furtum autem fit [...] generaliter cum quis alienam rem invito domino contrectat.'

1605 Lines dealing with the third branch of *larrechin* seem to be missing from the manuscript, probably between 1613 and 1614. The question would doubtless be resolved by reference to the source, but this has not been traced. The attribution to Gregory seems to be a mistake; certainly no parallel to this passage has been found in the collected works (Migne *P.L.* 75–76).

1609 *Pourchacier* is used intransitively in the sense "act to one's own advantage". The progression seems to be from stealing oneself, through profiting from the thieving of others, to selling things that are not one's own to sell (including simony). Perhaps we are to understand that the beneficiary here has made a deal to share his takings with members of the household in exchange for their complicity, or even to act as a fence for goods that they have stolen.

1613 The emendation assumes that the author intended another example of the monosyllabic past subjunctive (see Introduction p. 25). One might equally read *le bien* in 1612 and *l'eüst* here.

1616 "For this branch is very much a Church concern"(?).

1623 *A force faite* is a fixed collocation, attested in T-L, meaning "using force".

1625 *Que* after a negative is attested in the sense "than if it were".

1629 *prestance*: seems to be a hapax; T-L has only this example, and the word is absent from Gdf., *FEW* and *AND*. (Mod. Fr. *prestance* meaning "bearing, presence" is a Renaissance borrowing from Classical Latin *praestantia* < *prae-sto* not *praes-sto*.)

1636 T-L lists many examples of *de bone/franche/bele/pute part*, and very many of *de male part*, which seems to mean little more than "bad"; *as leur* must mean "(bad) for their followers" i.e. the people that are in thrall to these sins.

1645 *chu*: cf. 842*n*.

1653 *que* for *qui*. The sense is: "there is nobody who practices one of them [these five kinds of lechery] whom it does not lead straight to hell".

1655 *un*: see 191*n*.

1659–60 The manuscript reads: *Fornicacion est noncie Qui est de grant non marie*. It does not seem possible to make sense of *marie* as either the name *Marie*, or the feminine of *mari* ("lost, afflicted"), and besides, the line is hypometric. Suchier suggests *Cui est de grant nonbre manie*, which seems strained, and is open to the objection that *noncier* does not mean "name, call" in any of the many quotations in T-L, but always "announce", hence our rather radical emendation. (Given the general corruption of the line, one might even read *Qu'est entre gent non mariee*.)

1671ff. This means that there are four more kinds of lust apart from these first five (hence the plural *les premieres*) that will not be discussed. These will include homosexual activity, etc. Didactic works of the period typically draw a veil over the topic, not out of 'delicacy' but, apparently, so as not to put ideas into the heads of the laity. Cf. *Manuel des Pechez* ed. F. J. Furnival, EETS OS 119, 123 (1901–03), 83–84:

> Des privitez ne troverez ren,
> Kar mal peot fere, ou poi de bien.

or Mirk, *Instructions for Parish Priests*, ed. E. Peacock, EETS OS 31 (1902), 221–24:

> Also wryten wel I fynde
> That of synne aȝeynes kynde
> Thow schalt thy paresche no þynge teche
> Ny of that synne no thynge preche.

or Peter of Fecham, *La Lumere as lais*, ANTS 56–58 (1996–2000), 3553–56:

> Dunt l'en put peccher tant avant
> Ke nul pecché ne sereit tant,
> Cume peccher cuntre nature,
> Mes de teu pecché parler n'ai cure.

(See also E. J. Arnould, *Le Manuel des Péchés* (Paris, 1940), 53–54.)

1680 *matire* is altered from manuscript *matere*; cf. *matere* (: *clere*) of line 90 (the only other occurrence of the word in the text).

1681 One of the main advances in the approach to penance in the late twelfth and early thirteenth centuries was the increasing emphasis placed on the circumstances of the sin in determining the penance to be given by the priest. Peñafort deals at length with this topic, introducing the mnemonic verse 'Quis, quid, ubi, per quos, quoties, cur, quomodo, quando, Quilibet observet medicamina dando' (III.xxxiv.31 — similar verses appear in other works), and the idea appears in many contemporary vulgarizing works dealing with confession, e.g. *La Lumere as Lais* (10,023ff., 10,079ff.), or the *Manuel des Pechés* (95–100, 1541–44, 5915–16, 9379–99, 9953ff., etc.). (In fact the first appearance in French of the word *circonstance* in its modern sense dates from around 1265.) Jehan similarly goes into quite some detail in the following lines, in a way that suggests a learned source (cf. 1744), treating the estate of the penitent (whether wealthy, aged, ordained, married, noble, educated, 1699), the type of sin (public or private, mortal or venial, simple or compound, 1743), the cause (whether sought out, the result of temptation long resisted, etc., 1757), how and for how long the sin took place (1771), the number of sins (1797), the time (1807), and the place (1817 — see *La Lumere as Lais* 3529*n* for a consideration of the circumstances of time and place), in other words covering most of Peñafort's points. See further 1927*n*.

1685 The line is somewhat unexpected; *mais* must be a rare example of the prepositional use in the sense "except, besides". It is just possible that the original read *chist vii* for *chiaus qui* (assuming a scribal eye-slip), or even *Mais chiaus sont li plus renoumés*.

1686 I.e. the other potential sins can be related/reduced to the ones just discussed.

1692 The general sense of the text and (particularly) the pronoun *les* of line 1694 suggest that *cas* is intended as plural and thus that *fait* of the manuscript should also be plural. The line is still a little awkward, however: "that cause the sin to be made worse" is a possible sense (*faire* was commonly used in Old French where *rendre* might be expected in Modern French, cf. 2230). *Faire* + infinitive can also be used as a periphrasis for a finite verb (e.g. *fai moi escouter*, "listen to me"), so the line might mean no more than "that make the sin worse".

1703–04 *chiaus*: i.e. poor people, *ses*, i.e. of the powerful man.

1721 See 1023*n*.

1731–32 *miroir* = "model, example" (as at 781); *mirent* must mean something like "observe" or "see exemplified".

1733 T-L has two examples of *portement* in the sense of "the carrying of a hunting bird on one's hand"; ours is the only specimen recorded in the sense "behaviour", though the one remaining example ("gesture") is very close in meaning.

1735 *airont*: for *aront* (see Introduction pp. 8–9).

1746 *apairaument*: for the spelling, see Introduction p. 9; the sense appears to be "openly, in public view". The dictionaries do not gloss this meaning, but certainly most of Gdf.'s examples (especially the earlier ones) seem susceptible of this interpretation.

1763–64 "And, if he set out to do it, who urged him on/put pressure on him."

1767 *Sorc(h)erie* seems to have only the expected, literal meaning "sorcery". Why it should be linked with feasting and drinking is not clear, unless the witchcraft is intended to inflame (their own or their paramours') lust.

1774 *enfers* = "infirm, sick person".

1775 The manuscript has *a trie*, which is not in T-L; *FEW* (13, 2 p. 304) gives both a masculine *a tri* and a feminine *a trie* from Occitan in the sense "d'une manière exquise", connected with O.F. *trier*, "distinguish, pick out". In our text the expression seems to have the sense "carefully, in detail", which might be connected with the same verb. (T-L's suggestion *a tire* (cf. 1508), fails to notice the rhyme.)

1780 T-L records that *ame* can be masculine, but this is extremely rare. Under *plain* there are many examples of non-agreement, but only when the adjective precedes a noun for a container or unit of measurement ('plain les mains', 'du blé plain ses greniers', 'plain mesure'), hence our emendation.

1789 *ses*: for *c(h)es*.

1791 *alonge* seems to mean "addition" in the context, though the commoner sense "excuse" might just fit; cf. 1916.

1797 *nombre* is attested with a singular noun in the sense "quantity, magnitude".

1802 *esmanche*: (from *esmer*) = "estimation, calculation"; T-L has two examples of the term.

1807 *Ses*: for *c(h)es*; *entans* is presumably imperative, the analogical *-s* providing a rhyme for the eye.

1814 The context rather requires a singular *la* for *les*, but this would make the line hypometric; *les* must be a licence in the sense "such *folies*".

1815 *autres termes* is probably scribal for *autre terme*, given the rhyme.

1816 This allusion to Bernard has not been tracked down.

1823 *propres* is a noun here, meaning "property, possession".

1827 *croissanches* is ambiguous; it may mean "outgrowths, offshoots, branches" here, or "things that increase the sins, that make them worse" (i.e. the circumstances just discussed). Note that, in this and the following lines, the author seems to be assimilating his work to contemporary manuals, or to some model, stressing what he has covered, and suggesting the completeness of his treatment, even in such a short space. Sins were commonly presented in the manuals using the framework of the five senses, or the seven sacraments, or the ten commandments.

1833 *Qui* = "if anyone".

1844 *avesra*: the future of *avenir*, not *avoir* (which is *ara*, *arons*, etc. and never has a *v* on any of its twenty-five appearances in this text); see Introduction pp. 15 and 24. This means that *l'en* is the normal unstressed form equivalent to stressed *lui en aviendra*.

1850 The manuscript has *encreus*, but *encroistre* does not fit here in any of its senses, while *enchëoir* typically collocates with *mal*, *pecché*, etc.

1852–54 *aie* for *ait*, cf. 1250. Among the many senses of *maniere* are "habit" and "intention", either of which would fit at 1853, leaving the sense "manner, nature" for the equivocal rhyme.

1856 *sembler a* = "resemble".

1868 A play on words between the literal sense of *espeluquier* ("cleanse") and its figurative sense ("examine [critically]"); cf. 1757. (Cf. also 1175ff.)

1882 Although this noun phrase is masculine nominative plural, the syllable count suggests that the author expected the final *-s* that appears everywhere else to apply here too. (A more sympathetic emendation would be to attribute the final *-s* to the scribe and read *[Et] nechessaire*, but, as is pointed out in the Introduction, the scribe is probably more, not less, rigorous in the matter of declension than the author.)

1899–1900 Another of the equivocal rhymes which the author enjoys so much; the first *fais* probably meaning "deed", the second "done".

1912 The emendation is not strictly necessary, since the scribe often writes *dont* for *donc*; he does not write *donc* for *dont*, however, except in this line.

1915 Cf. 1252*n*.

1915–16 These lines appear to be a reflex of the celebrated passage from Augustine's *Sermon 181* (Migne *P.L.* 38, 981), often quoted by medieval writers on penance: 'cum humilitatis causa mentiris, si non eras peccator antequam mentireris, mentiendo efficeris quod vitaras.' The French remains rather opaque, however, especially since *alonge* is such an ambiguous *cheville*. Cf. 1791*n*.

1924 "is [now] more laden down (with sin) than he was when he unburdened himself (in his partial confession)."

1927 The sixth 'article' is omitted. It is not clear what source is behind these lines (the passage starts at 1875), but it is not the *Summa de Paenitentia*, which has a different set of articles arranged in a different order. These so-called 'points of shrift' appear in most of the confessional manuals and vary from source to source, but one might expect the missing point to be that confession should be frequent (particularly given Payen's convincing argument — see Bibliography) or possibly that it should be humble. See further 1979*n*.

1934–35 There is a mark on the membrane obscuring line 1934, and the *f* of ?*fieus* is scarcely discernible. The mark intrudes onto line 1935, where the membrane appears furthermore to be rubbed, and the letters *ers* of *persone* are very difficult to read.

1959 There is another mark on the membrane here; the words *sains* and *et* (the Tironian *nota*) are scarcely legible.

1960 T-L has examples of ditransitive *pardoner* in the sense "excuse someone from something, spare someone something".

1979 Here Jehan begins the third major section that he announced in line 979, namely his description of satisfaction. After his definition (divided into necessary and voluntary satisfaction), he begins, at 2032, an extended metaphor or allegory (which continues for nearly 900 lines), depicting the World, the Flesh and the Devil as military leaders waging war on good men, each of the three having certain specific sins under their command. The Devil has pride and sloth (2054), which we must combat by prayer; the Flesh has lust and gluttony (2130) which we must combat by fasting, and the World has avarice, envy and wrath (2390), which we must combat by almsgiving. (It will be seen that this is the same allocation of deadly sins that appeared in lines 663ff. For more information about the 'Three Enemies of Man', see Wenzel in the Bibliography, and *Le Besant de Dieu de Guillaume le Clerc de Normandie*, ed. Pierre Ruelle, Brussels, 1973, pp. 56–61.) This basic framework has been considerably elaborated with divisions and subdivisions, suggesting again a scholastically inspired source, and the table below gives a more detailed picture.

The Devil is in league with pride and sloth; we fight them with	2054
prayer	2069
1 must be sincere	2086
2 we may ask for:	2096
a pardon for our sins	2100
b grace from God	2102
c may also ask God: i to relieve temporal suffering	2106
ii not to put temptation in our way	2110
iii to grant worldly goods	2112
but all of the above must be conditional on what we need	2114
3 must also be prompt, open, humble, entire, devout	2118
4 may take place anywhere, but church is the best setting	2122
The Flesh is in league with lechery and gluttony; we fight them with	2130
fasting	2141
there are three branches, but we should try to combine them:	2148
1 avoid worldly pleasure	2154
2 avoid mortal sin	2170
3 abstain from food	2202
a enforced fasting (no use unless borne with patience)	2222
b reprehensible fasting:	2232
i as misers do to save money	2238
ii as hypocrites do (?for outward show — lines missing)	2280
iii as gluttons do to sharpen their appetite	2342
c praiseworthy fasting (as penance), requires four things:	2356
i cheerfulness	2365
ii duration	2370
iii moderation	2380
iv almsgiving	2386
The World is in league with avarice, envy and wrath; we fight them with	2390
almsgiving	2412
1 what can we give as alms	2645
2 who can give alms	2645
3 to whom should alms be given	2693
4 how should we give alms:	2757
a out of the kindness of our heart	2759
b humbly, as humility protects against:	2769
i vainglory	2778
ii despising the recipient	2793
iii believing almsgiving is enough without confession	2801

c	with a cheerful countenance	2811
d	speaking pleasantly	2817
e	making almsgiving durable	2841

1980 *Mener* may seem a little contrived here, but there are in fact various senses in T-L that might fit, "carry out, perform, go through, etc.", and there are standard collocations with *joie*, or *duel*, for example, which support the manuscript reading.

1983 The manuscript has *le* for our *se*. The dictionaries do not list this verb in this construction, but T-L has an example (from Adam de la Halle) of the reflexive of *amender*: 'N'enver aus ne se daigne amender n'escondire', glossed as "Buße tun (do penance)".

1985–86. It is difficult to see what the scribe understood when he wrote *ki la male porte* in 1986; the emendation assumes a sense "the pain/penalty that the sin brings with it"; Suchier suggests reading *ki le mal amorte*. (Breymann emends *si porte* of 1985 to *suporte*, though the verb is extremely rare at this date.)

1992 *maugré sa faiche* (= *face*): "despite himself, (even) against his will", the only example of this precise expression in T-L, though there are many similar collocations with *vis*, *visage*, *dents*, *nez*, etc.

1995 *assaus* = *assous*.

1998 The form *assolicïons* has been retained on the assumption that it represents a change of suffix, but it is quite possible that the scribe simply omitted a minim and that one should read *assolucïons*.

2005 Supply *assoume* again ("when he counts his sins and then calculates the penance he should do").

2009 *faire* seems to be a 'pro-verb' here, standing for *monter*, i.e. he finds that his sin amounts to more than his penance could do [i.e. could amount to].

2015 "Whatever is supererogatory, he offers it up to Holy Church"?

2018 *qu'* = *qui*.

2020 There is a line missing between 2019 and 2020, no doubt caused in part by there being four lines on the same rhyme in the original (perhaps even involving some equivocal rhyme such as *el plus haut degré*). The subject might well change from the penitent (who acts willingly) to the penance (which has great worth), though it is quite plausible that it is the penitent who is worthy.

2028 *Apoursivir*: although written by the scribe as *A poursivir*, this looks like an unattested verb with a double prefix (cf. *aporpenser, aporseoir*, etc.), probably in the sense of "seek after, strive for". One would be more confident if *affection* of 2026 (meaning "inclination, desire") were not followed by *a* + infinitive on two of its four appearances in T-L.

2029 The masculine nominative singular *chis* (for Central Old French *cist*) is a well known typically Picard form (see Introduction p. 20). The form *ches* as masculine oblique singular, however, is not picked up by the standard reference works, and does not figure in Gossen. On the other hand the scribe writes this form nine times in our text (never before a vowel), the same number of times as he uses the form *chest* (which appears once before a vowel). This suggests that the spelling might well have been intentional, and the emendation is possibly otiose.

2035 The manuscript is clear, and makes good sense, but this is almost certainly a mistake for *du Maufé*.

2044 *Que* here presumably means "for, because"; *cascuns* must mean each of the 'warriors', rather than each man or each sin, i.e. these three warriors split up/go their separate ways and share out the sins between them, for each one has a large share of them (i.e. sins).

2053 *s'* = *si*; cf. 2231*n*.

2058 The dictionaries have various collocations of *tenir* with *lieu*, but perhaps the most likely sense here is "be important (for), be of use (to)".

2060 *chist ·ii· raim*: i.e. pride and sloth.

2068 The form *faisons* appears seven further times, always as an indicative; there is no other instance of the *nous*-form present subjunctive, *fa(i)che(nt)* being the subjunctive form for the other persons. It is possible that the author wrote *et* for the scribe's *que*.

2070 The source of this metaphor has not been identified, but it does not appear to be Biblical.

2075 Röhrs (p. 320) suggests that the rhyme represents *besoin : seloin*, but T-L has not a single instance of a palatalized *seloi(g)n* in four and a half columns of examples, suggesting that the rhyme is defective. S*elon* is sometimes an adverb meaning "accordingly", e.g. 'quant avercz vent, siglez sulunc', or 'Dont li fait blasme gentillece, Quant il ne se maintient selonc'. The emendation assumes that *besoig* has the sense "struggle, hard work", though the line is still rather uncomfortable.

2091 Cf. 372*n*.

2117 *besoigne* is an impersonal verb here, with the sense "be necessary"; *nos* is the indirect object pronoun.

2135 The manuscript has *moustre* for our *metre*. T-L lists *metre pais, metre chalenge, metre defense*, but not *metre guerre*, which generally collocates with *(em)prendre, faire, mener, movoir* and *rendre*; perhaps the scribe started to write *mouvoir*.

2138 *raconfortee*: T-L has one other example of this triple prefix; the verb, of course, means "strengthen".

2155 The dictionaries do not list the form *esquier*, which appears again at line 2174; the rhyme *esquive* (manuscript *esquiee*) : *vive* in the next line suggests that the form is scribal.

2160 The expression looks proverbial, but no other example has been found. The sense is perhaps that it is better to have a little of one's own property than to have a lot that one will have to pay for.

2165 *vassaument*: T-L has our example with the suggested sense "wisely"; perhaps "nobly" might be a better translation in context. As the following lines make clear, *prendre le mains* here refers to choosing transitory, earthly joy and *laisser le plus* to neglecting eternal joy.

2184 The author draws a distinction between commandment and advice. This distinction also underpins the next lines, which suggest that it is worse to break a commandment (*la* = *Loi*) than to disregard a simple recommendation.

2207 It seems unlikely that any lines are actually missing here, but the construction is rather loose, the *li* must refer to a penitent/confessant who is not explicitly mentioned.

2208 *Pour che*: "for this reason" i.e. because he was not undertaking the other two kinds of fasting (cf. 2204).

2209 *voir* is of course the adverb, "indeed".

2224 For this rhyme, see Introduction p. 15.

2218 *qui* is for *quë*, or perhaps *cui*.

2230 *Chele* refers back to *passcience, faire* is used in the sense that would require *rendre* in Modern French (cf. 146, 1692, 2242); *le* is a Picardism for *la (june)*.

2231 *s'* is not a reflexive pronoun, but a licence for *si*, which the author also permits himself at line 2053.

2242 The expressions *estre bien de* and *estre mal de* ("to be in (dis)favour with") are well attested; here *faire* is used in a causative sense.

2251 Intransitive *amender* is glossed by T-L as "Förderung haben, gefördert werden (receive support, be helped)"; the sense must be "a friend from whom he cannot receive support/assistance".

2259 *espargne-malle*: this is the only example in T-L; Gdf. has two others from problematic, undated sources. (Early 'piggy banks' were pottery jars — not yet in the shape of a pig — with a slot to receive the coins, but with no other opening; consequently they had to be broken before the coins could be removed.)

2269 The same expression recurs at 2616; T-L has several examples.

2271 Perhaps a reference to Isaiah 58:3ff.

2276 The idea is that while fasting may make the body thin, it makes the soul fat, i.e. mortifies the flesh but is good for the soul.

2292 *cache*: a Picardism from *casser* rather than *cacher*.

2295 *son* = God's.

2296 *cunkie* = *conchie* = "deceive, trick". It seems likely that there are some lines missing here; it is not said explicitly what is hypocritical about this behaviour (in fact it seems laudable enough), and it is similarly unclear which *paroles* are intended in line 2300. Perhaps the original had a couplet (? before 2292) that explained what words hypocrites use to deceive people about fasting. The *s* of *recors* in 2300 is also hard to account for, unless it is purely an eye-rhyme; one might perhaps read *et recors* as a noun in the sense "tales". Suchier suggests *et retors*.

2309 The rhyme here (which spans a page-turn) is a further indication that the scribe's language is more Picard-coloured than that of the author.

2312 *Car* = "flesh", i.e. someone in the flesh, the real thing, is better than a picture. The expression looks proverbial, but no other examples have come to light.

2317 I.e. everyone prefers (genuinely) good people to those who (merely) resemble/appear to be good people.

2324 *Que* = "for, because".

2328 The subject of *tournent* is *si bien* of line 2326. Manuscript *lor* for our *li* seems to be due to the plural idea of hypocrites in general overriding that of the single exemplary hypocrite we have elsewhere.

2338 The reference is to Matthew 6:16–18:

> Cum autem ieiunatis nolite fieri sicut hypocritae: tristes demoliuntur enim facies suas ut pareant hominibus ieiunantes. Amen dico vobis quia receperunt mercedem suam. Tu autem cum ieiunas ungue caput tuum et faciem tuam lava, ne videaris hominibus ieiunans sed Patri tuo qui est in abscondito, et Pater tuus qui videt in abscondito reddet tibi.

2344 *haskie*: a Picardism for *haschiee* ("torment").

2345 *aigrie*: see Introduction p. 12.

2350 *Grigores*: the manuscript has *gg* with a titulus. (The word is written in full on its other appearances.)

2359 *Vengier* has two constructions: either some evil deed is the object (*vengier mautalent*, etc.), or a person is object, with the evil deed optionally introduced by *de*. Here we seem to have both constructions in a kind of zeugma; it might be better to read *de* instead of *et*.

2360 *souffraint*: the manuscript has *souffroit*. One sense of *souffrir* (at least of *soi souffrir de*) is "abstain, go without", and this might be what was intended here, but the awkwardness of *que* (rather than *dont*), and the tense of *souffroit* would argue against it.

2365 The manuscript appears to have *nos epsce*, with a titulus over the *p*. One would be tempted to read *mos* for *nos*, but for the gender problem. Cf. 2338*n*.

2369 The scribe writes *se i oinst* for our *s'esjoïst*, presumably expecting some form of *oindre* to go with line 2366 and with *encraisser* of 2368, whereas in fact the verb takes up the idea of *leeche* from 2364.

2377 Cf. I Samuel (I Kings) 14:24–47.

2382 *outragier*: ours is the only example of the adjective in T-L.

2388 *eoule*: the sense seems to be "oil"; *lumiere* appears to mean "lamp" here, a very rare sense in French (T-L has another example, as does *AND*), and one that suggests a calque on a Latin source. This has not been identified, and consequently it is not easy to see why almsgiving should be mentioned here. Could the idea be that one should give alms from the food that one would have eaten had one not been fasting?

2392 T-L has only three examples of *grevable*, including this one, plus one adverb *grevablement*.

2398 The first *i* of *fuissiemes* is carefully formed with a 'dot' above it. Gossen does not mention this form in §73 ('formes faibles des parfaits en *-ui* et l'imparfait du subjonctif'), though he does note the forms *euissiens*, *puissions*, etc., and he cites four further examples of *fuissiemes* in his discussion of the (apparently western Picard) ending *-iemes* in §79. One might compare the spellings *suistanche* (2847) and *pluiseur* (397, 872, etc.) and Röhrs' remarks on pp. 307 and 341.

2399 For the rather idiosyncratic form *queme* see Introduction p. 13.

2403 I take *le hounie* to be in apposition to *ire* (i.e. *ire la honnie*, "wrath the accursed one, accursed wrath"), and *aveukes* to be adverbial "also, therewith". Suchier's suggested *gloutounie* instead of *la hounie* fails to notice that gluttony is a sin connected with the flesh (672, 2131) not the world, and also overlooks the evidence of lines 729–31.

2404 It is possible to make sense of the manuscript: "so that avarice or envy or accursed wrath (since it would come to do battle) could not harm us". However, it is tempting to make *venrroit* plural, to cover all three deadly sins, perhaps *Puisque venrroient batellier*.

2409 In prose: *que l'amistie de nous et de nos proismes fust toute brisie*. "Nonetheless, even if it happened that the world had such power over us that the love between us and our neighbours were completely destroyed, we could regain our freedom by the means that I shall describe to you: that is by almsgiving."

2412 *esscache*: under *eschacier*, T-L has a sense "aufjagen, verjagen (drive away)". Our example is not listed, but there is one from Gilles li Muisis: 'Ja mais, se n'est par grasce, [sins] ne seront escachiet', and half a dozen others, though none that mentions ice or snow.

2414 *tant que*: can mean "concerning, regarding". T-L has four examples including this one, and two more of *en tant que*; the expression is followed by a preposition in every case. The rather vague sense is probably because *en chest liu* ("under this heading"? cf. T-L "Stelle in einer Schrift (passage/reference in a text)") is little more than a *cheville*, to provide a rhyme for *Dieu*.

2416–18 "So in almsgiving, when one does it, it is necessary that one gives an appropriate gift ..."

2425 This spelling seems to combine elements of *combien* and *quant*; cf. 1304*n* and 2399*n*.

2431 I.e. generosity rewards whatever he has contributed to society for her (generosity's) sake(?).

2440 The expression looks proverbial, but no other example has come to light.

2443 After this line the scribe repeats line 2430 (*Ou en avoir ou en amis*), which is evidently out of place. In Breymann's edition this forms line 2444. It seemed sensible to retain Breymann's line numbers to facilitate comparison with his edition and with subsequent studies (particularly that of Röhrs); consequently our edition lacks a line 2444. Cf. notes to lines 2456, 2913 and 3027.

2448 A common proverbial expression, Morawski n° 1229.

2453 Again, no other example of this proverb has been found.

2454 *li*: manuscript *le* seems hard to defend; *li* must refer to the almsgiver.

2456–58 These lines repeat lines 102–04; cf. notes to lines 2443, 2913 and 3027.

2461–63 The sense of these lines is rather obscure. Perhaps *largue* in line 2460 is a noun meaning "a generous person", who would also be subject of the verb *sache* in 2463: "the wealth of a generous person will never be lessened by any gift that he knows how to make appropriately". The construction *qui ... sera* is nonetheless odd in this context, though it may be influenced by the rhyme.

2485 I.e. "if there is any (good) in me".

2493 The transitive use of *renomer* is not uncommon in the sense "give someone a good reputation", and T-L lists examples with an inanimate subject, e.g. 'ome | Que sens e proëce renome'.

2509–10 I take *destrois* to mean "afflicted, overwhelmed"; manuscript *seront*, however is more problematic, since there is no obvious plural noun that could be its subject. The rhyme (though not conclusive) suggests a nominative singular rather than a plural, and the idea of *on* from line 2506 may still be in the author's mind. As emended, I take the text to mean "he will never be so afflicted by them, particularly by the three [that are particularly combated by almsgiving, namely avarice, envy and wrath (see line 2390)]". It is quite likely that lines 2509–10 have been interverted with 2511–12.

2512 *embramé*: the dictionaries know only *embrami* in the sense "burning, ardent, etc." (and their examples suggest a figurative rather than a literal sense, though the verb is very rare). T-L does have one example of *embramer*, the result of an emendation, glossed as "verlangen, ersehnen (long for)". Notwithstanding, one is disinclined to emend to *embrasé*.

2513 *estainte*: this is the only example of the noun in T-L, though Gdf. has a few later examples.

2514 *li*: must refer to *amosne*.

2517 *Che* appears as a determiner on only four other occasions in the text (524, 2926, 3078, 3292), and never before a following vowel. It is possible that the scribe here misunderstood *chest* of his exemplar as a pronoun (= "for this reason, hence") rather than an adjective qualifying *amor*, and 'corrected' it to *che*.

2519 *douner*: (our) giving alms.

2528 See 1979n for the topics that Jehan actually deals with. Even allowing for *quant* in 2530 meaning "how much", and thus perhaps being part of How one should give alms, Jehan's first topic, namely Who can give alms, is notably absent from this introductory list, and a couplet may be missing from our copy.

2534 *la secussïon*: T-L has four examples of the word in the phrase *metre a secucïon*; three are about carrying out the terms of a will, and one is about dealing with complaints. Our word probably means "the way in which it [almsgiving] should be carried out". (Suchier suggested emending to the extremely rare *discussïon*, but he mistakenly believed this to be supported by line 2801, where the manuscript actually has *desfencion*.)

2540 *sans lui*: i.e. without his overlord's knowledge/consent.

2545 This passage contains some legal terminology, especially in its distinction between movable and immovable property. (The rather opaque form *fiés* is, of course, the nominative singular of *fief*.)

2548 In this equivocal rhyme, the second *devise* probably has its rarer sense of "will, testament", though it may simply mean "division".

2549 The verb is usually *moitier* or *moitoier* ("halve, divide, ?reduce by half"), the double *i* in the spelling here presumably indicating this extra syllable, cf. *otrïier* 2690 and *crucefïiés* 393.

2562 The author appears to use *frankise, segnourie, pöoir* and *poissanche* more or less interchangeably in this section in the sense "right of possession, power/freedom to dispose of something".

2568 This well attested proverb is Morawski n° 1571.

2577 *conquerant*: Gdf. hints at a legal sense for this noun (glossing it as "plaignant"), but otherwise, the dictionaries list only the sense "conqueror". However, one of the senses of the verb *conquerre* is "gain, obtain", and the noun here appears to mean "the person obtaining it". The passage is still not easy to follow. A comparison with the *Summa de Paenitentia* II.viii.7 will clarify the sense, and incidentally show the relation between our work and its (ultimate) source:

> Item quaeritur, utrum de illicite acquisitis possit aliquo modo fieri eleemosyna. Ad hoc dicunt quidam generaliter quod non [...] Alii, quibus assentio, ponunt distinctionem trimembrem, videlicet, quod in illicite acquisitis aliquando non transfertur dominum [sic = dominium] in accipientem, ut in rapina et furto. Aliquando transferetur, sed illi, qui dedit, competit repetitio, ut in usura et simonia.

> Et idem videtur in pecunia acquisita in ludo aleae, scilicet quod competat repetitio. Et dicit graeca constitutio, quod usque ad quinquaginta annos potest repeti. Quod qualiter intelligam, tangam forte in fine huius tituli. [The author does this in chapter 11, which provides the stuff of our lines 2623–38.] Aliquando vero transfertur dominium et non competit repetitio; exemplum de pecunia acquista de meretricio vel histrionatu vel ex improbitate officialis qui interdum extorquet a subditis aliqua. In primo membro, scilicet, cum non transfertur dominium, et in secundo, scilicet, cum transfertur dominium sed competit repetitio, non potest fieri eleemosyna, sed praecise debet restitui iuxta formam positam supra in titulis specialibus. In tertio autem membro, scilicet, cum transfertur dominium et non competit repetitio, licite potest et debet fieri eleemosyna. Et hanc distinctionem probat Ambrosius.

Manuscript *prendre* has been emended to *rendre* in 2578, the idea "keep or take" making no sense in the context. One might read *Qu'i[l]* for *Qui* in 2578.

2579 *gäang*: the scribe has written *gaignie*, presumably for the past participle. This, of course, makes excellent sense, but on its ten other appearances the verb and its derived forms are always spelt with double *a*, which counts as two syllables. Even allowing for this being a solitary monosyllabic variant, a feminine agreement is required here, and both *gaignié[e]* and the Picard *gaignie* would make the line hypermetric. *Com est gäang* (the form appears at 1587) also has the advantage of offering a closer syntactic parallel to *Com est simonie* in 2573.

2580 *hyraus* is the normal word for "herald", and very commonly (perhaps even usually) has a pejorative sense. Typically linked with minstrels, singers, *ribaus*, dice players, and people feigning illness to beg for money, heralds were originally poor and often disreputable people, employed by knights to keep a tally of their successes in tournaments, and to announce their prowess to anyone who would listen. They are consequently associated with lying and boasting for payment, and the entry in T-L has various examples of heralds behaving in uncourtly, dishonest and sometimes venal ways. Although *jongleur* does not usually have such negative connotations, nonetheless there are a few examples of the term being used with overtones of lying, and money and other gifts are very frequent themes when jongleurs are being discussed. (Cf. A. Långfors, 'Le Dit des hérauts' in *Romania* 42 (1914), pp. 216–25.)

2581 *conqueste*: this is the only example in T-L of a feminine derivative of *conquerre* with final *–e*; Gdf. has one further example dated 1263. T-L also prints *la queste* for our *l'aqueste*, though it has two examples of *aqueste* from other sources.

2590–93 For differences between the medieval game of chess and the modern one (including the possibility of playing using dice), see J.-M. Mehl, *Les Jeux au royaume de France du XIIIe au début du XVIe siècle* (Paris, Fayard, 1990), chapter VII. For the game of *tables*, see chapter VIII. As for *hazart*, Mehl reports (p. 92): 'Le sens générique de "jeu de dés" devait se maintenir jusqu'à la fin du Moyen Age [...] Parallèlement cheminait le sens plus restreint d'un certain type de jeu.' Either the general or the specific sense would fit here. *Hazart* in the specific sense was rather a complicated game (played, it will be remembered, in Bodel's *Jeu de saint Nicolas*), using three dice, in which one player rolls the dice both for himself and for his opponent. If the first player scores a *hazart* with the first throw, he wins the round; if he does so on the second throw, his opponent wins. If no *hazart* has been thrown, the first player can still win if he throws his initial score a second time. *Hazart* here refers to any of the statistically unlikely scores 3, 4, 5, 6, 15, 16, 17 or 18. *Plus de poins* (more commonly called *les plus points*) is a very basic dice game with one or more dice and two or more players, where the highest score wins (see F. Semrau, *Würfel und Würfelspiel im alten Frankreich*, Beihefte zur *ZrP* 23, 1910, p. 43). *La grigoise* (nearly always known as *la griesche*, though the form *grijoise* is also found in Jubinal's *Jongleurs et trouvères*, Paris, 1835, p. 34) is a slightly more complex game whose rules are obscure, but which uses three dice, and, according to Semrau may involve trying to predict what score will fall with the next throw (Semrau p. 58). (Mehl, p. 91–92, believes that the game was the same as *les plus points*, using three dice, but the juxtaposition of the two games in our text — which Mehl did not know — perhaps makes this interpretation less likely.) *Per ou nonper*, on the other hand, despite appearances, may refer not to a game but to a type of rigged dice, to judge by Semrau's quotation (p. 30) from the *Livre des mestiers* of Estienne Boileau (ed. G. B. Depping, Paris, 1837): 'Nus deicier ne peut ne ne doit fere ne acheter [...] dez mespointz, ce est a savoir qui soient touz d'as, ou tous de ·II· poinz, out touz de ·III· ou (etc.) [...] ou dez a deus ·II· ou a deux as, ou a deus ·V· ou (etc.) [...], que on apele per et nonper.' (Cf. Mehl p. 82.) It is on this basis that I have assumed an accidental inversion in the manuscript, which reads: *S'en ai ·iii· dés a la grigoise A plus de poins per ou nonper*.

2595 *escakons*: the manuscript reads *escakeus*, and the emendation is rather tentative. T-L has one example of a word spelt *eschaçons* and glossed merely as "a game" ('As eschas ni a tables nul frere dou Temple ne doit jüer, ne as eschaçons', from a *Règle du Temple* quoted by A. Delboulle in *Romania* 33 (1904), p. 349). The game is not mentioned by Mehl. T-L (s.v. *merele*) suggests reading *estakes* here, a form of *estaches*, in the sense of "post or stake as target for shooting or throwing practice", but surely our author is dealing with indoor board games here. Line 2597 may suggest that our *eschaquons* was a dice game of some kind, and it may have been one that involved a chessboard and dice together (like *dringuet*: see Mehl p. 95). Given the rarity of the word one could understand a scribe's misreading *on* as *eu*. *Mereles* is the game known in English as 'nine-men's morris' (formerly also called 'merels'), in Germany, where it is still popular, as *Mühlen*, in France (ambiguously) as *la marelle* or *le jeu du moulin*. There appear to have been two basic versions of the game. One is played with dice, each player having nine small flat pieces like draughts. The board is marked with three concentric squares, with lines joining the mid-point of each side of the innermost square to the mid-point of each side of the outermost square. Players place their pieces in turn on a corner or an intersection on the board, according to the throw of the dice, with the aim of occupying any three points connected by a line. Every time a player joins three points, he or she may remove one of the opponent's pieces; the loser is the player left with fewer than three pieces. In the other (rather more challenging) version, each player has twelve pieces (sometimes fifteen) and no dice are used, the aim being to take the opponent's pieces by jumping over them into an empty position beyond. The game can be further complicated by the pieces being given different values. (Cf. Mehl pp. 149–51.) *La Vieille* (*Poëme [...] traduit du latin de Richard de Fournival par Jean Lefèvre*, ed. H. Cocheris, 1861) bears this out (ll. 1739–52):

> Ces gieuz sont nommez aux merelles,
> Dont jouvenceaulx et jouvencelles
> Se jeuent dessus une table.
> Douze ou neuf font le gieu estable,
> Mais a douze prent sans faillir
> Celle qui puet oultre saillir
> Dessus l'autre par adventure.
> A cest gieu n'a on des dez cure,
> Mais au neuf puet on bien jouer
> Avec les dez, et remuer

> Si comme la pointure la porte.
> Car trois merelles d'une sorte
> En ordre seulent gaaing faire
> Sur celles de leur adversaire.

2596 *sercos*: for this reduced vowel, cf. Gossen p. 91.

2597 *soulagier*: The normal word for "entertain, divert" is *solacier*; *soslagier* normally means "relieve". One would be tempted to emend to the expected *soulac(h)ier*, but the form appears again at 2631. Gossen (§38) mentions that there is a tendency in Picard to devoice final voiced consonants, leading to rhymes such as *forche : gorge*, *piece : siege*, and to reverse graphies such as *sagiés*; it is possible that the same phenomenon is in play here.

2598 *Le point de l'eskekier* is rather tantalizing. Mehl writes (p. 96) 'quant au "point de l'eschiquier", le nom fait référence aux dés et à l'accessoire sur lequel on joue. [In fact, *point* is the normal word for a square on a chessboard, and so need not refer to dice at all.] Faut-il y voir une façon élégante de parler du jeu de dés? La fréquence des mentions de ce jeu dans les lettres de rémission imposerait une conclusion inverse. En tout cas le jeu se joue sur un tablier. Par ailleurs, les circonstances du jeu rappellent les dés. [Mehl offers no support for this rather vague remark.] Le dringuet, le franc du carreau et le point de l'échiquier constituaient donc des jeux proches.' Later (p. 101), he describes *le franc du carrreau* as an outdoor game, played by throwing an object and making it land inside a square drawn on the ground. 'D'une certaine manière, il est l'extension aux normes d'un jeu d'extérieur du "point de l'échiquier" déjà évoqué. Il en reste encore proche, surtout lorsqu'il se pratique sur une table, comme en Touraine en 1497. Sans doute ce jeu a-t-il aussi été pratiqué à l'aide de dés.' Quite what prompts this assumption is unclear; at any rate, our author certainly seems not to anticipate the use of dice. One imagines a game where an object had to come to rest entirely within a square without touching or straddling the sides, where perhaps one player could knock his opponent's piece(s) out of the way, and where, conceivably, progress had to be made in a specified path across the board, but this is mere conjecture. Given that there were apparently indoor and outdoor versions of *le franc du carreau*, one wonders whether there was not also an outdoor version of *le point de l'eschiquier*, perhaps played on a paved surface. T-L has two examples of the expression, but again, no clear picture emerges of the game. One is from *Balaham und Josaphas* (ed. Appel) l. 7114:

> Al point jüent de l'eskekier
> Tant k'il el angle sont venu!
> Li clerc l'ont primes maintenu,
> Si l'aprisent as chevaliers.

(T-L adds the note 'hier verblümt von der Sodomiterei'); the other is from *La Vengeance Raguidel* (ed. M. Friedwagner, Halle: Niemeyer, 1909) l. 4914:

> Or sui au point de l'escekier,
> Or puis laissier, je sui a cois.
> Ke ferai jo? Par foi, j'en vois.

(The editor's note is of no help.)

2599 *toupet*: Walter of Bibbesworth, in his *Tretiz* (ed. W. Rothwell, ANTS, Plain Texts Series 6 (1990), line 37) has a parallel: 'En la rue juez au toup'. The form *toupet* appears to be relatively rare.

2600 *boute en coroie*: a game typically associated with duping the unwary, where a trickster would make skilfully arranged loops in a thin leather strap, and ask his victim to put a finger among the loops in such a way that, when the trickster pulled on the strap, the finger would be inside a loop, and not outside. See Gaston Paris's note in *Romania* 21 (1892), pp. 407–413.

2601 The sense of this line has resisted all investigation. On the basis of other forms in the text such as *saudee* (377), *taut* (381), *craulla* (398), etc., it is permissible to assume that *rauller* is for *rouler*, though it is not clear in what sense. The dictionaries know no collocation of *metre* and *chiere*, though one sense of *metre* is "to bet, wager". Is it possible that *metre sa chiere* simply means something like "have a good time"?

2602 *jeter pierre*: Mehl describes various games involving the throwing of objects at a target, and mentions specifically (p. 103) *le jeu de la pierre* (*du perrel/parreau*). 'Dans sa forme la plus fruste, il consiste à lancer des pierres, soit le plus loin possible, soit vers un but précis.' In a public *plache*, the latter seems the more likely.

2603–04 Mehl tells us (p. 48) 'Billes, boules et quilles se confondent sous la plume des clercs de la Chancellerie royale, des poètes, ou des notaires confectionnant des inventaires,' and gives many examples of ambiguous terminology in this semantic area.

However, *billes* were normally heavy, rounded pieces of wood (sometimes spherical, sometimes flatter in the form of a disc), thrown or hit with a stick (*billart, crosse*) shaped either like a hockey stick or like a croquet mallet. The aim was to hit a target (often a stick fixed in the ground), and/or to negotiate obstacles (such as croquet hoops). Typically several players were involved, apparently sometimes in teams. As for *quilles*, Mehl (p. 55) writes that the earliest written attestation of the game dates from 1317, which would make the presence of the term in our text all the more remarkable. Unlike the modern game, the (heavy) skittles were knocked down not with a ball, but with a stick, seemingly thrown from a distance with some force. The *court baston* mentioned in line 2604 might thus be the target for the game of *billes*, or the projectile for the game of ninepins (though it should be said that Mehl's — later — evidence mentions a stick for skittles of an ell in length, hardly *court*). Another (perhaps less likely) possibility is that the *baston* might be used for a third, different, game. T-L has a quotation: 'le berger [...] doit aussi eschever tous jeux, excepté le jeu des merelles et du baston', but what *le jeu du baston* might be is a mystery.

2610–11 *s'i[l]*: see 333*n*.

2620 *vous* is in all likelihood the reflexive pronoun, i.e. *un conseil où [auquel] vous vous attachassiez*. This reflexive use is rare but attested.

2629 *li = le + lui* (cf. Hasenohr §94).

2631 *soulagier*: see 2597*n*.

2638 I.e. a ward, who cannot legally act to his own disadvantage without his guardian's permission. This is T-L's earliest example of the word *tutor*.

2642 T-L has only one example of *talenter*, not taken from our text.

2645 This section appears to derive ultimately from the *Summa de Paenitentia*, II.viii.8–9, though considerably abridged. It follows on from the passage quoted in 2577*n*:

> Sed quaeritur circa hoc, utrum monachus vel alia religiosa persona possit facere eleemosynam. Videtur quod non, quia nihil habet, nec etiam voluntatem [...] Distingue, tamen quia aut habet administrationem, aut non. In primo casu, debet et potest facere [...] In secundo casu [...] non potest, nisi de mandato praelati. Monachus

enim non postest tractare, etiam utilitates monasterii sui, nisi de praecepto abbatis. Sed quid si videat monachus aliquem indigere ad mortem? In hoc casu, si non habet praelatum praesentem a quo petat licentiam, credo quod debeat dare, nam in tali casu omnis homo tenetur ex praecepto pascere proximum [...] Item, quid si petat licentiam et abbas expresse prohibeat? Videtur quod non possit dare, quia etiam a bono debet cessare propter bonum oboedientiae. Credo tamen contrarium, quia in tali praecepto, quod directe est contra Deum, non est oboediendum homini, sed Deo [...] Item, quid si monachus de praecepto vadit Romam, vel est in scholis, numquid ibi potest dare eleemosynam, non habita distinctione an egeat pauper ad mortem vel non? Credo quod sic; nam eo ipso quod praelatus dedit ei licentiam standi in scholis, vel eundi Romam, intelligitur ei concessisse licentiam faciendi ea quae honesti scholares et romipetae sive itinerantes solent facere [...] Item, quid de uxore, numquid potest facere eleemosynam sine mandato vel licentia viri? Videtur quod non [...] Ad hoc dico, quod si uxor habet res paraphernales, id est, proprias praeter dotem [...] potest de illis, etiam invito viro, facere eleemosynam. De rebus autem viri, ut de pane, vino et aliis quae bono et approbato more solent ad dispensationem uxorum pertinere, potest et debet facere eleemosynas, moderate tamen secundum facultates viri [...] Et debet semper sibi conformare conscientiam, quod non displiceat marito in corde, licet forte aliquando prohibuerit ore. Solent enim mariti facere tales prohibitiones uxoribus absolute, ut sic temperent eas, non a toto, sed ab excessu quem suspicantur.

2651 *il*: The expected form would be *eles*. Masculine subject pronouns are sporadically used for feminine ones in Old French (see Hasenohr §80), but this may well simply be a case of the semantics of *persone* prevailing over grammatical considerations. Cf. 2777.

2655 *especïalité*: T-L lists our example and gloss it as "besonderer Fall (special case)"; this is the dictionary's only example of this early word in this sense. It is also attested with the sense "special privilege, special favour", etc., and also as a legal term.

2687 *Qui* is for *Cui*, or perhaps *Quë*.

2668 As the entry in T-L shows, the form *prïeus* is not uncommon for *prïeur*, especially in rhyme with *religïeus*.

2689 For this use of *avoir*, cf. 2753.

2696 Cf. Tobias 4:7–12.

2700 This seems to be an example of the construction *torner* x *a* y, in the sense "interpret *x* as *y*", i.e. it would be considered a sin for someone to do this; *li* would thus be for *le + lui* (and *Qu'* would mean "for"). This line has no parallel in the Vulgate.

2701–02 "But even if it is the case about Tobias that/even assuming that Tobias did not know what he was saying…"

2706 Cf. Matthew 5:42, 'qui petit a te da ei, et volenti mutuari a te ne avertaris', or Luke 6:30, 'omni autem petenti te tribue, et qui aufert quae tua sunt ne repetas'.

2707 A difficult passage which, allowing for the one slight emendation, I take to mean: "But if anyone, in order to disprove what I say, should wish to show that someone who helps a sinner supports him in sinning (for it says in the proverb that 'assés escorche qui pié tient', and even though someone who persists in wickedness does a bad thing, someone who supports him does little less [i.e. a sinner is bad, but someone who supports a sinner is hardly better]), I would attach a condition to this fact/reasoning without delay…" The proverb is in Morawski n° 137 with a variant 'autant gaaigne qui pié tient comme qui escorche' (n° 207); the idea, *pace* T-L, seems to be that a peripheral involvement in an activity is (?morally) identical to playing the main part in it. *Tout* in this concessive sense nearly always takes the subjunctive, but examples can be found of its use with the indicative (see *AND* s.v. *tut*).

2716 *feroiie*: the manuscript is quite clear, with the *i* well formed and 'dotted' both times. Pope (§917) mentions forms of the imperfect ending without the final *-e* that first appear "in the thirteenth century, earliest in the Northern region, e.g. *P. Mor.* [*Poème Moral* ed. M. Cloetta, Erlangen, 1886], *sarroi* 98c, *voldroi* 167c, etc.", and we might read *feroi je* here.

2720 I.e. simply because he is a man.

2723 *ordurie* is unknown to the dictionaries.

2737 *souräagié*: T-L lists only two examples of this word, including ours. (The other example is from an Artesian source.)

2739 *el conte*: T-L does not list the expression with this meaning (only in the sense "precisely"), but the phrases *jeter fors de conte* ("leave out of consideration") and *metre en (son) conte* ("take into account, consider") show close parallels to the use of the expression in our text.

2741 *li encheü En povreté*: those who have fallen into poverty.

2743 The manuscript appears to have *Nest pas par leur o*. Röhrs makes the clever suggestion that the scribe's exemplar had *ne st par leur o*. with a titulus over the *st* (i.e. *sont*), which the scribe misread as *N'est*, adding the *pas* to make up the syllable count. It should perhaps be added that the first letter of the line is unlike the scribe's usual capital *N*. It resembles a large lower case *n*, and Breymann took it to be a capital *Y*; no other capital *Y* appears in the text for comparison.

2748 The manuscript has *grant merite* for *a merite* of the edition. The scribe perhaps understood *A l'aumosnier* as "the almsgiver has" (rather than "to the almsgiver") and thus interpreted a second *a* as a dittography needing correction.

2765 T-L has the expressions *metre a* and *en fuer*, but ours is the only example of *estre en fuer a*.

2777 Again, *il* is used for the expected *ele*, cf. 2651n.

2780 *seculiers*: the manuscript reads *en laniers*, but neither of the two senses of *lanier* ("falcon" or "cowardly, lazy", cf. 2266) fits here, and no simpler emendation suggests itself. For all that, even allowing for a hastily written long *s* being mistaken for an *l*, it is still not easy to understand the error. T-L has two examples of *los* used in the plural.

2783 "God does not want anyone who hopes/strives for His reward (i.e. a reward from Him) to look for it from someone else." *Tendre a* is attested with an infinitive, but T-L has no example with a noun object.

2785–86 Given the author's penchant for equivocal rhymes, we may perhaps assume that manuscript *dit ai* in line 2786 is intended as part of *dit(i)er* rather than part of *dire*, but line 2785 remains slightly cryptic. Presumably it means no more than "This is why I mention, or I have mentioned, the benefits of almsgiving that I wrote about".

2787–88 Once again, something seems to be amiss here. For our *Et che*, the manuscript reads *Estre*. The emendation produces a kind of sense ("for it fulfils its intention/plan, and this is necessary for salvation"), but it is hardly satisfactory. *Proposement* without an article is particularly suspect, and the couplet does not fit the argument that precedes and follows it. One might have expected an adverb meaning "modestly, discreetly", and it is possible that there has been some omission, conceivably due to the original having four lines rhyming in -*ment*.

2791 The reference is to Matthew 6:1–4:

> Adtendite ne iustitiam vestram faciatis coram hominibus ut videamini ab eis, alioquin mercedem non habebitis apud Patrem vestrum qui in caelis est. Cum ergo facies elemosynam, noli tuba canere ante te sicut hypocritae faciunt in synagogis et in vicis ut honorificentur ab hominibus, amen dico vobis, receperunt mercedem suam. Te autem faciente elemosynam, nesciat sinistra tua quid faciat dextera tua, ut sit elemosyna tua in abscondito et Pater tuus qui videt in abscondito reddet tibi.

The following lines from *Perceval* (ed. Hilka l. 42) offer a gloss on this familiar Biblical passage:

> La senestre, selonc l'estoire,
> Senefie la vainne gloire
> Qui vient de fausse ypocrisie;
> Et la destre que senefie?
> Charité.

2796 *s'en dechoivre*: T-L has three examples (though not ours) of the reflexive verb in the sense "sich verfehlen, irre gehen, das Verkehrte tun (go wrong, do the wrong thing)", and one of them has an object with *de* ('de rien ne vos decevrois', *St Jul* 3140).

2800 Isaiah 58:7 reads: 'frange esurienti panem tuum et egenos vagosque induc in domum tuam, cum videris nudum operi eum, et carnem tuam ne despexeris.'

2806 *fes* = "burden [of sin]".

2814 *enpreigne*: possibly the verb has one of its usual senses ("undertake, begin") though it is slightly uncomfortable here; it may be that it is used in the sense of *apprendre*, with a change of prefix.

2816 The reference is in fact to Ecclesiasticus 35:11, 'in omni dato hilarem fac vultum tuum et in exultatione sanctifica decimas tuas.' (The work is not uncommonly attributed to Solomon at this period, cf. 2838*n* and *La Lumere as Lais* 9958.) The manuscript has ·*xxxiii·ime* here, and our scribe is quite punctilious about placing a 'dot' (actually a short stroke) over the letter *i*. However, in the context it is easy to see how a slip might occur involving one minim (i.e. *xxxɩɩɩme* instead of *xxxuɩme*). *Traitié* is not attested in the sense "chapter", though the word is rather rare; for the meaning here, compare line 2863.

2819 The source of this metaphor has not been identified, but it does not appear to be Biblical.

2824–26 T-L has many examples of *le message Dieu* (also *le message Jhesu*) in the sense "poor person, beggar". The idea is expanded on at length in the *Sermo de Sapientia* (see 404*n*) vol. 1, p. 285. The basis of line 2826 is unclear.

2828 Morawski has the commoner 'Bonne parole bon lieu tient' as a variant to n° 278. T-L glosses *tenir bon lieu* as "einen guten Platz, Aufnahme, Entgegenkommen finden (meet a warm reception)".

2829–32 "This [*parole*] that is said to a beggar can better encounter a warm reception than any other expression could [encounter] that anyone might wish to say to someone else." *C'* is of course a perfectly standard spelling of *Qu'*, and *ascun* is by no means unknown for *aucun* (cf. line 1576), but it does seem possible that the scribe was confused at this point.

2838 The reference seems, in fact, to be to Ecclesiasticus 4:3, 'cor inopis ne adflixeris et non protrahas datum angustianti.' (Cf. 2816*n*.)

2847 This contrasting of substance and form belongs to the world of scholastic philosophy; the *Petit Robert* dates this sense of *sustance* at 1270.

2849–50 "Long carrying out is the correct organization of almsgiving", i.e. it is best to give alms over a long period of time. This is the only example in T-L of the aphetic form *complissement*, though Gdf. does have others.

2858 *Fraindre* is attested in the sense "break off, stop", though the intransitive use is very rare.

2859 The scribe simply omits the rhyming word (there is no erasure, no hole in the membrane); he has *as* where we have emended to *li*. Perhaps something more fundamental has gone wrong here, but the version as edited seems to make good sense.

2863 Tobias 4:8–9 reads: 'quomodo potueris ita esto misericors; si multum tibi fuerit abundanter tribue, si exiguum fuerit etiam exiguum libenter inpertire stude'; for *traitie* cf. 2816*n*.

2872 *paintëours*: a licence, of course, for *paintres*, see Introduction p. 18. (Suchier, with more zeal than common sense, suggests emending to *Boins paintre qui un ours veut faire*.)

2873 This is the only example in T-L of *ploumet* in the sense "plummet, lead pencil"; *AND* lists a further two.

2879 *apens*: T-L has only one example of the word ('Et cil qui n'avoit nul apens De jor ne d'oure ne de tens', *Perc.* 7635), glossed as "Erinnerung (recollection)", though here the meaning must be "reflexion, thought".

2885 The manuscript has *en* for our *de*, which surely must be wrong.

2888 *I* must mean in heaven; it is possible that *est* is a slip for *ert*, but it makes sense as a general statement. The author seems to be striving rather hard for his effect here; the sense appears to be that ending will be ended, i.e. all will be permanent/there will be no more death (cf. *fenir* in line 2936). *Afinee* in line 2890, another play on words, is probably from the adjective *fin* rather than the noun, and means that joy will be refined/pure.

2891 *dur[e]ra*: there are three other examples in the text of *-rer* verbs with a contracted future, and two (*ploureront* 1035 and *rentrera* 1437) of a non-contracted form.

2904 A reference back to line 625.

2913–14 These lines are very like 2923–24, and Suchier suggests deleting them as an accidental anticipation, but the sense is weakened without them, and it is not clear that they are inauthentic. (Cf. notes to lines 2443, 2456 and 3027.)

2922 *rechité*: the manuscript has *retinte*. *Tinter* is used transitively to mean "utter", but apparently only in a fixed collocation with the object *mot*, and usually in the negative. *Rechité* is Suchier's suggestion.

2927 Cf. *Sentences* II.xi.1: 'Hieronymus tradit unamquamque animam ab exordio nativitatis habere Angelum ad sui custodiam deputatum.'

2930 *le*: a Picardism for *la*, referring to *ame* of line 2928 (as does *l'* in 2927).

2946 Possible allusions are to I Thessalonians 5:17 ('sine intermissione orate'), I Timothy 2:8 ('volo ergo viros orare in omni loco levantes puras manus sine ira et disceptatione'), or Ephesians 6:18 ('per omnem orationem et obsecrationem orantes omni tempore in Spiritu et in ipso vigilantes in omni instantia et obsecratione pro omnibus sanctis'). Sinclair (see Bibliography) argues that this prayer is an adaptation of a specific sequence of "prone prayers", but the parallels are not close, and it seems far from impossible that Jehan could have compiled his prayer without reference to a specific model.

2947 *Son* is more likely to mean St Paul's than Jehan's.

2957 *Aposto[i]le*: the *i* has been restored for the sake of the rhyme, even though the form *Apostole* is well attested. Pope Honorius IV died in 1287, and Nicholas IV succeeded him on 22 February 1288 (see Steven Runciman, *A History of the Crusades* (Cambridge: C.U.P., 1951–54, repr. Harmondsworth: Penguin, 1978) 3, 400). However, the prayer here is likely to be generic rather than personal.

2959 The scribe has written four minims in the middle of *maronier*; one could equally read *maronn[i]er* or *maroun[i]er*.

2962 *subjeus*: On p. 328, Röhrs claims that the development of Latin *c* + consonant to *u* is dialect feature, but Gossen does not mention it, and it is unlikely to operate on a learned borrowing like this. The form may be influenced by the verb *gesir*, and cf. *sougieuz* listed in T-L under *sogire*.

2964 We must assume that *tout* is intended as an adverb. Naturally, this phrase is still dependent on *prïons* of line 2953.

2971–72 The manuscript has *Chil* for our *Ne*. Perhaps the author meant that the poor man will find the door open, and be expected to leave by it; the dictionaries do not support this interpretation, however — rather the reverse. Perhaps the scribe's eye slipped back to *Chil* in 2970. An alternative emendation might be *Chil ne trouvera porte ouverte*.

2974 According to T-L, *usage* is occasionally feminine, though apart from our example only one other is listed, and that not particularly convincing. The word appears marked for gender only once more in the text (32) where it is masculine. One might here emend to the rare *usance*.

2976 I am at a loss to explain this line. At this period, Romans seem to have had a reputation for being mean, e.g. G. de Coinci *Ste Leocade* 917 'Trop covoitex sunt li Roumain' (cf. Rutebuef, ed. Faral, I 365, 716, I 467, 112), and Tobler (*Vermischte Beiträge* II, 225) recounts a widespread joking etymology that derives *romain* from *rore* (< RODERE) and *main*. The charge was particularly levelled at the papal court. However, this is not sufficient to explain the reference here.

2980 "So it is two thousand years since [covetousness] came to stay in the town"; intransitive *herberger* is not uncommon in the sense "find shelter, stay", etc., cf. line 843. According to tradition Rome was founded in 753 BC, and the present work was written in 1288, a gap of 2041 years.

2992 The verb *maistrier* is attested, and we must assume that this is what the scribe had in mind, *la* referring to Rome. It is, however, possible that the author intended the less surprising *i a mestrie*, with *mestrie* as a noun.

2995 The scribe writes *quela* (or perhaps *que la*) *arendre*, thus giving rise to the only appearance of the form *el* (well attested, but more characteristic of western than eastern dialects) in the text.

3005 The manuscript has *capiteles* here; at 241 *capitle* rhymes with *title*. One sense of the word given in T-L is "Punkt (point)"; we may understand: "after the aforementioned points".

3027–34 The passage is repeated as lines 3143–3150. It is impossible to say whether this is deliberate, but if it is a slip, as seems highly likely, the lines would better be suppressed here than on their second appearance. T-L notes another example of *oïr clamor* (as well as a standard collocation *plainte et clamor*), where *clamor* seems to have the sense "complaint, lament". Cf. notes to lines 2443, 2913 and 2456.

3035 Rudolph I of Habsburg, the most powerful landowner in Germany, was elected king in 1273 and recognized by the pope in 1274 after having promised to mount a crusade (a promise that he was not to fulfil). He was never crowned Holy Roman Emperor. (See *Lexikon des Mittelalters* (Munich: Artemis, 1977–) 7, 1072.)

3051 Philip IV ('the Fair') came to the throne on the death of his father Philip III ('the Bold') in 1285. Breymann sees this prayer, which praises only Philip's physical beauty, with no mention of any moral or intellectual qualities and with the suggestion that the king lacks both sense and goodness, as thinly veiled criticism. Moreover, *roiauté* of 3056 is rather ambiguous, since it might mean either "kingdom" or "kingliness, royal dignity".

3057 *biaté*: an attested Picard form (see Gossen §58).

3061 Sancho IV ('the Brave'), King of Castile from 1284 to 1295, apart from his troubles at home, spent most of his reign in struggles to push back the Moors of the Emirate of Grenada, including his recapture of Tarifa in 1291. (See *New Cambridge Medieval History* (Cambridge: C.U.P., 1994–2000) 5, 698.)

3068 *sevree*: the manuscript has *finee*, which finds no explanation in the dictionaries; cf. T-L's 'tot certainement ne croie Que l'ame soit dels cors sevree' (*Clig.* 5457), 'Kant le cors ert de l'alme severé' (*Deux coll. Mir. anglon.* 16,152), 'les almes ke severé sunt Del cors divers habitaciuns unt' (*Lumere as Lais* 12,029).

3071 The Lord Edward had arrived in Tunis too late to join the eighth crusade, but pushed on to Acre in 1271 (an expedition sometimes known as the ninth crusade), negotiating an eleven-year truce with the Mamluk sultan Baibars. He set off for England in 1272, the year in which he became king on his father's death, arriving home in 1274. He took the cross again in June 1287, but his plans for an alliance between a unified Europe and the Mongols came to nothing, and he was not to return to the Holy Land. (See Henry C. G. Matthew and Brian Harrison (eds.), *Oxford Dictionary of National Biography* (Oxford: O.U.P., 2004), 17, 809a.)

3074 *Voloir* seems odd here, and one is tempted to assume that it is a mistake for *valoir* (which appears at line 3282). If it is a mistake, however, it is one which the scribe makes again at line 3216. Perhaps we are to understand that God should send the king all he desires?

3075 *decha mer*: the work was written in Nicosia, so the expression refers to the Holy Land; hence the use of *venir*. Cf. 3121, 3141*n* and 3152.

3077 For *soi avancer* with *de*, cf. 'chascuns de bien fere s'avance', 'd'armes se vousist avancer', 'la dame de parler s'avance', all noted in T-L s.v. *avancier*. The expression is glossed as "sich hervortun (distinguish oneself)", though other senses might well be possible.

3079 The subjunctive is normally *otroit*, but the form here is remodelled for the sake of the rhyme; see Introduction p. 23.

3081 Peter III of Aragon ('the Great') had himself crowned king over the island of Sicily after the Sicilian Vespers in 1282, usurping Charles I of Anjou, and was promptly excommunicated by the (French) Pope, Martin IV, a keen supporter of Charles. His sons Alfonso III ('the Benevolent') and James II ('the Just') ruled Aragon and Sicily respectively after his death in 1285, and were in turn excommunicated (hence our lines 3086–87). Just before he died in 1291 Alfonso was reconciled with the Pope as a result of the Treaty of Tarascon, which ceded Sicily to Charles II. James (now King of Aragon and Sicily) was finally persuaded to relinquish his claim to the island four years later. (See Jonathan Riley-Smith, *The Crusades: a history*, (second edition, London: Continuum, 2005) pp. 203–4, and *La Grande Encyclopédie de l'histoire* (Paris: Bordas 1968) 4, 278c.)

3091 This prisoner must be Charles II of Anjou ('the Lame'), son of Charles I, who was taken captive in a sea battle by Peter III's admiral Roger of Lauria in 1284, during the troubles which followed the Sicilian Vespers. (See *NCMH* — note 3061 above — 5, 517.) He became King of peninsular Sicily (Naples) on his father's death in 1285, and was released, thanks in part to the intervention of Edward I, on 27 October 1288 (our text presumably being completed before this date).

3098 Röhrs rightly points out (p. 285) that *li* does not appear elsewhere in hiatus with *en*, (always being reduced to *l'en*), and that consequently the verb here should be read as *enporter*. However, this does entail difficulties with the sense, unless we are dealing with a change of prefix, the verb having the sense of *aporter* (cf. *enfichié* 1137, *encreüs* 1850, *enpreigne* 2814, and perhaps *enportera* 2929).

3099 Robert II ('the Noble'), Count of Artois, took part in the eighth crusade and joined the campaign on behalf of Charles I of Anjou after the Sicilian Vespers. On Charles's death in 1285 he became governor of Sicily during Charles II's captivity, thus the enemies of lines 3106–08 must be the Aragonese. (See *Lexikon des Mittelalters* 7, 890 and Runciman, *op. cit.*, 3, 292.)

3105 The manuscript reads: *i ait* instead of *l'ait*. As edited, the line must mean "that he and his friends may still have it", though it seems rather awkward. A more radical emendation would be to read *Qu'encor laient si anemi* and to suppress the semi-colon. For the scribe to misread *laient* as *i ait et* would not be too implausible an error on its own, and *encore* for *encor* would be quite unremarkable, though a misreading of *anemi* as *ami* is less likely. Three such errors coming together, however, rather strain credulity.

3115 Edmund, Earl of Lancaster, took part in the 'ninth' crusade with his brother the Lord Edward in 1271, thus earning his nickname of Crouchback (cross-back). When Edward took the cross in 1287, Edmund almost certainly did the same. (See *ODNB* 17, 755b.)

3119–20 I.e. has prepared and is still preparing/keeps preparing.

3130 I.e. "his worth increases as his wealth decreases" (because the latter is the result of his generosity). (Both *empirier* and *amender* can be either transitive or intransitive, so one might equally understand "he is eating into his wealth, but increasing his worth".)

3139 *se*: perhaps for *si*.

3141 *dela mer*: from the point of view of someone writing from Cyprus, the expression refers to Europe. The prayer for the lords currently in the Holy Land follows at 3151.

3143–50 See 3027n. The emendation of *ne aie* to *n'en oie* in line 3150 is suggested by line 3034, and is made more likely by the fact that *ne* < NON does not appear in hiatus in this text, and that *aie* as pres.sbv.3 of *avoir* appears only twice more (1250, 1852) compared to twenty-eight appearances of *ait*.

3153–55 *Patriarche*: T-L glosses this only as "der Papst in Rom (the Pope)", but since *decha mer* here refers to the Holy Land we must be dealing with the Latin Patriarch of Jerusalem (though after the loss of Jerusalem in 1187 the seat of the patriarchate had moved to Acre). For the first part of 1288, a certain Elijah was patriarch, being succeeded by Nicholas of Hanapes, who remained in the post from the latter part of 1288 until he died escaping from Acre in 1291. (See Runciman, *op. cit.*, 3, 419.) The expression *gouvreneres de l'arche de sainte Eglise* does not appear to be a specific title. Churches, monasteries, municipalities all had their *arche*, or strongbox, to keep money, documents and so forth safe, and doubtless the keeper of the *arche* was synonymous with the head of the institution.

3157–58 The first *sens* must mean "(in such a) way/manner" and the second "(through his) wisdom/good sense/prudent behaviour".

3158–60 *clergiés*: the article and the syllable count strongly suggest that we are to read *clergié* as a masculine noun, a suggestion supported by the use of *du* in 3160. The form *clergie* in 3160 would thus be another example of the Picard reduction of *ié* to *ie* (see Introduction p. 9).

3163 Henry II of Lusignan became King of Cyprus and titular King of Jerusalem on the death of his brother John II in 1285. Most of the former possessions of his kingdom had consequently been lost well before his accession, but it was during Henry's reign that the few remaining crusader strongholds fell in rapid succession to the Muslims. (See *NCMH* 5, 606.)

3164 *maint*: This could be the normal pres.sbv.3 of *mener*, though the sense seems very strained. Given that the graphies *ai* and *a* were thus to some extent interchangeable in Picard (see Introduction p. 8), *maint* here is probably a hypersophistication representing *mant*, pres.sbv.3 of *mander*. Cf. 3196 and especially 3283.

3175 The subject of *ont* is, of course, *Sarrasin* of 3168.

3175–82 The year 1291 saw the loss of all the strongholds listed here. The fall of *Acre* on May 28 effectively marked the end of the crusaders' hopes in Palestine. *Saiete* (Sidon), finally fell on July 14. *Castiau Pelerin*, in Athlit, between Haifa and Caesarea, was never captured, and was lost only when the crusaders abandoned it on August 14. *Sur* (Tyre) had already been abandoned, without resistance, on May 19 (cf. 3265n), and *Barur* (Beirut) was surrendered on July 31. *Cayfas* (Haifa) had, of course, been lost as long ago as 1265, twenty-three years before our text was composed. (These dates are mostly extracted from R. L. Wolff and H. W. Hazard (edd.), *The Later Crusades, 1189–1311*, (1969), vol. 2, cap. 16.)

3181 Of the senses of *frankise* listed in T-L, perhaps the one that fits best here is "edles Verhalten oder Tun", i.e. the walls are only standing as a result of noble actions/deeds of prowess.

3196 See 3164n.

3213 *sourparllers nuist* is proverbial, and also appears in the forms 'trop parler nuist', and 'sorparlers nuist, sorgraters cuist' (see Morawski nos 2275, 2276, 2426, 2428).

3216 *voloir*: see 3074*n*.

3221 The King of Armenia in 1288 was Leo III, who died in 1289. In *The Cambridge Medieval History* vol. IV part I (Cambridge: C.U.P., 1966), we read: 'Between 1274 and 1305 this Christian bastion in the Near East was continually invaded, pillaged and laid waste by the Mamluks of Egypt and Syria and by the Seljuqs from the north.' The Turkomans and the fanatical Syrian sect of the Assassins certainly fought in the huge armies of the Egyptian Muslims. However, the reference to the Tartars here is an error. Leo's father had been at pains to establish good relations with the Mongols, and in 1281, for example, the Armenians fought alongside them in the battle of Hons. It is true that the Mongols seem to have provided relatively little support to Armenia after this period, but there was never hostility with them in Leo's time. It is not clear whether the error is factual or merely due to a misreading; however line 3234 shows that our author is not claiming any first-hand knowledge of the Armenian situation.

3226 *Turquemans*, curiously, does not seem to have been picked up by T-L. The *Trésor de la langue française* notes one earlier example than ours (spelt *turckeman*) in *Robert le Diable* (ed. E. Löseth, Paris: SATF, 1903), dating from the end of the twelfth century, though it, too, does not cite the *Disme*.

3235 Although Antioch had fallen to the Sultan Baibars in 1268, the titular princes of Antioch continued to be counts of Tripoli. When Count Bohemond VII died without an heir in October 1287, the title should have passed to his sister Lucy, but, Lucy was absent in Apulia, and their mother, the princess Sybil, at the request of the nobles, took over the regency, but attempted to appoint the unpopular Bartholomew, Bishop of Tortosa, as her bailiff. When this was discovered, the nobles and citizens of Tripoli formed a commune which deposed Sybil and declared itself sovereign. Lucy arrived early in 1288, expecting to assume the position of Princess and Countess. However, the commune would not accept this at first, and sought instead the protection of the Genoese. (This seems to be broadly the position described in our text, though I have found no other reference to the commune's threat to besiege the princess.) Only when the Genoese insisted on installing their own *podestà* to take over the government of the county, did the commune recant and acknowledge Lucy's claim, whereupon a deal was brokered between all three parties, before the end of 1288. The Prince of Antioch referred to here must be Lucy's husband, Narjot of Toucy, Admiral of Sicily and Captain-General of Morea. After all these efforts, Tripoli was to fall to the Mamluks on April 26 1289. (See Runciman, *op. cit.*, 3, 403–04.)

3236 *espi[n]ce*: The verb has various senses (T-L's entry is rather jumbled, and may represent more than one lemma), many of them shared with the simplex *pincier*. Here we seem to be dealing with a sense "steal, take away from", with the construction *espincier a* x *de* y. If this is correct then *qui* is for *cui*, unless we should read *quë*.

3248 *le*: a Picardism for *la*.

3250 The manuscript has *qui* for our *qu'on*. The emendation is based on the assumption that the scribe has misread an abbreviation for *con* (= *c'on*/*qu'on*) in his exemplar as an abbreviation for *qui*. The sense would be *qu'on le lor conseille*, remembering that *le* is omitted before *li* and *lor*.

3253 "for at the very least they should leave off this course of action because of the blame/damage to their reputation for good faith/loyalty, on account of which people are speaking ill of them".

3265 In *The Kingdom of Cyprus and the Crusades, 1191–1374* (C.U.P., 1991), Peter W. Edbury writes (p. 98):

> John of Montfort lord of Tyre had died childless in 1283. By the terms of Hugh III's enfeoffment, the lordship should have escheated to the crown, but Hugh was unable to find the 150,000 Saracen bezants due to John's heir by way of compensation for the expenses incurred by the Montfort family in fortifying their lordship. The king therefore came to an agreement with John's next of kin, Humphrey […], whereby Humphrey should hold Tyre until Hugh paid the compensation; if Hugh had not paid by the end of May 1284, Humphrey was to have the lordship on a permanent footing. In the event both Hugh and Humphrey died before the term expired. Humphrey's heirs, however, acquired no rights in Tyre, and so presumably they were indemnified. In 1285 John of Montfort's widow, Margaret of Lusignan, the sister of Hugh III, concluded a truce with the Mamluks to cover the lordship, and so at that point she must have been regarded as possessing legitimate authority there. But at some stage in the late 1280s Henry II conferred Tyre on his brother Amaury who remained seised until its fall in 1291.

He adds in a footnote: 'Amaury is named as lord of Tyre in a description of the events of 1289 [i.e. the fall of Tripoli] [...] and in papal letters of 1290 [...]'. Since our author says that the lord of Tyre has just started some endeavour in 1288, it might well be to Amaury's taking over the lordship that he refers. If this identification is correct, then the father mentioned in line 3273 would be Hugh III of Cyprus, I of Jerusalem, who died in 1284.

3269 The first word of this line in the manuscript is quite clearly *En*. The most natural emendation would be to *Eu*, except that the form does not appear in this text, indeed *el* appears only once (2739), the normal form being *u*. The passage seems to mean "[pray] that in whatever he has started God in his mercy may send him perseverance/the ability to persevere always in the best/at his best/as well as possible" (*perseverer* typically collocates with *en*). For the rather uncommon use of *mieus*, cf. *La Lumere as lais* 7233ff.: 'Parfit put estre en treis maniere: Lesser le mal est la premiere, E l'autre est en bien profiter; Le tierz est en le meuz ester.' T-L cites our example but glosses it as "immer mehr (more and more)", a sense suspiciously not shared by any of the other examples.

3276 T-L has many examples of the expression *soi sentir de* (including ours), "feel the effect of, be influenced by". It recurs at 3279.

3278 This proverb is not listed in Morawski, though his n° 520 reads: 'De mauvés arbre mauvés fruit.'

After line 3296 in the same hand: *Hic liber est scriptus; qui crixit [sic] sit benedictus.*

REJECTED READINGS

22 renge] rende; 28 li] le; 107 sensauche; 112 onquens namenrrie; 113 ne] le *subpunctuated and partially erased*; amenrrier; 114 Fu pour pour c., alumier; 185 beu *inserted in another hand*; 202 suagir] *orig.* sauoir, o *made into* g; 213 Qui; 214 li fus; 253 Av; 314 se] sen; 340 as] ad; 345 liauge *with second minim of* u *erased, cf. l. 363*; 348 ne erent; 361 assom q.; 363 liauge *with second minim of u erased, cf. l. 345*; 391 Encore; 404 proceuns; 405 deueroit; 420 serront *with first r subp.*; 430 sesforte; 439 top *with abbreviation mark, strictly* terop *or* treop *cf.* 1245; 443 leetre, *cf. 1565, 1837*; 444 Quil; 446 ferme; 450 quar f.; 455 que *of* quemant *rubbed*; 485 sient; 486 coulun *or* cousun *altered to* coulon; 495 Et;

500 ueons toute jour prestes; 547 looee; 548 son courage; 589 as] es; 633 tous; 645 *orig.* De lui encontre nous desfendre, *corrected by scribe (and* De nous encontre *written again in left hand margin by another hand)*; 647 tost] tout; 680 penssant; 705 quil; 731 MS *has* maine *altered to* maint *or perhaps* maint *altered to* maine; 749 *see note*; 805 **P**uis; 830 Que] Con; 908 p.] repentanche; 911 gaires; 949 p.] pie *crossed through and* pitie *added in different hand*; 970 pproprement; 986 apesse *with abbreviation mark, strictly* aperesse *or* apreesse;

1008 v] plouvoir; 1022 ?mereuelle; 1035 pourriront; 1037 la] lor; 1039 Quant ilasentent ou ileuoient; 1041 Pour; 1092 P. s. atourner a n. b., *corrected by scribe*; 1101 P. cheest d. *with first* e *of* cheest *ins.*; 1108 rempdencion; 1120 fornoie; 1126 faites; 1141 prioons; 1143 n. d.] nous de ches; 1156 a. t. pris auons, *corrected by scribe*; 1159 faites; 1160 nara ia pite de nous, *not corrected by scribe*; 1165 qui or g. v., *not corrected by scribe*; 1166 arriere; 1179 il e. ·ii· coses faire; 1181 force; 1182 aporce; 1210 l'a.] la boine; 1240 presinst; 1245 top *with abbreviation mark, strictly* terop *or* treop, *cf.* 439; 1269 *apparently* eschll *with top of first* l *erased* =? eschil; 1276 ichi; 1289 maint; 1301 lors vies; 1314 entre *with final* r *ins. in another hand*; 1337 puis *one supernumerary minim*; 1339 deerrain; 1427 ki] si, *see note*; 1443 deerraine; 1453 enondevant; 1455 a ensoume; 1493 Si ai] Que iai;

1511 i] qui; 1525 d. et retraire, *see note*; 1544 p.] pais; 1546 Sont; 1550 a. puis g.; 1555 En o.; 1563 La tierche rest;

1565 leetre, *cf. 443, 1837*;   1638 Et;   1659 noncie;   1660 grant; 1671 deesraines;   1672 gies *with abbreviation mark, strictly griies or geries*;   1680 matere;   1697 Quantres *(or* Quautres);   1705 mesfait;   1725 as] ad;   1780 peccies et de;   1837 leetre, *cf. 443, 1565*; 1850 encreus;   1863 a.] asamble;   1912 Donc;   1920 Dieu;   1921 a] as;   1927 **Si** *with* **S** *crossed out, perhaps by another hand — orig. guide-letter clearly visible*;   1934–35 *see note;*   1939 **D**es coses ·vii·, *word order corrected by scribe*;   1970 Que] Com;   1983 se] le;   1986 ki la male porte;

2018 prent;   2019 qu'il le] qui li;   2023 en Dieu plus amarme; 2073 ecoutre;   2075 on lamende;   2097 enquerre;   2135 moustre; 2156 esquiee;   2164 perpeutuaument;   2198 en] len;   2238 avers] autres;   2244 venuee;   2299 haiene;   2312 que sa p.;   2321 uoie ou on lencontre;   2328 li] lor;   2333 ruee;   2360 souffroit;   2365 v.] nos;   2369 s'e.]   se i oinst;   2395 tournons;   2411 Reuenries; 2434 Que   2436 *letter (probably p) erased between* Mais *and* ains; 2440 pourete;   2443 *see note;*   2454 le;   2459 finent;

2501 Qua amosne;   2507 amosme;   2509 seront;   2522 tenre; 2578 r.] prendre;   2579 gaignie;   2592–93 *see note;*   2604 guilles; 2623 *final* -s *of* juastes *added in another hand*;   2624 uos conpagnons   2636 s *inserted in another hand*;   2652 autre; 2657 faiere *with first* e *subp.*;   2710 *final* t *of* soustient *inserted, prob. in another hand*;   2710 Sil;   2718 ·iii·;   2723 lor o.;   2743 *see note*;   2748 a] grant;   2780 s.] en laniers;   2788 Et che] Estre; 2795 requerre;   2806 son fes] confes, c *changed to* s *by another hand and* son fes *written again in this hand in margin*; 2815 ·xxxiii·ime;   2847 moustrers;   2856 si qui;   2858 s.] seul; 2859 li] as;   2885 de] en;   2897 quil;   2910 p.] *one supernumerary minim,* ?peinitanche;   2922 retinte;   2928 boine euree;   2959 m.] *one supernumerary minim,* ?marouner;   2970 Ne] Chil;   2989 que] con;

3005 capiteles;   3044 puisse;   3068 s.] finee;   3088 deboinaine; 3150 ne aie;   3166 C. et crestiens;   3209 si] qui;   3250 qu'on] qui; 3269 En;   3286 puissent

GLOSSARY

This glossary is selective. It omits words that are common in Old French, unless the form in the text is likely to cause confusion. It also omits words that have survived into Modern French with their meaning largely unchanged, except where the text furnishes an early or otherwise interesting example. Common variant spellings are often ignored, particularly those involving *c/ch, o/ou, ie/e, m/n* or doubled consonants. The abbreviation *etc.* is used in the few cases where line references are not exhaustive. Apart from a few anomalous forms, nouns and adjectives are listed under the (masculine) oblique singular. Verbs are listed under the infinitive; where the lemma does not appear in the text, it is followed by a semicolon, and its form is inferred by analogy. Participles are also listed under the infinitive, unless they appear only in adjectival function. An asterisk before a word or line number indicates that the entry is the result of emendation, and the abbreviation *n* after a line reference draws attention to the Notes.

äatie, *s.* challenge, provocation 3246
abandouner; *v.r.* give oneself over 1127, 1136, 1707, 1747, 2375, 2451, 2855
abhominacion, *s.* **faire a.** disgust 1208, 1374
abonder; **abunder**; *v.i.* abound, be found (in abundance) 79, 1510, 1717, 2467
achesmer, *v.r.* deck oneself out 1355
aclin, *adj.* subservient, obedient 1476
acliner; *v.i.* give in, submit 66, 2298
acoisier, *v.r.* to become calm 360
acorderresse, *s.* reconciliatrix 1224
acoster; *v.t.* come into contact with, hit 133
acusement, *s.* indictment, reproach 1348
acuser; *v.t.* divulge, confess 1654
adés, *adv.* straightaway 1326, 2254
ade[se]r; *v.i.* approach, touch 508
adrecher; *v.r.* go, turn 518, 1408
aërdre; *v.r.* hold to, stick to 1646
aësmer; *v.i.* judge, think 1557
afaire, *s.* affair, matter 1790; **de ... a.** of a ... nature 863, 2002, 2170, 2194; **avoir a. a** be dealing with 775
afermeement, *adv.* firmly, strongly 2918

affichié, afikié, *p.p. as adj.* firm, determined 1436, 2175 (*see also* **enfichié**)

afiert, *pres.ind.3 of* **aferir**; *v.i. & impers.*, be appropriate, befit 474, 1199, 1487, 3170, 2566

aflire, *v.t.* afflict, distress 2840

afoler; *v.t.* harm, injure 2061, 2241

agaiter; *v.t.* watch, lie in wait for 640

agreer; *v.i.* please 1081, 2621

aguiser; *v.t.* prick, goad 1033

ahaitier; *v.t.* please 2611

aidanche, *s.* help 165, 857; **estre en a. a** help 28; **faire a. a** help 873, 1358

aigrier; *v.t.* spur on, stimulate 2345

aigrure, *s.* bitterness 1191

aiue, *s.* help 656; *s.pl.* auxiliaries 635

ajourner; *v.t.* put off, defer 1321, 1325

aleganche, *s.* alleviation, remission, pardon 1895

alegier; *v.t.* lighten 2806

alieve, *pres.ind.3 of* **alever**; nurture, cultivate 1814

alonge, *s.* delay, **sans a.** without further ado 153, 1916, 1957; addition 1791, 2116

alumer, *v.t.* light 114, 828; *v.i.* give off light, be bright 1028

amaritude, *s.* bitterness, sorrow 995*n*

amende, *s.* reparation 1067, 2015, 2030, 2069

amendement, *s.* reparation 1956

amendise, *s.* reparation, penance 1996, 2009

amenrir; *v.t.* do down, take money from 2594, **a. de** rob of, take 3168; *v.i.* diminish 2461

amenuisier, *v.t.* lessen, reduce 57, 103, 1772, 2457 *inf. as s.* reduction, impoverishment 1590

*****amermer**, *v.i.* diminish, grow less *112, *113, 2023

amesurer, *v.r.* behave with moderation 2446, 2881

amordre, *v.t.* lure, draw 1200, 1280

amorter, *v.r.* die, die off 458; amortize oneself (fig.), put oneself in the hands of, become the vassal of 616

amounester; *v.t.* exhort, demand 1313

anoier, *v.impers.* **a. a** sadden, grieve 58, 283, 1022, 1126

äombrer; *v.t.* darken, cloud 3210

äouvrir; *v.i.* open, gape 396

aparaument, apairaument, *adv.* plainly, clearly 369, ?openly 1746*n*

aparellier; *v.t.* prepare 306, 3120; *v.r.* resemble, compare 822

aparoir, *inf. as s.* appearance, seeming 2311
apartenanche, *s.* appurtenance, estate, land, premises 2988
apens, *s.* reflexion, thought 2879*n*
apenseement, *adv.* thoughtfully, advisedly 2878
apensement, *s.* intelligence, thought 906, 2731
apenser; *v.r.* consider, decide 870, 3085
apert, *adj.* clear, visible 308, 1562, 2323
apertement, *adv.* clearly 437
apoursivir, *v.t.* ?seek after, strive for 2028*n*
appoiaus, *s.nom.* support, 3124
apresse, *s.* **par grant a.** ?at speed 530*n*
apresser; *v.t.* harass, be at one's heels 766, 1418, 3184; weigh down, oppress *986; crush, torture 1274*n*
aqueste, *s.* acquisition, obtaining 2582
aquisist *impf.sbv.3 of* **aquerre**, 1596, **aquiere**, 2521 *v.t.* acquire, 1596, 2304, 2521
arche, *s.* (Noah's) ark 489; ark, chest, strongbox 3154*n*
arestison, *s.*: **sans a.** without delay 2643, 3093
argüer; *v.t.* harass 2394
argument, *s.* argument, proof 1232
arramir; *v.r.* swear to fight, fight 3106, 3107
arresner; *v.t.* try to persuade 763
arriereban, *s.* horde, host 745
article, *s.* point, item 1883
asambler, *v.r.* join together 309, 1751; *v.t.* attack 758
ascentir; *v.t.* assent, agree 2091
asesront *fut.6*; **asesist** *impf.sbv.3 of* **assäoir**, *v.r.* sit 419, 487, 549
aspret, *adj.* rough, 136*n*
assaure, 1425, 1964; *p.p.* **assaus** 1995; *v.t.* absolve
assëurer; *v.t.* bring certainty 816; guarantee, safeguard 1306
assolicion, *s.* absolution 1998*n*
assoumer; *v.t.* add up 2004
atalenter; *v.t.* please 1663, 2862
atapir, *v.r.* hide 1255, 1260
ataquer; *v.r.* hold to 2620
atardanche, atarjance, *s.* delay 1243, 2118
atargier, *v.i.* delay 1381 (*see also* **targier**)
atendanche, *s.* delay 589; hope, trust 1066
atendue, *s.* delay 2063, 3132
atenir, *v.i.* belong, be related 1935
atiser; *v.t.* drive, inspire 926, 1423, 1592
atouker, *v.t.* reach 1522, 2094

atour, *s.* ?fuss, ?delay 808*n*
atourner, *v.t. & r.* prepare 664, 1092, 1863
atout, *prep.* with 1828
aüner, *v.t.* unite 2151
avancement, *s.* advantage 902
aversier, *s.* adversary 836
aviser, *v.t.* advise 1841, 2947; *v.r.* consider, reflect 818, 2639
avoier; *v.t.* lead, guide, 190, 2984
avoutire, *s.* adultery 1665

baillie, *s.* power, control 1302, 3007; possession: **avoir en b.** possess 1564, 2867
ballier, *v.t.* give 2583, 2692
barat, *s.* deceit, trickery 651, 1502
barater; *v.t.* deceive, trick 652
bastir; *v.t.* create 924
batalle, *s.* battle, fighting, attack 709, 740, 838, 847, 2392; battalion, company 711, 729, 730, 733, 2052
batoir, *s.* beetle, dolly or paddle for beating laundry 1865, 1871
berele, *s.* ?game, ?attack 1603*n*
besoigner; *v.i.* do, conduct oneself 2351; **b. a** have dealings with, 3096; *v.impers.* be necessary 2117, 2416
beubanche, *s.* pride, arrogance 756, 2179, 2359, 3107
beubant, *pr.p. as s.* arrogant person 746
bille, *s.* wooden ball or disk 2603*n*
boufoi, *s.* arrogance, vanity 1542
boute en couroie, *s.* a trickster's game 2600*n*
brehaigne, *adj.* barren 379
büee, *s.* laundry 1176
büer; *v.t.* launder 1185
bueverie, *s.* drinking bout 1768

cane, *s.* can, bucket 184
capitle, capitre, *s.* chapter 241, 2864; point 3005*n*
cardonal, *s.* cardinal 2963
celestïen, *adj.* heavenly 3166
cete, *s.* whale 478
challe, *pres.sbv.3 of* **chaloir**; *v.impers.* concern 1535 (*see also* **quaut**)
charoigne, *s.* flesh, body 1984
cheïr 67; **caïr** 1138; *pres.ind.3* **kiet** 866; *pret.3* **kaï** 176, **kaÿ** 1093, **keï** 2437; *p.p.* **keü** 860; *v.i.* fall (lit. & fig.) 1090, 1948

chescer 1381, **chesser**; *v.i.* cease 765, 1285; rest 1381

chief, kief, *s.* head 1475, 1480, 2366; **au premier ch.** in the first place 759, 1553; **venir a ch. de** get the better of 1544, 2215

chier, *adj.* dear 2587, 2758; **avoir ch.** like, appreciate 2246, 2756, 2944

chiere, *s.* face, countenance 2699, **faire bele ch.** welcome 2247; **metre sa ch.** ? 2601*n*

chifler; *v.t.* mock 380

cibole, *s.* onion 1038

clamour, *s.* lament, complaint 3034, 3150 (*see also* 3027*n*)

clergie, *s.* learning 886, 2617, 2968

clergié, clergie, *s.* clergy 3158, 3160

coi, *adj.* calm: **soi tenir c.** keep still 541

col, *s.* neck: **c. estendu,** headlong, rashly 700

comenchalle, *s.* beginning, first steps 3280

comparer; *v.t.* compare 1175

comparison, conparison, *s.* comparison 416, 825, 1187, 2516

complexion, *s.* disposition 853

complir; *v.t.* carry out 1365, 2787, 2905

complissement, *s.* accomplishing, carrying out 2850

condiction, *s.* condition 2716, **sous c.** conditional 2115; ?situation 1148*n*

conduire; *v.r.* behave 3015

confermer; *v.t.* confirm, state 111, 358, 1345, 2022

confés, *adj.* confessed 2805

confessant, *pr.p. as s.* person making confession 1936

confesse, *s.* confession 1246, 1250, 1273, 1362, etc.

confessor, *s.* priest hearing confession 1395, 1781

confondre; *v.t.* overthrow, destroy 648, 729, 2035

confusion, *s.* shame, embarrassment 1892

co(n)nissanche, counissanche, conuissanc(h)e, *s.* sense, understanding, wisdom 27, 200, 1722, 2003, 452, 562, 593, 677, 2397, 2920, 3295

conmandise, *s.* command 2039

conmune, *s.* alliance, league: **faire c. contre** gang up against 3244

conquerant, *pr.p. as s.* obtainer 2577*n*

conquerre 635; *pres.ind.1* **conquier** 2603, *3* **conquert** 1603; *p.p.* **comquis** 3175, **conquis** 2596; *v.t.* overcome 635; conquer, take 3175; get hold of, acquire 1603; win 2581, 2596

conquest, *s.* winnings 2609

conqueste, *s.* acquisition 2581

conte, *s.* sum 3290; account: **faire c. de** show consideration for, value 1301, 1625, 1644; **estre el c.** come in for consideration 2739
contemdre, *v.t.* resist 1972
contraire, *s.* contrary, opposite 2485; disadvantage, harm 2638; enemy, adversary 669, 787
contralier; *v.i.* resist 1725
contrit (*nom.* **contris** 1427, **contrius** 1375, 1380), *s.* contrite person 1425
coraille, *s.* heart, entrails 2258
***coree**, *s.* heart, mind 548*n*
coreument, *adv.* cordially, from the heart 2822
coroie, *s.* strap, leash 542, 2600 (*see also* **boute**)
cotele, *s.* short coat 2596
coulon, *s.* dove 486
coupaule, *adj.* guilty 1495
***courner**; *v.t.* sound (horn): **c. la recreüe** sound the retreat, admit defeat 2395
court, *adj.* short 161, 2604; **tenir c.** harass 762
couvenable, couvenaule, *adj.* suitable, fitting 573, 1155, 1168
couvenenche, *s.* promise, agreement 1628
couvine, *s.* affairs, business 767
couvreture, *s.* pretence, imitation 2313
couvrir, *v.t.* cover 829; conceal 1790; *v.r.* protect oneself 699; keep a secret, fail to tell all 1793
crauller; *v.i.* shake, quake 398
crïer = **créer** 969
criminal, *adj.* deadly, capital (sin) 1547
croissanc(h)e, *s.* growth 451, 453, 463, 465; ?outgrowths, branches *or* ?ramifications, circumstances 1827
croistre, *v.i.* grow (older) 1711; increase, get worse 614; *v.t.* increase 56, 875, 2723
cuitanche, *s.* acquittal, forgiveness 1100
cuivre, *s.* attack 744
cultiverresse, *s.* female cultivator, nurturer 1223
cunkier; *v.t.* deceive, trick 2296
curé, *s.* parish priest 1386, 1857

dant, *s.* (honorific title), Mr, my Lord 539
decha, *prep.* this side of 3075*n*, 3121, 3152
dechevable, *adj.* false, deceitful 630, 1908
dechevant, *adj.* deceitful 2762

decré, *s.* canon law 1384
defenir; *v.i.* die 971
definanche, *s.* end: **sans d.** perpetually 737, 1453
dehait, *s.* illness 1292
dehaitié, *adj.* sick 2738
dela, *prep.* that side of 3141*n*
delaianche, *s.* delay 3051
delaie, *s.* delay 1851
delaiement, *s.* delay 1461
delaier, *v.t.* delay, postpone 528, 1249, 1394, 1473
demaint, *pres.sbv.3 of* **demener**; *v.r.* behave 3156
demoustraction, *s.* demonstration 1049
departir; *v.t.* divide 2043, 2219, 3245; separate, cut off 1922; *v.r.* be divided 1635
deputaire, *adj.* base, contemptible 2325
derechief, *adv.* also, furthermore 2367
desconfire, *v.t.* overcome, defeat 400, 718, 723, 741, 836, 839, 2052
descuser; *v.t.* exonerate, pardon 1796
deserte, *s.* deserts, something deserved 69, 1561
deseure, *prep.*: **de d.** over and above 2015
desfen(s)cion, *s.* defence, resistance 854; prohibition 2801
desirier, *inf. as s.* desire 3050
despens, *s.* expenditure 3188
despiter; *v.t.* despise, disdain 2794
despoire, *s.* despair 1086
desraignier, *adj.* last 760
desrainable, *adj.* wrong, wicked 2232, 2393
desraison, *s.* wrong behaviour, wickedness 374
destraindre; *pret.5* **destrainsistes** 2625; *v.t.* force 2231
destreche, *s.* coercion, force 1898
destroit, *adj.* afflicted 2509
desvoier, *v.i.* go astray 2925; *v.r.* do wrong 3252
determiner, *v.i.* give a definitive scholarly answer to a question 894
detrenchier; *v.t.* rend (*scindere* of Joel 2:13) 1198
deut, *pres.ind.3 of* **doloir**; *v.r.* grieve 1073
devise, *s.* distinction, division 2569, 2640; arrangement, plan 1350; (?) will 2548*n*; **par tel d.** on condition 1995, 2228; **a (sa) d.** = as one would like 833, 2547
deviser, *v.t.* describe 817, 1615, 2029, 2410, 2948; ?distinguish 1581, 1675

dïaublie, *s.* devilry, wickedness 1570

diffamer; *v.t.* speak ill of, disparage 2989, 3254

dilac(t)ion, dilassion, *s.* delay 2715; **faire d.** delay, prevaricate 1363, **metre d.** delay 1237

discrection, discression, *s.* discrimination, discernment 2750, 2752, 3216

disnee, *s.* dinner, meal 2378

distinction, *s.* distinction: **faire d.** subdivide, break down 2559

diter, ditier, *v.t.* write, versify, 36, 1525, 2786, 1171; *inf. as s.* writing, composition 17, 2689

ditié, *s.* composition, treatise 2949

douer; *v.t.* endow 2931

droiture, *s.* rightful fee, duty 7; right to remain 2982; **par tel d.** on condition 2663

durra *fut.3 of* **durer**, *v.i.* last 2891

efforchivement, *adv.* forcefully, strongly 499*n*

element, *s.* one of the four elements (earth, air, fire and water) 402

enbatre; *v.r.* rush into, plunge into (fig.) 270

enblerres, *s.nom.* thief 1608

enbramé, *p.p. as adj.* burning 2512*n*

encarkier; encarquier 1968, **enkerquier**; *v.t.* impose, enjoin (penance) 2207, 2212

encaucher; *v.t.* drive 1764

encherkier, *v.t.* look for, enquire about 1698

enchëu *p.p.*, **enkaÿ** *pret.3 of* **encheïr/enkaïr**; *v.i.* fall (fig.) 2741, *1850; *v.impers.* befall 1094

encombrier, *v.t.* harass 3209; *inf. as s.* harassment, distress, affliction 1762, 3227

encomencier; *v.t.* begin 3267

encontremont, *adv.* upwards 187

encraissier; *v.t.* fatten, nourish 2277, 2279; anoint 2368

*****endever**; *v.t.* rave, be mad 1453

endroit, *s.* way, manner 607, 1526

enfichié, *p.p. as adj.* firm, determined 1137 (*see also* **affichié**)

enfourmer, *v.t.* instruct 592

enporter; *v.t.* ?bring 3098*n*

enpregne *pres.sbv.3 of* **enprendre**; *v.t.* learn 2814

*****ensacher**, *v.r.* 107*n*

ensaucher; *v.t.* exalt, raise up 196

*****ensoinne**, *s.* excuse, reason for delaying 1455

entalenté, *p.p. as adj.* desirous, inspired 3024

entechier; entekier; *v.t.* defile, taint 871, 1912, 2491
enten(s)cion, *s.* intention 2326, 2519; opinion, thought 2749
enterin, *adj.* entire 2677; whole, intact 3180
entredeus, *adv.* mid-way: **en e.** ?as a compromise 551*n*
envaïr, *v.t.* assault 1079, 1499, 1759
envoiser; *v.r.* amuse oneself 2591
eoule, *s.* ?oil 2388*n*
erraument, *adv.* straightaway 1745
e(s)rrement, *s.* behaviour 1734, 3264
escakons, *s.pl.* 2595*n*
escarsseté, *s.* meanness 1583
eschar, *s.* mockery; **faire e. de** mock 934
esclarchissure, *s.* explanation 192
escoler; *v.t.* teach 2817
escondir; *v.t.* refuse 2836
escorcher; *v.t.* flay, skin 2712 (*see* 2707*n*)
*escuel, *s.* difficult situation 1269*n*
esforch, *s.* strength 857
eskekier *see* **point**
eskernir; *v.t.* scorn, humiliate 935
eskiele, *s.* body of troops 750, 753
esmanche, *s.* estimation, calculation 1802, 1806
esme, *s.* estimation, opinion 1335, 1741, 2645
espargne-malle, *s.* piggy-bank 2259*n*
espars *p.p. of* **espardre;** *v.t.* shower (fig.) 84
especï**alité,** *s.* special case, special privilege 2655*n*
espelukier, *v.t.* examine 1757; *inf. as s.* examination 1868*n*
esperanche, *s.* hope 1065, 1084, 1114, 2919; **sour e.**: in the expectation 1323*n*
esperassion, *s.* hope 1104*n*
espi[n]cier, *v.t.* steal 3236*n*
espoir, *adv.* perhaps, possibly 1448
esrachinement, *s.* eradication, purging 1222
esrranche, *s.* error, sin 2006
esscacher; *v.t.* drive away 2412
essüer; *v.t.* dry 1186
estainte, *s.* extinguishing, snuffing out 2513
estour, *s.* battle, attack 850; **atendre l'e.** stand one's ground 657*n*
estous, *adj.nom.* hard, cruel 748
estovoir, *inf. as s.*: **par e.** necessarily 2420
estre, *inf. as s.* state 1442; situation, way of life 1471
estriver, *v.i.* struggle 1369, 1972

estude, *s.* study, application: **metre son e. en** apply oneself to 996

ëur, *s.* fortune 654

eure, *s.* hour 318; moment 1307; time 2370, 2373, 2374, 2379; **nostre e. est morte** ?our time is up, our hour has come 1311; **de e. en e.** ceaselessly 837; **en l'e.** immediately 526, 720; **toutes eures** ceaselessly 766

fac(h)e, faiche, *s.* face 127, 1252, 2103; **maugré sa f.** against one's will 1992*n*

fache, faice, faiche *pres.sbv.3*, **faichent** *pres.sbv.6 of* **faire**

faconde, *s.* eloquence, ability to speak (clearly) 1640

faintise, *s.* pretence 2953

femer; *v.t.* manure 515

feste, *s.* feast, festivity 1314; (relig.) feast 1334; **faire f. ains que vegile** do things the wrong way round, put the cart before the horse 1810

fin, *s.* end 1242, 1286, 2840, 2925, etc.; **aler a f.** die 947

finanche, *s.* end; **faire f. de** end, finish 2941

foursser; *v.t.* spawn, shed 473

fraindre; *v.t.* break, destroy 2056; *v.i.* break off, end 2858

frontiere, *s.* front line (of battle) 728

fuer, *s.* value, esteem: **estre en f. a** be valued by 2765

garant, *s.* protection: **a g.** in safety, unhindered 557

garde, *s.* care, keeping 1001, 2225; **metre en g.** keep, save 2353; **prendre g.** observe, have as a model 1740

garder, *v.t.* regard, consider 2763; have charge of, watch over 2670, 2972; take care 2814; **g. de** keep from 2276, 2774; *v.r.* take care 1852; look after oneself 681; **soi g. de** keep (oneself) from, avoid 201, 800, 1016, 2012, 2341, 2776

garnir; *v.t.* endow 30, 2772, 3127

gehir; *v.t.* confess (sins) 126, 1695

gerpir; *v.t.* abandon: **g. camp** run away, flee 742

gerrier, *s.* warrior 2042

gerrier, gerroier, *v.t.* wage war on 797, 2036, 3207, 3228

gisoit *impf.3*; **gist** *pres.ind.3 of* **gesir**; *v.i.* lie: **g. a** to have sexual intercourse with 1664; **g. en maladie**, lie sick, be on one's sick bed 3294

glose, *s.* gloss 304, 2367; **en g.** as an explanation 2387

gloutounie, gloutenie, glouternie, gloutrenie, *s.* gluttony 672, 1550, 1633, 2131, 2348

gouvreneres, *s.nom.* person in charge 749, 3154

gré, *s.* will 484, 2683; **de g.** willingly 1898, 1900, 2019; **par sun g.** with one's consent 1613; grace 608, 2293; **en g.** graciously 44, 2017
grevable, *adj.* harmful, painful 2392*n*

haskie, *s.* torment 2344
hazart, *s.* 2591*n*
herbegier, *v.i.* lodge 843*n*, 2980*n*
honte, *s.* shame, 1873, 1893; shame, disgrace, scandal 1516, 3201; **a h.** for shame 2292; **aler a h.** go to perdition 1643; **avoir h.** be ashamed 2740; **faire h. a** insult, offend 1075
hyraus, *s.pl.* heralds 2580*n*

lai(s)denger; *v.t.* beat, injure 21; insult, deride 1577, 2824
lanier, *s.* craven 2266
las, *s.pl.* snares, traps 67
lau, *conj.* where 99*n*, 751, 3294
leeche, *s.* happiness 1544, 2364, 3261
legier, *adj.* easy: **de l.** easily, unresistingly 1760, 1761
legistre, *s.* lawyer 223
lescive, *s.* lye 1175, 1180, 1188, 1201, 1370
***letre**, *s.* something written, textual authority 443, 1565, 1837
leus, *adv.* straightaway 385, 720, 788, 1288, 1388, 2970
loiable, *adj.* honourable, noble 2357
loier 531; *pres.sbv.1* **lie** 537; *imperat.2* **lie** 526; *pret.3* **loia** 542; *v.t.* bind, tie up
loier, *inf. as s.* reward, recompense 226, 385, 602
loquenche, *s.* eloquence 32, 82; ?ability to speak 1292
louage, *s.* renting 2161
lumiere, *s.* light 317; ?lamp, lantern 2388*n*

maire, *s.* ?mother 576*n*
maisnie, **maignie**, **manie**, *s.* household 285, 1610*n*; followers 351, 790
malle *see* **espargne**
manechier = **menacer** 2257
***maronier**, *s.* seaman 2959*n*
maugré, *s.* displeasure, ill will 2295; **m. sien/eus** against his/their will 1399, 2223; **m. sa fache** *see* **fache**
meche *pres.sbv.3 of* **mener**, *v.t.* lead 3257
medechine, *s.* ?medicinal plant 929*n*
megnier = **mengier/mangier**

memoire, memore, memere, *s.* memory: **de m.** in one's memory, mind 1105; **tenir en m.** remember 1504; **aver en m.** remember, think of 2777, 2790, 3065
mension, *s.* mention: **faire m.** mention 3215
menuier, *adj.* ungenerous, mean 581
mereles, *s.pl.* nine-men's morris 2595*n*
mesra *fut.3 of* **mener,** *v.t.* lead 197
message, *s.* message 1890; messenger: **Dieu m.** poor person, beggar 2824*n*, 2830
mestier, *s.* estate 1720, 2897; **avoir m.** need 2107, 2584, 2694; be helpful, be necessary 1697, 1878, 2084, 2362, 2470; **estre m.** be necessary 2524, 3197
meuble, *s.* movable property, chattel 2546
mire, *s.* physician, doctor 1775
miseranche, *s.* wretchedness 1422*n*
miudre, *adj.comp.* better 588
moitïier; *v.t.* halve 2549
moleste, *s.* wrong, injury 1809
mouvoir, *v.i.* move 450, 466; arise 2003; **m. de** spring from, stem from 1074, 1683, 1859, 2421, 2501, be inherited from 2545, 3272

nasse, *s.* net or trap for catching fish 1090
nekedent, nequedent, *adv.* nevertheless 1283, 1305, 2124, 2162, 2190, 2205, 2406, 2621
niche, nise, *adj.* stupid, ignorant 231, 555, 1235, 1512, 1586, 2343
nicheté, *s.* stupidity, ignorance 1226, 1510, 2079
nombre, *s.* quantity, magnitude 1797
nonper *see* **per**
noter, *v.t.* notice, discern 3241
noumeement, *adv.* particularly 1858, 2957, 3018, 3238

obeïssanche, *s.* obedience 590
offendre, *v.t.* offend 1077; attack 618
oir, *s.* heir 2541, 2550
ordo(u)ner, ordener, *v.t.* set in order, arrange 1294; appoint, establish 1351, 2379; ordain, admit to holy orders 1713
ordurie, *s.* vileness, immorality 2723
orendroit, *adv.* now, currently 2965
os, *adj.* bold, daring 504
oublïance, *s.* act of forgetting 1247; **metre en o.** forget 954, 1244
ourer, *v.i.* pray 868

outragier, *adj.* excessive, immoderate 2382
outre, *adv.*: **d'o. en o.** through and through 2072
outreement, *adv.* above all 2104
outrer, *v.t.* overcome, defeat 838

paie, *s.* reward 2782, 2784
paier; *v.t.* pay 7; *v.r.* be satisfied, be rewarded 2781
paine, *s.* suffering, pain 889, 1024, 2109, 2290, 3070; punishment, penance 1986, 1987; effort 1880, 3188; **mener p.** undergo punishment, do penance 1979; **metre p.** strive 606, 2047; **soi metre en p.** put oneself out 3203; **a paines** hardly 1091, 1846, 3194
paire *pres.sbv.3 of* **paroir**; *v.i.* appear 1178*n*; *pres.sbv.3 of* **parer**; *v.t.* enhance, do credit to 1342*n*
pantain, *s.* mud, mire 134*n*, 137, 139
parfurni *pret.3 of* **parfurnir**; *v.t.* finish 3291
parrochien, *s.* parish priest 1383*n*, 1407
passable, *adj.* transitory 2158
passer, *v.t.* cross, walk across 347, 356; break, fail to comply with 329, 460, 485; *v.r.* behave 469; **soi p. de** cross, walk across 349
pechavour, pechevor = **pechëour** 121, 2709
pener, *v.r.* strive 575, 841, 1354, 2152
per, *s.* peer, equal 412; fellow, neighbour 2594; **dés p. ou nonper** ?rigged dice 2593*n*
pereche, *s.* sloth, acedia 1551, 1641, 1649, 2055
*****perecheus**, *s.* slothful person 404*n*
peur *see* **puer**
plaisaument, *adv.* pleasantly 2821
ploumet, *s.* plummet, lead pencil 2873*n*
point, *s.* moment 1240; detail, item, matter 304, 631, 1741, 2671; situation, position 1431, 2916; (*neg. part.*) not at all 460, 848, 1028, etc.; (+ **de**) no 64, 317, 320, etc.; **p. de l'eskekier** a (board) game 2598*n*; **plus de poins** a dice game 2592*n*
poissanche, *s.* power, might 76, 267, 322, 786, 2913, 2923; power, virtue 976; ownership 2575; strength 561; **en sa p.** in one's prime 1444*n*
portement, *s.* behaviour 1733
pourre, *s.* dust 221
pourtraire, *v.t.* draw, sketch 2872
pourveïr, *v.r.* think about, give attention to 565; *pr.p. as adj.* careful, provident 3273
poverte, *s.* poverty 2971

pregne *pres.sbv.3*; **prendés** *imperat.5*; *****prensist** *impf.sbv.3 of* **prendre**, *v.t.* take, 1420, 3130, 1240
premerain, *adj.* first 1017, 2154; superior 2169
prestanche, *s.* loan 1629*n*
prïeus, *s.* prior 2668
priver; *v.t.* remove 960; *p.p. as adj.* close, intimate 687, 713; *as s.* intimate friend 959
proi(s)me, *s.* fellow, neighbour 1576, 1595, 2409
proisié, *p.p. as s.* renowned person 1197
propre, *s.* (fig.) private property 1822
puchier, *v.t.* draw (water) 88, 104, 183, 2458; *inf. as s.* drawing 170
puer, peur, pueur, *adv.* outside: **jeter en p.** cast out, destroy 612, 1032, 1173, 3258
puisor, *s.* bucket 88*n*, 97, 160
puterie, *s.* prostitution 2579

quanbien = **combien** 2425
quaut, *pres.ind.3* of **chaloir**, *v.impers.* concern 1597, 2122 (*see also* **challe**)
queme = **comme** 2966
queure = **courre** 719
*****quille**, *s.* skittle: **·ix· quilles** nine pins, skittles 2604*n*
quinsaine, *s.* fortnight 1353

raconforter; *v.t.* strengthen 2138*n*
racordanche, *s.* recollection 1443
rage, *s.* madness 1296
raim, rain, *s.* branch 488; branch, subdivision 1591, 1599, 1614, 1616, 1618, 1619, 2060, 2150
rainssiaus, *s.nom.* subsidiary branch, subcategory 1605
ramener; *v.t.* relate, reduce (to) 1686
rasques, *s.pl.* (fig.) mire, morass 1299*n*
ratiere, *s.* rat trap 1598
rauller, *v.i.* ? 2601*n*
reclamer, *v.t.* pray, beseech 3151
recreant, *adj.* overcome, ready to admit defeat 764
recrëue *see* **courner**
recuert *pres.ind.3 of* **requerre**, *v.t.* ask for 906, 1392
recuevre, *s.* remedy, help 983*n*, 2959
regehir; *v.t.* confess (sins) 1376, 1872, 1888 (*see also* **gehir**)
remaindre, *v.t.* stop, put an end to 2857

rench *pres.ind.1*; **renge** *pres.sbv.3 of* **rendre** *22, 251, 1495
rencheïr, *p.p.* **rencheüs** 122, *v.i.* fall, fall back 63
renoumer; *v.t.* give a good name to, cause to be praised 2493; *p.p. as adj.* renowned, well known 447, 733, 1685, 3126
reposer, *v.t.* not do, abandon, forsake 505
reprendre, *v.t.* rebuke, criticize 1464, 1523, 1739, 1874, 2235
rescourre, *v.r.* defend, justify oneself 222, 722
resgardanche, *s.* consideration: **faire r.** consider, examine 1721
resgardeüre, *s.* consideration 1023
resoig, *s.* worry, concern 522, 2196
resoigner; *v.t.* worry about, be concerned for 1590
restif, *adj. as s.* resistant, unresponsive person refractory 1766
restoble, *s.* stubble 214*n*
retaut *pres.ind.3 of* **retolir/retoldre**; *v.t.* take back 382
reter; *v.t.* accuse 510
retraire, *v.t.* tell, say 1396, 1691, 1789, 2031, 2082, 2119, 2477, 2528; reproach, admonish 2087; *v.r.* **soi r. de** desist from, renounce 1163, 1527
retraite, *?s.* reproach 1152*n*
reube, *s.* possessions 1622
reuve, reve *pres.ind.3 of* **rover**; *v.t.* demand 1384, 2696
rikeche, riquech[e] = **richesse**
roi, *s.* net 481, 483
roiauté, *s.* ?kingdom *or* ?kingliness 3056*n*
roiste, *adj.* hard 131
rout, *adj.* broken 161, 2907; destroyed 1084, 2136
route, *s.* troop, company 738, 2908; **sire de la r.** leader of the troop, 703*n*
ruer; *v.t.* throw 1183, 2333

sablon, *s.* sandy shore 388
salir, *v.i.* leap, rush 700
sam(b)ler; *v.i.* seem 256, 1296, 1333, 1570, 1910, 2811, 2893, etc.; resemble 1856; cause to seem, present as 1792; *pr.p. as s.* one who resembles 2317; appearance 2812
sara *fut.3*; **saront** *fut.6*; **sevent** *pres.ind.6* of **savoir**, *v.t.* know 238, 794, 1064, 1409, 1736, etc.
satiffaire, satiffassion = **satisfaire, satisfacion** 144*n*, 147
saudee = **soudee**, *s.* reward 377, 3067
secussion, *s.* execution, way of carrying out 2534*n*
seel, *s.* bucket 150, 151, 156, 178
segnourage, *s.* authority, power 2660

segnourie, *s.* power, authority 671, 2163, 3220; power, virtue 939; ownership 2563, 2570; domain 3170, 3245

semont *pres.ind.3*; **semounés** *pres.ind.5* of **semo(u)ndre**; *v.t.* encourage, incite 180, 2633

sené, *adj.* wise 2997

sentence, *s.* judgement 208, 251, 883, 1978, 2995, 3003

sentir; *pres.ind.1* **sench** 2309; *v.t.* feel, experience 3230; feel, opine 2309; smell 1039; *v.r.* **soi s. de** feel the effect of, be influenced by 3276*n*, 3279

septesme, *s.* septuagesima (Sunday) 1351

sequere, sequeure *pres.sbv.3 of* **secorre**; *v.t.* help 125, 1402

sercot, *s.* surcoat 2596

serjant, *s.* servant 412, 420, 425, 431, 1592

seront = **selonc** 503, 913

*****seut** *pres.ind.3*; **seulent** *pres.ind.6 of* **soloir**; be accustomed to 1514, 2858, 3129

siege, *s.* (fig.) seat, throne 52; **s. saint** Holy See 3020

sodoier, *v.i.* fight as a mercenary 3233

so(u)mme, *s.* main points, gist 2551; **en s.** in sum, briefly 78, 1088, 2681

souatume, *s.* sweetness 827

*****souffraindre**, *v.t.* lack, do without 2360

soulagier = ?**soulacier**, *v.t. & r.* entertain (oneself) 2597*n*, 2631

souräagié, *adj.* very old 2737*n*

sourmener; *v.t.* overwhelm 1714

sourparller; *inf. as s.* excessive talking 3213

soutillanche, *s.* cunning, cleverness 204*n*

souv(e)rain, *adj.* supreme 1018, 3069; important, chief 1600; *as s.* superior 1401, 2669, 2683, 3015

souverra *fut.3* of **souvenir**, *v.impers.* remember 1945

souviner; *v.t.* throw down, knock flat 768

*****suagir** = ?**soagier**, *v.t.* relieve, ease 202*n*

suistanche, *s.* substance 2847*n*

tables, *s.pl.* form of backgammon 2590

tai, *s.* mud, mire 487, 2333, 2334

talenter; *v.i.* be pleasing 2642*n*

targement, *s.* delay 477

targier, *v.i.* delay 1877 (*see also* **atargier**)

taster, *v.t.* taste 435

taut *pres.ind.3*; **taur(r)oit** *cond.3 of* **tolir**; *v.t.* take away 375, 378, 381, 695, 1088, 1640, 1932

teche, *s.* moral blemish, vice 1642
tendre, *v.t.* hold out (hands) 2254; **t. a** be drawn to, 2630, 2200; hope for, strive for 2783
tenëure, *s.* right of occupation 2981
tenir 25; *cond.3* **terroit** 1206; *v.t.* hold 632, 2712; hold (property) 3103, 3204; hold (in position) 1475; have a hold over 1327, 2407; keep to, hold to 193, 560, 977, 3003, 3021; **t. a, pour** consider as, take for 25, 2889, 2315, 2488, 2494, 2823; **estre tenu de** be obliged to 2, 2680, 2684, 2945; **t. justiche** uphold 3028, 3144; **t. lieu** ?form part of, ?stand for, represent 2058; **t. boin lieu** encounter a warm reception 2828, 2829; **t. penitanche** carry out 941; **t. pourfit a** be good for 898; *v.r.* hold out 3178; **soi t. en** persist in 1284; **soi t. de** resist 1206 (*see also* **coi, court, memoire**)
terme, *s.* period of time 1813, 1815; **metre t.** delay 1368
terrïen, *adj.* earthly, of this world 417, 418, 3140, *3166, 3202
tesmoignier, *v.t.* give testimony, swear 3234; (of written document) bear witness, relate 264, 300, 2350; **t. a** describe as, swear to be 218, 226, 3095
theologie, *s.* theology 885
tire, *s.* set, series, list 1508
title, *s.* chapter 242, 2799
toupet, *s.* (spinning) top 2599
tourner, *v.t.* stir 1864; **t. a** contribute to 1895; result in 2328; regard as 2700; *inf. as s.* stirring 1867
traire, *v.t.* draw (water) 162, pull out, draw 2258; entice, drive 2628; *v.i.* **t. arrier** draw back, retreat 532; *v.r.* **soi t. a** turn, betake oneself 1395
traitie, traitié, *s.* chapter, section 2815, 2863 (*see* 2816*n*)
trespasser, *v.t.* break (commandment), disobey 470; *v.i.* die 1657; *inf. as s.* death 684
tressime, *adj.* third 241 (*see* 246*n*)
trie, *s.*: **a t.** ?in detail, punctiliously 1775*n*
tristre, tristreche = **triste, tristesse** 922, 985
tutor, *s.* guardian 2638

un = **en** + **le** 191, 241, 282, 370, 759, 1655

vaillanche, *s.* value, worth 2853
vaineglorïeus, *adj.* vainglorious 236
vassaument, *adv.* ?wisely, ?nobly 2165*n*
venrra *fut.3*; **verroit** *cond.3 of* **venir**, *v.i.* come

veoul *pres.ind.1*; **volut** *p.p. of* **voloir**, *v.t.* want
veu, *adj. as s.*: **de v.** of old 2172
veu, *s.* vow 2173
vicaire, *s.* vicar: **v. de saint Piere** vicar of St Peter, pope 3026, 3087
vies, *adj.* old 287, 370
vieutanche, *s.* vileness, wickedness 1630
vieuté, *s.* vileness, wickedness 1568
vieuteche, *s.* vileness, wickedness 2054
vix, *adj.nom.* vile 672
*****voier**, *v.t.* send, direct 1008
voluntaire, *adj.* voluntary 1901, 1988, 2001
vuis, *adj.nom.* empty 179; devoid 2308

INDEX OF PROPER NAMES

References in this index are exhaustive, and cover the names of books and places as well as people in one alphabetical list. Names are listed under the oblique singular form, unless only nominative or plural forms appear in the text.

Acre 3178, Acre
Adan 303, Adam of Genesis
Alemagne (roi d') 3038, Rudolph I of Habsburg, King of Germany
Anemi 93, 224, 596, 621, 801, 856, 1082, **Anemis** 629, 2054, 2903, 2913, 2923, 3209, The Devil.
Antioche (prince d') 3236, Narjot of Toucy, Prince of Antioch
Aposto[i]le 2957, the Pope (Nicholas IV)
Arragon (roys d') 3083, Peter III, King of Aragon
Artois (conte d') 3099, Robert II, Count of Artois
Augustin 1229, **saint Augustin** 229, **Augustins** 2387, **sains Augustins** 1419, 1913, St Augustine of Hippo, bishop and doctor
Barur 3180, Beirut
Bede 1230, The Venerable (since 1899 St) Bede, historian and theologian
Bernart 1230, **sains Bernars** 1816, St Bernard of Clairvaux, abbot and theologian
Castele (roy de) 3062, Sancho IV, King of Castile
Castiau Pelerin 3179, Castle Pilgrim (now known as Athlit), see 3175*n*
Cayfas 3182, Haifa
Chaÿm 1093, Cain of Genesis 4
Chipre 3193, 3293, Cyprus
Corrintiens *(pl.)* 239, Corinthians, recipients of Paul's epistle
Cris(t) see **Jesu**
Daniel 509, Daniel of Biblical Book of Daniel
David 1452, King David, psalmist, of Book of Psalms and I and II Samuel
Dïauble (le) 847, 1167, 1496, **li Dïaubles** 629, **li Dïauble** 298, the Devil
Dieu 11, 16, 22, 33, 62, 70, 77, 116, 125, 153, 165, 173, 186, 232, 233, 244, 252, 283, 332, 344, 356, 366, 371, 372, 375, 380, 381, 383, 399, 402, 407, 420, 424, 438, 445, 454, 456, 468, 470, 484, 497, 498, 501, 560, 566, 571, 591, 611, 675, 799, 807, 857, 862, 870, 874, 904, 913, 938, 949, 956, 959, 1066, 1072, 1075, 1089,

1102, 1106, 1140, 1168, 1172, 1224, 1252, 1338, 1360, 1413, 1488, 1648, 1809, 1819, 1822, 1922, 1926, 1956, 1982, 1983, 2041, 2059, 2063, 2071, 2074, 2085, 2094, 2097, 2103, 2110, 2112, 2119, 2127, 2129, 2201, 2226, 2242, 2294, 2299, 2331, 2337, 2349, 2359, 2415, 2515, 2524, 2558, 2610, 2634, 2642, 2650, 2654, 2668, 2766, 2767, 2776, 2782, 2824, 2830, 2860, 2862, 2870, 2900, 2917, 2930, 2932, 2952, 2973, 2993, 2997, 3017, 3032, 3036, 3042, 3076, 3079, 3116, 3132, 3142, 3148, 3151, 3156, 3164, 3195, 3208, 3222, 3229, 3256, 3266, 3288, **Dieus** 28, 45, 59, 196, 258, 265, 290, 294, 301, 316, 323, 338, 368, 376, 382, 478, 493, 729, 812, 1005, 1014, 1073, 1107, 1160, 1312, 1414, 1544, 1554, 1587, 1650, 1794, 1796, 1855, 1905, 2018, 2035, 2050, 2068, 2269, 2365, 2381, 2452, 2517, 2574, 2616, 2756, 2763, 2777, 2783, 2826, 2940, 3002, 3034, 3046, 3053, 3058, 3065, 3073, 3084, 3103, 3109, 3138, 3150, 3268, **Dieu[s]** 2023, 3172, **Diex** 3050, **Diu** 3, 5, 9, 250, 253, 272, 282, 313, 328, 503, 810, 2107, 3114, **Dius** 245, **Dix** 2896, **Deu** 1000, 2123, God

Disme de Penitanche 2942, 3296

Edmons (mesire) 3125, Edmund Crouchback, Earl of Lancaster, brother of King Edward I of England

Elye (saint) 331, Elijah of I Kings (III Kings) 17

Engletere (roy d') 3071, 3118, Edward I, King of England

Ermenie (roi d') 3221, Leo III, King of Armenia

Espurgatore 2024, Purgatory, cf. **Purgatoire**

Estievene (saint) 310, St Stephen, protomartyr (see Acts 7)

Evain *(obl.)* 1110, Eve of Genesis

Evangile 2338, ***Evangille*** 1164, New Testament

Ezechïas 945, Hezekiah of II Kings (IV Kings) 20/Isaiah 38

Franche 440, 3090, France (and see **Phelipe**)

Franchois (saint) 491, St Francis of Assisi

Gomorre 275, Gomorrah of Genesis 18–19

Grigore (saint) 1230, **sains Grigoires** 1085, **sains Grigores** 1582, 1615, 2022, 2350, St Gregory the Great, pope and doctor

Guïs see **Juïs**

Haussasi[n]s *(pl.)* 3226, Assassins, fanatical religious sect

Henri (monsegneur le roi) 3167, Henry II of Lusignan, King of Cyprus and titular King of Jerusalem

Jehan 516, 518, 525, **Jehans** 522, 528, 534, Joannes of *Vitae Patrum* III, 27

Jehans 2941, 2947, **Jehans sires de Journi** 29, **Jehans de Journi** 3292

Jeromes (sains) 1076, 2272, St Jerome, doctor
Jerusalem 3175, **Jherusalem** 3199, Jerusalem
Jesu Crist *(obl.)* 461, 804, 869, 991, 1321, 1522, 1561, **Jhesu Crist** *(obl.)* 390, 2703, 2953, 3162, 3214, **Jesu Cris** *(nom.)* 297, 964, 1477, **Jhesu Cris** *(nom.)* 970, **Jesus Cris** *(nom.)* 335, **Jhesus** *(nom.)* 393, 1329 (always written as one word in MS), Jesus Christ
Johel (li proisiés) 1197, Joel of Biblical Book of Joel
Jonas (le prophete) 479, Jonah of Biblical Book of Jonah
Jonatas 2377, Jonathan of I Samuel (I Kings) 14
Journi *see* **Jehans**
Judas 1077, 1097, Judas Iscariot
Juïs 347, **Guïs** 309, the Jews
Lucifer 51, 269, Lucifer of Isaiah 14
Marie 1477, **sainte Marie** 106, 3222, **la benoite Marie** 41, the Blessed Virgin Mary, Mother of Jesus (cf. **Pucele**)
Mars (sains) 358, St Mark, evangelist
Mathés (sains) 300, **sains Matheus** 354, **saint Mathieu** 2789, St Matthew, apostle and evangelist
Maufés 709, the Devil (cf. 2035*n*)
Nicossie 3293, Nicosia
Nöe 280, 285, 1052, Noah of Genesis 6–8
Papes (li) 2960, the Pope (Nicholas IV)
Paradis 20, 52, 191, 967, 1019, 1021, (heavenly) Paradise
Pastoral 2351, The *Regula Pastoralis* of St Gregory
Patrïarche (le) 3153*n*, the Latin Patriarch of Jerusalem
Paus *see* **Pol**
Pharäons 351, Rameses II, the Pharaoh of Exodus
Phelipe (le roy de Franche) 3052, Philip IV, King of France
Piere (saint) 3026, **saint Pierre** 3087, St Peter, apostle
Pol 514, **Paus** 518, 525, Paulus of *Vitae Patrum* III, 27
Paus (saint) 111, 238, 826, 961, 1887, 2946, St Paul of Tarsus, apostle of the Gentiles
Proclus 448, the philosopher Proclus
Proverbes 1346, Biblical Book of Proverbs
Pucele (la) 294, the B.V.M., cf. **Marie**
Purgatoire 2885, Purgatory, cf. **Espurgatore**
Romme 2965, 2978, **Roume** 2552, 2986, 2989, 2994, 3112, Rome
Saiete 3179, Sidon
Salemon 2838, **Salemons** 1345, 2813, Solomon (see notes)
Sarrasin *(pl.)* 3168, **Sarrasins** *(pl.)* 3064, 3225, Saracens, Muslims

Sodome 275, Sodom of Genesis 18–19
Sur 671, 2273, 3180, 3285 Tyre, **segneur de Sur** 3265*n*, ?Amaury of Lusignan, Lord of Tyre
Surie 3135, Syria
Tartars *(pl.)* 3225, Tatars
Thobie 2696, 2701, 2864, Tobias of Biblical Book of Tobias
Triple 3237, 3257, Tripoli
Tulles 685, (Marcus Tullius) Cicero
Turquemans *(pl.)* 3226*n*, Turkomans
Vicaire (de saint Pierre) 3026, 3087, the Pope (Nicholas IV)
Vie des Peres 512, *Vitae Patrum*
Ysaïe 209, **Yzaïes** 2797, **Yzaÿas** 946, Isaiah, Old-Testament prophet
Ysidore 1229, (since 1722 St) Isidore of Seville, doctor

MHRA Critical Texts

This series aims to provide affordable critical editions of lesser-known literary texts that are not in print or are difficult to obtain. The texts will be taken from the following languages: English, French, German, Italian, Portuguese, Russian, and Spanish. Titles will be selected by members of the distinguished Editorial Board and edited by leading academics. The aim is to produce scholarly editions rather than teaching texts, but the potential for crossover to undergraduate reading lists is recognized. The books will appeal both to academic libraries and individual scholars.

Malcolm Cook
Chairman, Editorial Board

Editorial Board

Professor John Batchelor (English)
Professor Malcolm Cook (French) (*Chairman*)
Professor Ritchie Robertson (Germanic)
Dr Derek Flitter (Hispanic)
Professor Brian Richardson (Italian)
Dr Stephen Parkinson (Portuguese)
Professor David Gillespie (Slavonic)

Titles

For a full listing of titles available in the series and details of how to order please visit our website at www.criticaltexts.mhra.org.uk

www.ingramcontent.com/pod-product-compliance
Lightning Source LLC
Chambersburg PA
CBHW070546170426
43201CB00012B/1739